FRANK COSTELLO
Prime Minister of the Underworld

Other books by Joseph DiMona

Fiction
LAST MAN AT ARLINGTON
70 SUTTON PLACE

Non-fiction
GREAT COURT-MARTIAL CASES

FRANK COSTELLO
Prime Minister of the Underworld

by George Wolf
with Joseph DiMona

WILLIAM MORROW & COMPANY, INC., NEW YORK, 1974

PHOTO CREDITS:

United Press International: 5, 6, 7, 9, 10, 11, 13, 15, 18, 21, 22, 24, 26, 28, 29, 32; Wide World Photos: 8, 12, 14, 16, 17, 19, 23, 25, 27, 30, 31.

PRINTED IN THE UNITED STATES OF AMERICA.

1 2 3 4 5   78 77 76 75 74

DESIGN BY HELEN ROBERTS

Library of Congress Cataloging in Publication Data

Wolf, George.
    Frank Costello: prime minister of the underworld.

    1. Costello, Frank.   2. Crime and criminals—Biography.
3. Mafia.   I. DiMona, Joseph, joint author.
II. Title.
HV6248.C67W6   364.1′09′2′2 [B]   74-1128
ISBN 0-688-00256-0

*To my dear wife, Mina, and my dear daughter, Blanche,
who gave me so much encouragement and help*

CONTENTS

Photos appear between pages 194 and 195.

Author to Reader

In 1943 Frank Costello stood astride the criminal world, the undisputed *capo di capo re,* Boss of all Bosses of the Mafia. Charles "Lucky" Luciano, his sadistic predecessor, was in jail. Vito Genovese, his ambitious superior in underworld eminence, was in Italy, hiding out from a murder indictment. Meyer Lansky, brilliant and innovative, was at his side. Frank Costello had it made. Or did he?

Surely he had come a long way from his childhood home on a dirty, windblown street in Harlem; in 1932, at the age of forty-one, he sat in an elegant suite in the Drake Hotel in Chicago with New York's Tammany leader Jimmy Hines and worked for the nomination of Franklin Roosevelt as a presidential candidate; by 1943 he literally owned New York, appointing judges and district attorneys and even mayors. His slot machines in Louisiana and his gambling clubs in several states were pouring millions into his pocket. And his share of the money taken from underworld rackets such as numbers and bookie joints added to his wealth and power.

And yet, trouble was brewing. First from the law; a nationwide scandal exploded when a wiretap placed by New York District Attorney Frank Hogan on Frank's telephone revealed a conversation with a newly nominated New York Supreme Court Justice, Thomas A. Aurelio, thanking Frank for his nomination and swearing "undying" loyalty to the criminal leader.

And the Mafia was restlessly stirring beneath him. Costello wanted peace and nonviolence; the other leaders wanted action. Costello warned them to stay away from narcotics; they wanted in, anyway. Friction began, and soon it would explode when a lean, handsome man named Bugsy Siegel, the West Coast Mafia leader, stood on a road in Nevada and decided that this place in the desert would be the next capital of the gambling world.

This was in 1946, three years after I was hired by Frank. I was to be his personal lawyer for thirty years, and his friend for just as long. And that friendship is why I intended this book to be more than a study of a Mafia "Boss of all Bosses," as I learned it as the result of my unique relationship with him. Such a study, I hope, will in itself be of interest because the code of silence has prevented the telling of the inside details of the lives of the Mafia "Bosses of all Bosses" before and after Costello.

But Costello was different, and that is why this book has a second dimension. He was not "soft," by any means. On many occasions, I myself found him frightening. But he was "human," he was civilized, he spurned the bloody violence in which previous bosses had reveled.

My book will not glamorize or even apologize for Frank Costello. He was a lawbreaker all of his life, and caused financial and physical harm to many law-abiding citizens.

Nor do I fear that young boys may read this book and emulate Frank Costello. Too much will be revealed: the constant terror, even at the top; the knowledge that potential treachery and death lurk behind every "friend's" eyes.

But I believe that the life of Frank Costello is a moving story, a story of a man whose life might have taken a different direction if he had been born under happier circumstances. For he was intelligent, and he was just. To this day his former underworld associates speak of him with respect, as one of a kind, a man who gave everyone a fair shake from the lowest numbers runner in Harlem to the leading "Mustachio Petes" of the great underworld families.

This book presents my own inside look at the man who ruled over the Mafia. It is, as it must be, a bloody, violent tale in which killers prowl, and men live in fear. How did Frank Costello, who loved most of all to dine quietly every day in the Waldorf Astoria's elegant grill, become a part of that murderous world? Even stranger, how did he become its boss?

In my thirty years with Frank Costello I could not conceive of his carrying a gun, much less killing anyone with it. Yet, as he once ordered me to tell a reporter who wanted some facts on Frank's character, "Don't claim that I sell Bibles." And the world he ruled was filled with bloodshed.

So, in my book, the guns must speak too, as they so often did during Frank's lifetime, mostly against his advice.

Where they do, in the murders and intrigues described, it is —as we lawyers say—hearsay evidence. But it came from a very high source.

A book about the Boss of all Bosses of the Mafia must begin with a description of the underworld's oldest organization.

The word "Mafia" as I use it here refers to the nationwide interlocking group of underworld "families" of Italian derivation. This is in distinction to what is usually referred to as "the syndicate," which describes the informal relationship between the Mafia and the Jewish underworld families. These Italian and Jewish families, as I understood it from Frank, coexist on an equal level.

Where there is overlapping, there is bloodshed, but this happens very rarely. The two groups have always worked in surprisingly good harmony, the Italians respecting the Jews for their financial brains, and the Jews preferring to stay quietly behind the scenes and let the Italians use the "muscle" where needed.

Of course there are exceptions, as we shall see, where Italians called on the Jews for their "muscle," as in the Maranzano killing, and, on the other side, where the Jewish groups called on the Mafia for their "brains," as in the use of Frank Costello to handle political corruption in New York.

I must also say, at this point, that I never heard Frank—or any of my other high underworld clients—mention the word Mafia, or Cosa Nostra. The key word that always denoted the Mafia was not a noun but a verb: "connected." In describing a stranger to me Frank might say, briefly, "He's connected." And then I knew.

The Mafia is not organized like a business corporation. A more apt comparison would be to a sort of United Nations council, where the Boss of all Bosses rules over a "commission" of regional leaders ("family bosses") acting with common consent, trading with each other, and obeying certain rules for the benefit of all.

The first time the commission was called together, as we shall see, was in Atlantic City in 1929 where, in effect, it was created. Later, other meetings were held in New York, and when Lucky Luciano was in Cuba in 1946 and the Bugsy Siegel trouble in Las Vegas was breaking wide open there was a gathering of all family leaders again. The Apalachin meeting in 1957 was the last I ever heard of.

Meetings were called only when a nationwide matter of urgent necessity arose. Otherwise, the rules were set—Miami, Florida, and Las Vegas, Nevada, were "open" territories where all mobs could operate *and no violence must ever take place*. Other rules were simple and sensible: no New York gangs in the Chicago rackets, no Chicago gangs in Cleveland, what you might call laissez-faire all the way. National properties such as the "racing wire" would be shared equitably.

Jewish gangs in each of these areas cooperated with the Mafia gangs on a local basis, but I have never heard of a Jewish-Mafia "commission." When the well-publicized nationwide Mafia council meeting at Apalachin was exposed, there wasn't a Jew among them.

But even though the Mafia bosses operated as equals among equals, by tradition the leader of the Manhattan family was "first among first," "the Boss of all Bosses." This is because Manhattan was—and is—the center of the underworld, the capital of crime. When bank robber Willie Sutton said he robbed banks because "That's where the money is," he might also have been referring to the underworld's respect for Manhattan. Money and action all stem from the island seaport on the East Coast.

The breadth and depth of crime in New York may be seen in the fact that the Mafia has no less than five families there, all operating profitably. In New York the various rackets, ranging from labor extortion to loan sharking to numbers, are all strictly apportioned. And it is this apportionment—and various attempts to "take over" someone else's area—that is the most troubling element for a Boss of all Bosses to handle, and that usually results in bloodshed.

THE GUNS

Ernie "the Hawk" Rupolo felt the gun heavy in his belt, wedged against his stomach. The goddam movie would never end. He sat with his friend Bill Gallo in the Loew's theater in Brooklyn and watched Gary Cooper crawl hand over hand on a rope above a waterfall. Gallo laughed, and the Hawk joined him. The stunt man was so obvious.

A stunt man was just what the Hawk needed. He always got the beautiful jobs while the man who ordered the hit, Vito Genovese, took it easy in New Jersey.

When they emerged from the theater, the Hawk saw it was a warm night and dark. The moon was with him, anyway. "Let's go see Colonni," he said. "We can walk."

Late on a quiet street in Brooklyn, shabby two-story houses sitting behind shabby little lawns protected by iron railings. Two weeks on this "hit" and the Hawk never had a chance to do his job. Gallo had been ducking him. Did he suspect?

Gallo wouldn't be with him if he did. Halfway down the block, Rupolo pulled out his .38, stuck it against Gallo's head, and pulled the trigger.

CLICK!

"HEY! WHAT THE HELL ARE YOU DOING?" Gallo yelled, jumping aside so fast he bounced off a tree. The Hawk pulled the trigger again. Again it clicked. Jesus Christ! The piss-eyed gun jammed! To Gallo the Hawk said, "Scared ya?"

15

"Put that away!" Gallo said. "What are you trying to do?"

Gallo was white, shaken. The Hawk said, "Just a little joke. Some guys pulled it on me the other day and I went through the roof."

"Some goddam joke," Gallo said, and for the rest of the walk to Colonni's home he stayed carefully behind the Hawk.

But when Colonni heard about the incident he laughed, and finally Gallo managed a weak smile. They sat around over drinks for quite some time, and at one point the Hawk managed to sneak out of the room unnoticed. In the bathroom he opened the pistol and saw that the firing pin was rusty. What the hell should he do? He found some hair oil in the cabinet, which he used to oil the pin. But by this time his hands were shaking. There was one person, he knew, who would not find any of this funny, Vito Genovese.

The Hawk stuck the gun in his belt. An hour later Rupolo and Gallo were on the sidewalk again, walking back toward the theater where their car was parked, and Gallo was taking no chances, staying behind the Hawk. And so it was now or never, and the Hawk grabbed the gun again, turned and fired point-blank at Gallo's head, once, twice . . . five bullets in all. Blood spurted from Gallo's head; he crashed backward on the pavement, arms outflung, and the Hawk took off. He ran down the street, jumped into his Chevrolet coupe and sped away, his heart beating fast, his hands so shaky he could hardly control the wheel.

The trouble was that Gallo lived despite the three wounds in his head. And that the Hawk was arrested and started talking about the man who ordered the hit.

And that Vito Genovese was indicted for murder, and had to flee the country. This was in 1934, and Genovese's forced departure was the reason Frank Costello, who was next in line, eventually became "Boss of all Bosses" of the Mafia.

BOOK I
Early Secrets

1

September, 1971. I made a terse phone call to Frank Costello at his apartment on Central Park West. "Frank, I have something important to talk to you about."

Actually in those years, even though the newspapers kept saying he had "retired," after he had almost been killed, I knew better than anyone else that Frank was still active. Frank was in my office every week on different matters. But I had called this meeting for personal as well as legal reasons. Both Frank and I were getting old, and that posed a legal problem.

In fact we were the same age, eighty, but as Frank entered my office I had to smile ruefully at the difference between us. Frank still looked marvelously healthy. He always took such good care of himself, no matter what, was always so proud of his appearance. He was a habitué of the Biltmore Hotel's steam room and health club. Today he looked ruddy and fit, dressed conservatively in a single-breasted blue suit with a white shirt, a modest blue tie, and elegant gold cufflinks peeping out of the ends of his coat sleeves. How often in past hearings and trials had I pleaded with him to "wear a *cheap* suit, for God's sake!" but Frank would have none of it. He didn't want the jury's sympathy; he wanted their respect.

Now he sat down in a leather chair across from my desk, and said, "Where's your Scotch?" In those days of my own semi-retirement, my office was in my apartment on East 63rd Street in Manhattan, so my wife was available as a bartender, and she quickly got Frank his favorite, Scotch and soda.

I told him about the money he had asked me to borrow from an "old friend" of his. Frank had wanted $200,000. The friend had said he could come up with only $10,000. "Tell him to keep it," Frank said. "I put him in business, and now he plays games."

I noticed that Frank, as always, had placed his drink on my antique mahogany desk. A nice stain was developing. "Damn it, Frank, pick up that drink. You're ruining my desk."

Frank smiled. He loved to needle me, and he never seemed more happy than when I got exasperated and spoke sharply to him.

He said, "So get another desk."

I pulled out Frank's will in which I was named as the sole executor. The will had been drawn in 1949, twenty-two years ago. I said, "Frank, I want you to draw up a new will and name a new executor."

"Why the hell can't you remain as executor?"

"You'll need a younger man, Frank. I'll be too old to handle it, and I may even predecease you."

For the first time Frank dropped his blustering air and really looked at me. "Hell," he said, "I want *you* as my executor. I can trust you."

"But I'm too old, Frank. I'll advise the new executors. I'll testify at probate."

"OK, if you say so," Frank said. He took the will and slipped it into his inside coat pocket. I could see the reference to age had touched him.

He said, "When did you first come to work for me, George?"

"I helped Morris Ernst's firm represent you in Louisiana in your tax case in 1939. But I wasn't on a regular basis until the Aurelio case in '43."

Frank thought a moment, then he said, "If it wasn't for Aurelio, I might never have needed a full-time lawyer. Things were going pretty good until then."

Frank and I went into the living room. He had another drink and chatted with my wife about his summer home in Sands Point, Long Island, where his wife Loretta was a frequent hostess to us. Then he left. I was to see him many more times before he died, but that visit remains fixed in my memory. When he left with the will, his departure seemed to reflect the end of a personal era, an era that had begun with such excitement in 1943, for in that one year I represented both the infamous Lucky Luciano, the former No. 1 man in the Mafia, and Frank Costello, Luciano's successor. From that moment on I was with Frank while he faced a succession of legal actions, hearings, and trials as well as several dangerous Mafia intrigues. They were to culminate in a single bullet aimed at his head.

2

I first saw Frank Costello when I was conducting the defense of Joe Millstein, one of his bootlegging associates. At the time, prohibition had been a turning point in my life, as it was in Frank's.

I had graduated from New York University Law School in 1912 and received an LL.B., then in the next year an LL.M. After graduation my degrees did me little good, however, as far as income goes. I worked for two law firms, and specialized mostly in civil cases.

In 1917, I decided to go into private practice. As is normal for young attorneys, I had to struggle to make a living. One day I was sitting in the U.S. District Court, Room 318 in the old Post Office Building, awaiting the roll call of cases to which I might be assigned (and if lucky earn a fee). To my surprise, a close friend of mine appeared before the bench, charged with concealing assets in a bankruptcy case. Judge Goddard asked him whether he had secured an attorney, and when the defendant said no, the judge told him he would give him twenty-four hours to get one.

I went up to my friend and immediately got myself hired. I had one handicap, though—I didn't know a thing about the ins and outs of bankruptcy law. But I learned fast. The trial was before one of America's great judges, Augustus Hand. The jury returned a verdict of acquittal.

To my surprise, I soon became a specialist in cases involving concealed assets. Unfortunately there weren't enough of them to make me rich, or even solvent. Then prohibition came along and suddenly there were thousands of new types of cases for hungry attorneys. They called them "padlock cases."

When the federal agents closed a saloon for serving liquor, they would place a padlock on the door. The operators would hire an attorney to get the padlock removed so they could resume business.

The courts therefore found themselves inundated by thousands of padlock cases, and were only too eager to have a defense attorney make a deal with the U.S. Attorney's office to have the padlock removed after a few days of nonoperation.

And that is how I drifted into the area of criminal law. Most of these saloons were owned by underworld characters. My reputation grew; it was said I had "a way with juries," and my record of acquittals was almost perfect. I do admit here that I love to try a case in front of a jury, that I have a sense of the dramatic, and that I have, upon occasion, faced a jury, pointed at the defendant (usually a hardened criminal), and said in a deep shaking voice: "Send this man home to his wife."

But any lawyer knows there is more to success in law than talking to a jury. I was a demon for preparation, and would rent a hotel room before and during a trial so I could concentrate completely on the matter at hand.

Thus my fame spread, and soon I was counseling not just saloon owners but the greatest names in the underworld. The list of my clients included Johnny Torrio, who brought Al Capone to Chicago; Dutch Schultz, the brewery baron and numbers king of the Bronx; Lucky Luciano, the Boss of all Bosses of the Mafia before Frank; Vito Genovese, Frank's rival for years; Albert Anastasia, who controlled the Brooklyn waterfront; Willie Moretti, one of the top New Jersey dons; and Frank Erickson, described by the police as the all-time king of bookmakers.

I also became a defender of many unpopular clients, among them Jack and Myra Sobel, the Communist spies, and the notorious millionaire draft-dodger Serge Rubinstein.

Through it all I achieved something I treasure very much: a reputation for integrity among the judges and district attorneys I faced. In many cases, I was recommended by them (the most famous case concerned Governor Thomas Dewey's recommendation that I represent Lucky Luciano, no less).

But to this day people want to know the answer to one question: Why did I defend these notorious underworld characters, some of them murderers? My answer, which every attorney, I think, would agree with, is this:

I believe that every defendant, regardless of the degree of his culpability, is entitled to legal representation. In this belief, I felt that I was performing a public service and promoting respect for due administration of law. I believe I am supported in my view by the high regard in which I have been held by the bench, bar, and even the public.

I *did* feel certain qualms about representing criminals such as Costello, Genovese, Luciano, and the like. But I have always impressed upon them that I would not try their cases if they were to take the witness stand and testify untruthfully about the facts. In doing so, I knew that I was protecting not only myself, but the defendants from adding perjury and contempt of court to the crimes for which they were charged.

Though Frank Costello, among other criminals, wanted his lawyer to take orders from him, I remained adamant about my position.

My career as a criminal lawyer did not affect my personal life. My wife, Mina, and I lived in a lovely home in Saddle Rock Village, Long Island. During the Kefauver hearings I was on television every day, where, in full view of the public, I sat beside the No. 1 criminal in the land. Interestingly, during those hearings I was elected mayor of my home town.

Of all the colorful characters I ever counseled, there was none who approached my friend Frank Costello. I will say here that I became very fond of him personally despite all the storms and trials and rages we went through.

As I got to know him better, I used to talk with him about his past. I then began to understand what was behind his enormous drive. It was a long way from a poor little sun-baked village in Calabria, in southern Italy, to the No. 1 position in crime in the U.S.A. As you might expect, there were some contenders. Unlike Frank they were not born in Lauropoli, a very strange birthplace, indeed.

3

Francesco Castiglia, the son of Luigi and Maria Saveria Aloise Castiglia, was born on January 26, 1891, in Lauropoli, in Calabria, the mountainous region that occupies the toe of Italy.

A lifelong friend of Frank's, Frank Rizzo, whom Costello always called the Professor, is in Lauropoli today, where he also was born. Pictures he sends me show a charming whitewashed village gleaming in the sun. But this is a region of fierce heat which turns what little fertile land there is into dry baked gullies. For centuries farmers have struggled vainly to wrest a living from the stony land surrounding the village.

Recently I have had letters from the Professor about Lauropoli which throw a special light on the town and on Frank's forebears. Lauropoli, it turns out, was a village with a unique history. As the Professor tells it:

> The little Calabrian town where Frank was born is still there up the long hill in front of the Ionian Sea, where once stood the acropolis of Sybaris. Sybaris, founded by the Greeks, was the richest town of Magna Graecia.
>
> The acropolis ruins had been used "as a cattle and flock place" from the Middle Ages until 1776. Marchioness Laura Serra was the owner of two thousand acres of farms in the region. On the ruins of the acropolis she gave orders to build forty little one-room houses. To this little town, shaped like a cross, she gave her name, Laura-poli, which in Greek means town of Laura. After she built the town, she needed people to live in it, and, with the agreement of the King of Naples, she sent an edict:
>
> "Any one who has trouble with justice, or is wanted by the law, is free to come and live in the new town of Lauro-

poli where he and his family will have a nice house, work, and full protection."

In a few weeks many men and women came to Lauropoli from every part of the Kingdom of Naples, most of them petty criminals who wanted asylum and protection.

The fact that Frank Costello, who rose to head organized crime in the U.S., was born in a village founded by lawbreakers is intriguing.

Frank's father, Luigi Castiglia, was called to the army in 1865 and fought with Garibaldi's Legion for the new Kingdom of Italy. Luigi Castiglia distinguished himself in the battle of Tirob, got a medal for valor, and a pension of ten lire a month (two American dollars) for life.

In 1870 he married Maria Saveria Aloise. Frank's mother, according to the Professor, "was a very intelligent though an illiterate woman, very sensitive. She was stocky with black hair full of hairpins, a masculine woman with turned-down nose, and a dark complexion like her son Frank."

They had six children, four daughters and two sons, Eddy, the older, and Frank. Luigi, after his soldiering days, had become a farmer, but was unable to support his growing family. The poverty in the area was great, and the misery was greater. It was said that by crossing the Atlantic one could find a green, fertile land that welcomed immigrants. In 1895, Luigi Castiglia came to America, bringing with him his daughters and the older son. The letters he sent back disappointed his wife. Luigi had been in America six months and could not even find work. Finally he sent a letter which said that he had no money to take the family home, so Maria must bring Frank to America. "Sell everything," he wrote, "even the bed sheets, if necessary, even if you have to borrow some lire from someone, but come to America." Luigi, a man who could not even find a job, still thought of America as the land of opportunity.

The letter came on a special day for her son. Frank, who was five, had gone to the great wooded estate of Baron Francesco Compagna to steal wild berries and flowers. Frank's grandfather was the head watchman of the estate. Suddenly a group of hunters appeared. The smallest man in the group asked what the little boy was doing in the woods. Frank smartly told him he was the watchman's grandson and he was helping *watch* the estate. The little man, who was the King of Italy, smiled knowingly and turned to the watchman who was nervously standing nearby. "Here are five lire," said the King. "Buy this little boy a sailor suit. Your grandson has spirit."

A few days later, in August, 1896, Frank was dressed in a bright new sailor suit, clutching his mother's hand. They were on their way to America. Frank's instinct for meeting—and getting along with—the "better" people was already apparent.

Maria Saveria Aloise had left for New York with her red passport hidden in a handkerchief. The boy's name was also written in the same passport. She went first to Naples to board the ship, the port called by southern Italian people the City of the Seven Wonders. But Maria didn't see much of it because she had to watch over her son along with a mass of bundles. Only the black smoke of Vesuvius caught her eye, and the trams drawn by prancing horses.

Arriving in Naples early in the morning, she rushed to the dock, where she found the ship anchored twenty feet from the shore. To reach the ship it was necessary to go first in a small boat. Maria jumped into the boat with her son, and someone threw her bundles to her.

The sun shone on the blue water of the lovely bay of Naples. Maria was leaving for a new world, and she was happy. Little Frank looked smart in his dazzling whites, and euphoria overtook her as the boat came alongside the big ship. Then a deluge of dirty water came down from one of the bilges and inundated little Frank, ruining his new suit. Maria could not help thinking this was a bad omen for the future, but she knew she had to be strong. She took Frank in her arms and said, "Don't cry, my treasure, don't cry. It was your fortune. That thing means richness. You are leaving lucky. Blessed be St. Francis, who is protecting you."

But still, she worried.

4

Maria and Frank arrived in New York in 1896, one tiny ripple among the great waves of southern European immigrants washing into New York. Some of them pushed on to other communities, but most had no money and remained in New York.

East Harlem, where Frank's parents settled, was once a lovely valley between the Harlem River and the Morningside-Washington Heights bluffs. By 1896 it had already turned into a slum. The Italians took over the streets between Fifth and First avenues, and these immigrants who could not speak English were looked down upon by the area's former residents, the Irish.

No life of Frank Costello, or of other Italian Mafia leaders who grew up in the same circumstances, can be complete without an understanding of the Irish-Italian struggle. By 1896, when Costello arrived, the Irish who had preceded the Italians into the city owned New York. They founded and controlled Tammany Hall; they elected mayors; they controlled jobs and patronage; they made up the police force.

Poor Italian boys growing up among the Irish, who had gained so much power, found themselves in a dilemma. It was hard to get jobs, except on the lowest level of manual labor.

The job Frank's father got was one of those. In 1897 he went to work with a pickaxe at the reservoir in Westchester County. After fifteen days on the job, he received his first paycheck. But when he came home he had a bruised face and no money. Some Irish thugs had waited for him and two other Italians and taken their pay envelopes. Frank later said he never forgot his father's injured face and the look in his eyes when his father told him the thieves had called them "guineas" even as they stole their pay.

I have been asked what motivated Frank to go into crime. I must say Frank asked it of himself. And the answer, I believe, can be found in part in the world of East 108th Street, where

Italian families like Frank's faced a struggle for survival. Living there, if you had an Irish landlord who tormented you, you robbed the landlord. If you needed food to eat and had no job, you stole the money or the food.

And for protection, you organized in gangs.

Perhaps no one could explain Frank's genesis in crime as well as his lifelong friend Frank Rizzo, who wrote to me:

> I really think that it is important, very important, to put in evidence the education received by Frank in the streets of 108th and 109th. In a night of drowsiness came to my memory some Dante's verses in the *Divine Comedy*.
> "Tanto piu, silvestro e piu'
> "Maligno si fa il terreno col mal seme e non colto quando ha piu de buon vigore terrestre."
> "A good piece of fertile land not tilled gets more malignant and sylvan with bad seeds than land less fertile."
> An intelligent boy put in bad company at the end will be boss of that bad company because in him is all the stuff to be a boss. If we put the same intelligent boy in good company, he will be the boss because there is the stuff in him.
> There is Frank, a very intelligent boy, whose aim was to arrive higher, to get revenge, to get out of poverty, a pupil of that school of bad seeds, not controlled by parents busy working for a crust of bread, and some time without that necessary piece of nourishment.

Frank's brother Eddy was ten years older than he—and a wild one. Frank Rizzo, the Professor, writes that Eddy was in trouble all of his life, and always a headache to Frank, who later took care of him. In their youth he was constantly bringing Frank into the gang warfare on the streets.

But Frank, from his childhood on, had the instincts of a loner. And his cleverness was revealed in his first scrape with the law. He was fourteen years old when he first got into trouble.

5

Fourteen-year-old Francesco Castiglia's right leg was killing him. During the previous week his mother had sent her son to his aunt's farm. The farm was in Astoria, across the East River and not far from her house in Harlem. Frank had climbed a tree and fallen from a high limb, his leg twisting beneath him. The doctor had bandaged him from ankle to thigh, and told him not to move.

Now he lay in bed. He could hear his aunt moving around the house, turning off the lights, then she looked in on him. "You all right, Francesco?" He said he was, and she closed the door slowly.

But Frank was thinking. Last week his mother had said she couldn't afford the rent and the landlady had screamed that she was already two months behind. The family would be kicked out on the street.

Frank knew something about that landlady. He knew that she got up early every morning to clean the stairs and the bathrooms ("backhouses" they were called then), which were on each floor. Frank also knew that the landlady carried all of her money in her bosom because she didn't trust the banks.

Frank waited until very late at night, then got up, and limped out. He made his way through quiet roads to the 92nd Street ferry, crossing the East River and returning to his home. A half hour later he was in the cellar of his house, tying a black handkerchief around his face.

Heart beating fast, he heard the clump clump of his landlady's footsteps coming down the stairs. He waited behind the cellar door and when the landlady approached, he opened the door and found the woman was looking the other way. He threw his arms around her neck, seized the money from her bosom, and hobbled through the yard to 107th Street.

Unfortunately, the landlady recognized Frank. She cried out

"Thief!" and rushed to Frank's mother's door, which was on the first floor. Maria Saveria was stunned. "You're a liar! My son hasn't been home since Sunday!"

The landlady went to the police, where she got a surprise. The police investigated and it seemed the boy she recognized as Francesco Castiglia had been asleep with his leg in bandages in Astoria the night of the robbery.

6

Frank's mother started a little general store in East Harlem to help bring in money. She sold everything from sardines and codfish to candy, staying in the store from early morning to late at night.

With both parents working, Frank grew up uncontrolled, and determined to avoid his parents' lifetime struggle for money. The easiest way was to steal, and Frank did his share of petty thieving. He was becoming a young man without a future.

Then at the age of twenty-three he fell in love.

Loretta Geigerman, a pretty young woman, lived close by but, in effect, a world away. Her parents lived on upper Park Avenue, in those days a wealthy area populated mostly by Jews.

All of his life Frank admired and got along well with Jews, whom he respected. He once said to me, "When I met Bobbie [Loretta] it was like meeting one of my own people. She didn't talk Italian, but the German dialect of her parents was foreign, like mine. Bobbie and me got along great from the first, although neither of our mothers was too happy. Bobbie's thought her daughter could do better than a poor Italian kid from East Harlem. And my mother naturally was hoping for an Italian girl."

But the two were in love—and, may I say from my own knowledge, stayed in love throughout their lives together. Frank applied for a marriage license in 1914, using for the first time the name which was to become famous: Frank Costello, which he always preferred to his own name. It was one of several aliases he used in those early days.

The newlyweds were soon to meet their first test. On March 12, 1915, the police had been alerted that Frank was carrying a gun. They spotted him coming out of a barbershop and yelled for him to stop. Frank started to run up an alley. The police caught him in a hurry.

7

Judge Edward Swann saw standing before his bench a young Italian punk in cheap denim pants. The judge was angry. He started to pronounce sentence, and no doubt was certain he was making a routine effort to cleanse the streets of one more small-time hood.

In fact, every word he said was changing Frank's life.

"I find that in 1908 he was arrested for assault and robbery and in that case he was discharged. I find that in 1912 he was again arrested for assault and robbery and was also discharged in that case. I have looked him up and find his record is not good. I have it right here from his neighbors that he has the reputation of a gunman."

The prosecutors had obtained letters from neighbors of Frank's who knew he carried a gun at all times. Swann went on, "And in this case he certainly was a gunman. He had a very beautiful weapon and he was prepared to do the work of a gunman, and, somehow or another, he got out of it."

The judge then glanced briefly at Frank before pronouncing the sentence, "I now commit you to the penitentiary for one year."

Frank was transferred to the prison on Welfare Island and served ten months of the yearlong sentence. He had much time to think over the judge's words, "the reputation of a gunman." That reputation had put him in jail. Because of it, mere possession of a gun was enough to get him a year in prison.

"That's when I realized I was stupid," Frank once told me. "Carrying a gun was like carrying a label that says: 'I'm dangerous, I'm a criminal, get me off the streets.' I made up my mind I would never pack a gun again. And I never did."

What Frank did when he got out of jail showed his new turn of mind. He went legitimate—or, *almost* legitimate. He found a man named Henry Horowitz, a manufacturer of novelties, and proposed a "novelty" with a novel payoff. They formed a company on a capital of $3,000, most of it put up by Horowitz, to manufacture kewpie dolls, and other such items. But Frank did not intend to be a toy salesman. Their company, the Horowitz Novelty Company, manufactured punchboards, gambling devices much in favor then. The dolls were one of the prizes.

Official records show the company was formed in 1919, and one thing was quickly apparent: Frank, the Italian immigrant boy, was a clever businessman. Within a year the little company was grossing more than $100,000.

Frank's emergence as a businessman—perhaps the best who ever went into crime—was a revelation to himself, most of all. He found that he had a head for figures. A half century before computers he could remember to the penny information about inventories, sales, suppliers; he never used more than a scratch pad, on which he scrawled marks untranslatable by anyone else.

And his innate cleverness, shown in his first scrape with the law when he robbed a woman while supposedly three miles away with a bandaged leg, was revealed again in his business tactics. His very first business, the Horowitz Novelty Company, had a most successful bankruptcy.

The sudden folding of the company left creditors stuck for more than $14,000, even though the company had accounts receivable for more than that amount. But the attorney for the assignee made this statement to the referee:

"The debts which are due the company cannot be collected by the bankrupts as they were all East Side gangsters."

With his profits, most of them hidden, now protected by the bankruptcy ruling, Frank was on his way. Soon he was investing in other punchboard companies, and even real estate. He was growing more skillful in business every day, and there is no doubt in my mind he could have ended up a very wealthy man, perhaps even a legitimate businessman.

But just at the moment when Frank's talents and skills were growing apace an event occurred which was to change everything for him—and for lawbreakers throughout the country. On January 16, 1920, the Prohibition Amendment went into effect.

"It was," Frank once told me, "a whole new ball game. And we owned the ball."

Frank Costello was then twenty-nine.

Until prohibition, crime had been centered in local gangs. Organized crime began with that amendment—because never in history was there such a *need* for criminals to organize: smuggling whiskey into America was not a one-man enterprise. Whole fleets of ships, great convoys of trucks, warehouses, island bases off Newfoundland, even armed planes would eventually be needed to channel the flow of illegal alcohol past the stern guardians of the "saloonless nation" envisioned by the drys.

Never in history would crime be so popular; never would it be so cheered on by the people. A Hearst reporter named Damon Runyon found a new world in a restaurant called Lindy's, and soon characters like Hot Horse Herbie, Feets Samuels, and Nathan Detroit—based on real gangsters—became almost respected.

Frank Costello was quick to grasp this new opportunity, and soon, as he recalled later, he was in the middle of the action.

Great sea battles (never recorded, of course, in history texts alongside Lord Nelson) were to take place between armed smuggling ships and Coast Guard cutters, occasionally joined by seaplanes owned by the smugglers, armed with machine guns. Frank Costello bribed the Coast Guardsmen, but he couldn't bribe them *all*. And those who stayed honest wreaked havoc on his fleet when they could. Once Frank's brother gave him the bad news that one of his ships had hit an iceberg. Frank said, *"Too bad I can't buy the icebergs."*

But millions and millions of dollars were to be made, and suddenly the whole underworld was in a ferment. Who would rise to the top? Who would control and own the lion's share of this fantastic influx of gold? Gangs and families were formed expressly for bootlegging—many of them preying on each other, hijacking each other's truck convoys. Great underworld wars began. In Chicago Al Capone, whom Frank always hated, began a reign of terror, murdering and maiming.

Blood was spilled daily, and in New York the great names were Dutch Schultz, the brewery baron and numbers king, Arnold Rothstein, the underworld financier, Legs Diamond and Mad Dog Coll, two pathological killers who operated independently.

Young Frank Costello was almost totally unknown, but all he was doing was making more money than anyone else.

BOOK II
Bootlegging Battles
and Mafia Wars

1

Late in 1925 a man named Joe Millstein came to my office. He
was one of the fifty-two men arrested for bootlegging in what
was described as "the greatest roundup in the history of prohibition."

Millstein, whom I had once successfully represented in a
police bribery attempt, was small fry, merely one of the guards
who sailed on Frank's ships. The big fish in the net was Bill
Dwyer. Two lesser names, included in the list, were Frank Costello and his older brother Ed.

The trials were held in sections with six or more defendants
in each. It was while I was defending Millstein at one of those
trials that I first saw Frank Costello, my future client. He was
then in his mid-thirties, a young man with broad shoulders and
a quiet demeanor. While the government claimed Dwyer was
a "bootlegger," it described Frank as a "purchaser." In other
words, Dwyer owned the fleets and trucks and warehouses; Costello merely purchased the illegal booze.

The government was wrong. I learned this not only through
testimony at Frank's trial, but years later in conversations with
Frank, who always spoke of those bootlegging days with affection. I listened to fascinating stories, too, from a colorful character named Jim O'Connell, who was one of Frank's seagoing
captains, and who never tired in his later years of spinning
yarns about those wild days. It was in that era that Frank Rizzo,

the young Professor, arrived from Italy and came into Frank's employ. He soon became one of Frank's top administrative assistants.

If the phrase "administrative assistant" seems overly formal to use in connection with bootlegging, let me point out that Frank's operation was organized exactly like a corporation, with departments and staffs for all phases of the business. Not that these departments weren't unusual. Operating out of an office Frank leased at 405 Lexington Avenue, the "business" had a traffic department, a distribution department, a corruption department to handle bribery, a defense department employing gunmen to cope with rivals, and even an intelligence department to keep an eye on what prohibition enforcement agencies were doing.

In such a businesslike structure we can glimpse the approach to crime that was to raise the unknown Costello so rapidly toward the top of the criminal hierarchy. Underworld rivals could not help being impressed by the smoothness of Frank's operation. And when Bill Dwyer went to jail, and Frank amazingly went free, they knew they had an unusual talent in their midst.

Frank's tutor—the man who made him the business brain he was—was Arnold Rothstein, the underworld loan shark and financier who so fascinated Damon Runyon he named him "the Brain." Rothstein knew all there was to know about business practices, ethical and unethical. It was he who financed Frank when he got started, and showed him the way to success in business; how to organize, how to cut costs—and how to cut your rival's throat, if necessary. This was a continuing relationship throughout Rothstein's life, and when the famous loan shark died the executors discovered many notes on various deals between Frank and Rothstein. In fact, it was I who negotiated the final settlement of the legal claims that arose from those deals.

But Rothstein preferred to stay behind the scenes in those wild and chaotic bootlegging days. For one thing, a man could get killed! For another, his protégé, Frank, was soon making so much money he didn't need Rothstein's help.

A little background before we enter those wild sea battles and bootlegging wars ourselves as guests of Jim O'Connell, the Professor, and Frank Costello, whose memories make up my account.

The underworld saga of the prohibition days began early and on dry land. The liquor companies, aware of the imminence of the Volstead Act, stored up millions of bottles of liquor bonded in warehouses to be dispensed as "medicinal" alcohol or for special government uses. These warehouses were under government supervision.

They were also under constant attack. When the nationwide thirst began and the speakeasies began to sprout, they were the first targets for the underworld. Big Bill Dwyer, Legs Diamond, Owney Madden, Dutch Schultz, and others soon emptied the warehouses by using three techniques: forged government permits for "medicinal" alcohol, bribery of warehouse custodians, and open attack by bands of gunmen. The profits were so enormous that bloody rivalries broke out between the various gangs, who hijacked shipments of whiskey from each other.

Frank Costello was one of the "legitimate" bootleggers. By that I mean he imported the liquor which the "illegitimate" bootleggers attempted to hijack. An unofficial partnership sprang up between Frank and Bill Dwyer, although each maintained his own business.

The rest preyed upon them, swinging alongside trucks and forcing them off the road, then shooting and stabbing the drivers while the precious liquor was removed. Frank put armed guards on his trucks, but often they were not enough.

Frank fought back, as he had to, and he had to play rough, too, to survive. How well he succeeded may be gleaned from a remark an old friend of Costello's made to me recently: "If you're writing a book about how nice a guy Frank was, don't put too much in there about the Twenties."

While murders erupted on the streets, the bootleggers saw that the legitimate warehouse supply was drying up—and the era of smuggling from overseas began. Much of the liquor would be supplied from the British Isles. Frank immediately saw the complexity of the operation ahead. A secure base on this side of the Atlantic was needed, preferably an island off Canadian shores. From there the liquor would have to be shipped in large freighters to the U.S.A., unloaded at sea into small swift boats that could elude the Coast Guard, landed, and then trucked to "drops" where it would be cut and distributed.

I was told that some time in 1921 Frank Costello boarded an old freighter headed north toward Newfoundland. He had a date with the mayor of St. Pierre, capital of the small rocky Miquelon Islands, off Newfoundland.

Frank said he chose St. Pierre not only for geographic reasons, but because it was outside both American and Canadian jurisdictions, the only French possession remaining from the once great North American empire. Canada was working closely with the U.S. in those early days of the Volstead Act—but St. Pierre was working with nobody. Frank thought he might take a little trip.

2

An icy wind tore at the railings of the ship, and salt spray whipped across the bow. Frank Costello, in a red sweater, gray slacks, and boots, grabbed a railing on the bridge and held on. He was enjoying himself. The ship had been two days at sea, and the ocean was choppy. Two of Frank's men had been battling mal de mer, but Frank was unaffected. He loved it out here on the deck of the bucking ship with the waves buffeting the bow, and ahead a limitless horizon. Perhaps, he thought, one of his ancestors in Calabria had been a fisherman or even a merchant trader. All Frank knew for certain was that the sea *called* to him.

The captain of this old freighter was a rotund Dutchman who had been persuaded to re-route his normal trip back to Europe to drop Frank and his men off at St. Pierre. Now the captain came up to his passenger on the bridge. "A few minutes yet," he said. "Then you'll see it."

He handed Frank binoculars, and Frank put them to his eyes, sweeping the horizon. Nothing. He put the binoculars down. "It ain't going to be New York, I guess," he said to the captain, who laughed.

"Three hundred people on the whole island," the captain said. "I think you're crazy."

The captain had been probing for two days to find out why three men who did not resemble ordinary tourists wanted to go to that godforsaken island, St. Pierre. Was it another of those crazy rumors about buried treasure? "You fellows don't know of any sunken ships up there, do you?"

Frank was startled. "Sunk?" he said. "Already?"

That answer baffled the captain. He said, "I'm talking about treasure ships."

Frank looked at him a long time, and then smiled. "No, Captain. We ain't looking for Captain Kidd's loose change. We're strictly business."

The wind freshened, the ship took a sudden lurch as a wave crashed into her port bow, but the captain paid no attention, even though both of them were almost flung off their feet. The creaking of the plunging freighter and the wind in their faces forced the captain to shout. "What business could you have? There's nothing but codfish up there."

But his mysterious passenger had turned abruptly to face the sea and the conversation was over. The captain was startled when one of Frank's companions came onto the bridge and growled into his ear, "Don't ask too many questions, Skipper, or you might be seeing them codfish bottoms up."

The captain asked no more questions.

3

Huddled against the fierce North Atlantic winds, the granite masses of the Miquelon Islands emerged on the horizon as the red rusty freighter bucked her way north. Frank was having a cup of coffee in the wheelhouse when the helmsman gave him the word, "Dead ahead, Mr. Costello."

The captain bustled into the little wheelhouse and spread a chart on a chest-high desk. "I don't know these waters," he said, "and I don't want to catch any reefs. Damn fishermen up here don't even use charts—they *smell* a reef."

Frank said nothing to the captain but went out on the port bridge and watched in fascination as the island loomed larger. He didn't feel like asking that idiot captain for the binoculars, but even with his naked eye he could see this wasn't a grass-green paradise. The ship was turning slowly to port to come into the protected west side of St. Pierre, and Frank could make out other islands on the horizon.

Fifteen minutes later they were chugging slowly into a lonely port. A channel ran between crumbling wooden piers, which housed a few battered old fishing schooners and trawlers with nets out to dry. The village spread up from the port; from the roof of a government building at the far end a tattered French flag was flying.

Frank paid the captain, and walked down the gangway to be greeted by a young man in a fur-lined coat. The man said, "The mayor is expecting you, Mr. Costello. Your letter's been on his desk a week, and he still doesn't understand it. Cases of what?"

Frank smiled, but said he would elaborate only to the mayor. The deal he made with that mayor was to make St. Pierre rich. Two dollars per case of liquor—and by the end of prohibition more than two million cases would have passed through one little island.

Frank often said that if there was one place on earth that would ever build a monument to him it would certainly not be America, which regarded him as a criminal, or even Italy, which considered him a native son gone wrong, but St. Pierre, where he was regarded with only slightly less affection and awe than the Saviour.

A rocky outpost in the North Atlantic with only a few fishermen was transformed within weeks into a thriving, prosperous port. It was a boom town, as Frank once remarked, "with once in a while some *real* booms!" For the men who came in on those ships were rough customers. Gray fedoras instead of sea caps (the fedoras usually held with both hands in the icy North Atlantic winds), shaky sea legs happy to hit shore, guns in holsters, and very businesslike actions when they started to work. Warehouses had to be built, piers strengthened, loading equipment brought in, and workers ferried to the island. Meanwhile Frank was assembling his fleet, a most unusual collection of ships. Into the harbor day by day sailed ancient tramp ships, rust-streaked coasters, fishing schooners and yawls, anything that could sail and hold cargo long enough for at least one trip. Most of them had long since been condemned as unseaworthy, and had lain for years in derelict shipyards. Now prohibition gave them a new lease on life, and repairs hastily made them more or less whole again.

Big Bill Dwyer liked the looks of St. Pierre, too—as well as its cooperative mayor—and his motley fleet mingled with Frank's. Each of the ships sailed with a guard of underworld types, along with her regular crew, and they soon brought a touch of big city life to the island. Saloons and whorehouses sprang up along the docks, and incoming ships often had a line of prostitutes along the rails, to be greeted by screaming steam sirens, whistles, and bells.

4

His base secured in St. Pierre, Frank now turned his attention to the problem of transporting the liquor imported from the British Isles from St. Pierre to the U.S., finding a way to get it from the ships to shore, past the watchful eyes of the Coast Guard, and trucking it to warehouses where it would be cut and distributed. There were perils all along the line.

The bootlegging era evolved into two distinct phases. Before 1924 the Coast Guard had only a few rather old patrol boats, which could make no more than twelve knots in fair seas. Frank —as well as other bootleggers—assembled dozens of fast boats known as Jersey skiffs, handy little craft measuring forty feet, which could attain a speed of twenty-five knots and carry 200 cases.

These skiffs—known to the Coast Guard as the "Sunset Fleet" —would emerge from hidden coves toward dusk, heading for the big freighters anchored outside the three-mile U.S. territorial limit.

The Coast Guard boats were inadequate to deal with the fast-moving bootlegging skiffs. Worse, the "Guard" was despised by the very people it was supposed to protect. New York newspapers daily ridiculed the Coast Guard patrols and called them "pirates." When a Coast Guard cutter attempted to stop a bootlegging boat, and injuries resulted, the public was angry.

For the truth is America loved the whiskey that came from the great line of ships which was soon dubbed Rum Row by the press. Rum Row stretched from Chesapeake Bay in the south to Montauk Point in the north, with most of the ships standing off the New Jersey Highlands, convenient to the approaches to the port of New York.

Faced with public hostility and the apathy of local authorities, the Coast Guard did little or nothing to stop the transfer of liquor from Rum Row to the shore before 1924. A look at the economics of bootlegging will show what this virtually "free" opportunity to break the law meant during those bonanza years.

Scotch, for example, cost $8 a case at the port of origin, the British Isles. If an independent bootlegger purchased a case from one of the ships on Rum Row, it would cost him $65.

The landed price for Scotch was $120 a case. But this was not enough for the bootleggers. Each bottle of Scotch would be cut to one part liquor and three parts grain alcohol and distilled water.

In sum, the case originally purchased for $8 on the other side of the Atlantic ultimately brought the State-side bootlegger around $400. And, remember, many of these shiploads contained as much as twenty thousand cases of uncut whiskey.

Frank grew so rich so fast he was soon lending Arnold Rothstein money, instead of borrowing from "the Brain." His corporate empire stretched from St. Pierre in the north to Philadelphia in the south. His fleet of ships included everything from tramp steamers to former luxury yachts, as well as flotillas of Jersey skiffs to make the runs into the beaches. Trucks rumbled day and night from these landing spots to the warehouses. And along with his ships and yachts Frank introduced a new element into bootlegging, one that was to bring gasps of surprise in the courtroom in 1926: seaplanes for air coverage. These planes formed what might be called the air wing of Frank's defense department.

Such innovations were necessary. While the legal authorities generally ignored the bootlegging operations in those first years, Frank's ambitious underworld rivals did not. The ships at sea were rich targets for pirates; the trucks on the lonely roads at night were easy pickings for hijackers.

That very first year Costello's ships, trucks, and warehouses came under attack from every direction.

THE GUNS

5

Fog curled across the waters off Montauk, Long Island, at midnight as the *Nancy*, one of Frank's freighters, made her way carefully toward Rum Row, carrying ten thousand cases of Scotch and cognac. Periodically, the freighter would sound her fog horn.

Joe Collandra, the head of the armed crew Frank had placed on the boat, couldn't sleep. The continual blast of the horn tore into his nerves. Finally he got out of bed, threw on slacks and a sweater, and went up to the tiny officer's wardroom to have a cup of coffee. The second mate was sitting there, preparing to go up to the bridge to take over the watch.

Joe said, "Can't they switch off that goddam horn?"

The mate was a big Swede with blue eyes that didn't miss much. Joe didn't trust him, but what the hell. He could take care of him if he made any trouble. The mate said, "You can't see fifty feet out there. And it's a ten-mile swim to Montauk."

"Yeah, Jesus," Joe said. "Scare me some more."

Joe went over to the little galley and poured himself a cup of coffee, black. He was standing there, leaning against the wall, when a seaman came running down the corridor outside and stopped at the wardroom entrance. He said to Joe, "Captain wants you on the bridge."

"What?"

"The captain wants you. We're being hailed by the Coast Guard."

They were in international waters, so how could the Guard be bothering them? Joe quickly went back to his room, knocking on doors along the way to rouse Mike Gorla and Al Lazzeri, the two other guards. In his room he strapped on a .45 in a Navy belt and holster, picked up a submachine gun, and then went back toward the ladder to the bridge. Mike and Al were both looking out of their doors. "What's up?"

"The Coast Guard wants to see us. Get your guns and come up to the bridge."

The great engines of the ship had come to a stop as Joe came out on the bridge. The captain stood at the rail looking out over the side. "That cutter over there," said the captain to Joe, handing him binoculars. Joe quickly looked through the twin glasses and saw a gray patrol boat with sailors and officers, one of whom had a megaphone. This officer now called, "We're coming alongside!"

The captain had a megaphone on the deck beside him. Joe quickly picked it up and shouted, *"Like hell you are!"* Then he turned to the captain, "Get this goddam tub moving!"

The cutter was starting to swing toward them as the captain said, "But they're the Guard—"

"We're outside the international limit?"

"Yes."

"Get moving!"

The captain turned toward the wheelhouse and shouted, "Start the engines." He went back into the wheelhouse and started giving orders. Beneath Joe the old metal plates came alive as the engines began to work, and the ship slowly moved ahead, picking up speed. The cutter abruptly turned parallel to the ship's course. The officer over there was hailing them again but now he couldn't be heard. Then the cutter did an amazing thing. It swung away from the ship and disappeared in the fog.

The captain was back on the bridge. Joe said, "They took off."

"They'll be back," the captain said. "I got news for you, tough guy. You're in trouble."

The cutter, like a ghost ship in the fog, could now be seen about fifty yards away traveling alongside them. CRACK! A shot. The captain ran into the wheelhouse as Joe picked up the binoculars and saw, close up, a one-pound gun on the bow of the ship. Even as he looked it fired again, flame belching from its muzzle, and this time the shell connected. A crunch could be heard near the bow. CRACK! Another shell, another crunch, this time with a ripping sound.

In the wheelhouse the captain was shouting "Stop all engines" and the PA system came alive with his voice: "ALL HANDS TAKE COVER!" while the engines stopped dead, and the cutter started to swing toward the ship again. Joe was furious. He ran into the wheelhouse and saw that the two guards, Al and Mike, looking scared, were already there. Joe grabbed the captain and hit him on the jaw, knocking him back against the wall. "Christ, don't do that!" Al yelled, jumping on Joe and holding him back. "Let the stupid Guard come aboard if they want to."

"They ain't the Guard!" Joe said. *"They're phonies!"*

Al and the others rushed out on the deck just as the cutter came alongside and grappling hooks with rope ladders were thrown over the side. Dozens of men from the cutter swarmed aboard. But Joe had it all under control. His boys were on the bridge with submachine guns and the pirates were on the main deck below running towards them when Joe started firing his gun, ripping across the deck, hitting one of the pirates. The captain, knocking him aside with a bull-like rush and knocking the gun from his hands, shouted, *"You'll start a fire, you maniac!"* And two small objects arched from the deck below, hit the bridge, and ripping roaring explosions tore the bridge apart and sent Joe screaming in agony to his knees, his arm in shreds. Five minutes later the pirates were on the bridge and one of them, the phony lieutenant, was giving orders over the PA for quiet.

Twenty-four hours later Joe was in a hospital bed reporting to Frank the news that they had lost 10,000 cases to the pirates. But an angry Frank, as always, made a plus out of the situation. For he was to remember—and himself use in the future—the device of having bootleggers pose as the Coast Guard.

THE GUNS

6

October 29, 1924. The big Ford truck rumbled in the dark night toward Hoboken. Next to the driver was a guard with a .38 in his lap. He never let go of it. A submachine gun was on the floor at his feet. In the body of the truck behind him were "hams" of Scotch. These "hams" were large burlap bags lined with straw into which the bottles were packed when they were transferred to the skiffs. There was just room enough in the back for Tony Renni, another guard, also equipped with pistol and tommy gun.

Hijacking on the roads had become so prevalent that every trip was a potential fire fight. Tony had been through three of them already. He was batting .333. Once he had been tied up along with the other guards while the truck was hijacked. Another time he had been shot in the arm when a truck was hijacked. The third time they had successfully fought off the bastards.

Tony's wife wanted him to quit—but the money! Five hundred dollars a trip and he could work seven nights a week if he wished. Of course, nobody who did would have lived through the whole week.

What worried Tony most of all was the guard in front. One of those Jew boys that Costello was always hiring from Brooklyn. A tough kid, yeah, you could see that. But a kid! And crazy.

In the cab of the truck, looking steadily ahead as the lights picked up the road, the guard, an unusually handsome young man named Bugsy Siegel, was not nervous at all. He wanted to show these wops something.

He got his chance five minutes later. There was the car across the road and Bugsy knew that men with tommy guns would be in the forest on both sides. But this time the hijackers had made a mistake. They had set up the blockade on a straight stretch of road instead of just around a bend where they usually put it. The driver was standing on the brakes, the heavy truck was shuddering to a stop, and Bugsy was saying "BACK IT UP! BACK IT UP!"

The van had skidded part way around when the truck stopped. Bugsy opened the door, grabbed the tommy gun, and slipped into the woods just as the firing broke out. The driver jerked back against the seat, blood on his forehead. Then the back door of the van opened, and Renni came out, crouching. He almost made it to the woods when a flashlight flared from the trees, pinned him, and a burst of fire cut him down. He lay groaning on the road, a flare gun thrown from his hand. Bugsy scrambled behind the trees and saw the flare pistol lying on the road. He needed it.

That smart bastard Costello had thought up the idea of posting cars filled with armed men along the routes his trucks took, and the guard in back was ordered to open the back door and fire the flare if they hit a blockade. The cops along the roads were paid not to see the flare. Frank didn't want dead policemen, too.

But now lights were playing on the body and the flare gun, and men were moving through the woods quietly. Bugsy had to get that flare gun to alert Costello's cars. He aimed at one of the flashlights and fired. Red tracers pierced the night, somebody yelled and the light beam swung wildly against the sky as the man holding it jerked back in pain. The other lights went out fast, and Bugsy fired just in time as machine gun bullets ripped the place where he had been. He ran right across the road, scooping up the flare gun, and dived into the bushes on the other side.

Breathing hard, he found the flare gun loaded and he poked it up from the bushes and pulled the trigger. Nothing happened. He pulled again and this time a flare shot up into the sky and the whole area was filled with a ghostly white light. Bugsy saw a guy coming toward him from behind a tree, surprised by the light, and he cut him in two with a burst, the man doubling over and gurgling blood. But now the hijackers had Bugsy on three sides, the bullets ripping all around him. As he lay behind a tree, he fired wildly, cutting a swath back and forth in front of him, but one of those bastards would be behind him soon.

Then he saw the headlights coming fast up the road. Costello's men were here! The car stopped fifty feet up the road and Bugsy ran through the woods toward it. Inside, he saw not an armed crew, but one frightened old guy. The hijackers couldn't see inside the car, but they must have thought it was Costello's boys because suddenly they were running toward the abandoned truck and their car. They were going to flee with the liquor, and Bugsy earned his "bones" that night. He got one of the guys on his way to the truck. Then he shot out the right rear tire of the truck. And then, for good measure, he shot the old man in the car, jumped in and pushed his body aside, and went careening up the road toward the truck and the blockade. He veered crazily around the truck and into the bushes, then back onto the road where he saw the remnants of the hijacking crew in the car just starting to move. He rammed the front end of the hijackers' car, sending it sideways across the road, turning over as if in slow motion to crash on its side.

Bugsy's chest hurt from being slammed against the wheel, but he was out of the car, and when Costello's men finally arrived they found a nineteen-year-old kid standing guard over four frightened men and a full truck of liquor, untouched.

Tony Renni survived and—as he told me years later—treated Bugsy with respect after that. So did everyone else. You had to. He was . . . Bugsy. His escort service, the Bugs and Meyer gang, was hired often by Frank. "Meyer" turned out to be a quiet, intelligent young man named Lanksy who was to be Frank's friend ever after.

7

Despite the pirates on the high seas and the hijackers on land, Frank Costello by 1924 could look around him and feel a sense of triumph.

His mentor, Arnold Rothstein, had shown him how to make money out of business, instead of bullets, and he had taken what he learned from the master, added his own innate flair for dealing with people, and built a vast empire which was making him a multimillionaire.

His father had died of pneumonia in 1922; his mother was living in a comfortable seven-room house with a beautiful garden that Frank had bought her in Astoria. East 108th Street was far behind.

He told me his days were a torrent of work and decision-making. The vast industry of moving illegal liquor through all the intermediate steps was a complex operation, with or without the thieves and hijackers. Frank said he was never so busy in his life as he was during those years.

But he always found time to visit his mother in Astoria. One day in 1924 she called him. "Frankie, I want you to come over to see me today."

"Right now? I got fifteen things happening here. Maybe tomorrow, Ma."

"Now, Frankie. I got a boy needs help—from Lauropoli. His mother my best friend in the old country."

Frank's mother rarely bothered him at the office. So Frank knew this must be special. He hailed a cab and went out to the house in Astoria. His mother was in the kitchen when he arrived, with a stubby young man who was enjoying some lentil soup and huge chunks of bread. "This is Frank Rizzo," Mrs. Costello said. "And this is my son."

Costello grunted, but he was taken aback. The young man in his mother's kitchen was attired in a frock coat, a stiff bosomed shirt and high starched cuffs and collar, a black bow tie, and white spats over high-button shoes.

"What can I do for you?" Frank asked, but he was thinking he couldn't even be *seen* with this idiot in public!

"His mother writes me a letter. I find this skinny little lamb starving—"

"Skinny little lamb!" Frank said. "He's big as a truck."

"He's starving. He just get in this country and I promised his mother my son Frankie would help him get a little job."

"What kind of a job are you looking for?"

"A bookkeeper."

Frank said, "A *bookkeeper!* They're a dime a dozen."

Maria Aloise Costello waved her finger under her son's nose. "Now you listen to me. This boy was youngest teacher in college. He's a genius. He keep the books for you."

Frank took Rizzo back to Manhattan, then had one of his boys drive him out to a liquor warehouse on Long Island's south shore. Jim O'Connell, the giant sea captain employed by Frank, had just come in on a freighter with thousands of cases of Scotch, and was supervising the men stowing it away.

When he saw Rizzo, he almost turned purple. "You can't work here dressed like that. You a clown or moron?"

Rizzo said, "I buy new clothes when I make money."

"Jesus," said the captain, "you got to be kidding in that outfit."

He handed Rizzo some sheets of paper. Spaces on the sheets indicated the number of cases carried by each man. Rizzo's job was simply to keep an accurate record of the cases as they arrived and were stored.

The work was too easy. It was nothing for an educated man to do, sitting there making a mark on a sheet every fifteen minutes. Finally, Frank Rizzo couldn't stand it any longer. He stripped off his coat and his shirt, and—bare-chested—started helping the men carry in the cases of whiskey.

O'Connell didn't complain, but at five o'clock Frank Costello arrived and he was angry. "What the hell are you doing?" he said to Rizzo. "Your job is to stay in the warehouse and keep records. Now get back in there."

"But there wasn't enough to do—"

"Goddamit, I'll give you something to do. You go in there and sit at that desk and write your name ten thousand times. That will keep you busy—and meanwhile I'll have someone with brains take over your lousy bookkeeping job."

Frank Rizzo went back to that desk and spent the rest of the week writing his name. He didn't finish until Saturday, and when he did he brought the huge pile of papers with his ten thousand signatures to Costello. Costello just gaped at them. "What the hell's that?"

"My name, ten thousand times. You told me to write it."

Frank looked at him, and then broke out in laughter. "You didn't think I meant it! I was just *saying* that!" He was thumbing through the sheets. "This is a beauty," he said. "Ten thousand times. I tell him and he does it." He looked up at Rizzo and said, "Professor, I like you. I have to admit you've got guts— and you sure follow through." He pulled his check ledger over to him and wrote out a check. "Here's your week's pay."

The Professor was so relieved and happy he stuck the check in his pocket without looking at it. The first person he went to with the good news was Frank's mother. She looked at the check and said, "Humpph. Only $500. A genius like you deserves more!"

But the Professor was having a heart attack at the mention of the figure. He hadn't even bothered to look at the check. Five hundred dollars! For one week? And all he had done was write his name.

Frank's mother took him to the bank, cashed the check, and counseled him on what to do with these new-found riches. "You always got to have some money in your pocketbook," she said, putting $100 in small bills into his wallet. "Now you go to the big wop behind the desk over there," she said, pointing to a bank officer, "and you tell him you want to send $200 in lire to your poor family and $200 deposit for yourself. Tell him that if he don't give you enough lire, I break his head with my stick. But you no tell him where you get it. That's none of his business."

The Professor did what he was told and when he returned Mrs. Costello had some other motherly advice for him.

"Now, you go to store and buy some street suits. My son almost faint when he sees you in these monkey clothes."

But despite Rizzo's new suits, Frank never forgot his first sight of the man in the frock coat in his mother's kitchen. He called Rizzo "the Professor," and the name stuck ever after, from the bootlegging days on up through the Fifties. And the Professor came to be one of Frank's closest friends.

8

The Jazz Age was in full swing. Speakeasies were booming, Texas Guinan was New York's unofficial hostess, Jimmy Walker was doing the town every night with a blonde chorus girl named Betty Compton—and Frank Costello was quietly on top of the bootlegging world, which delivered the whiskey that fueled the Roaring Twenties.

Not that he was known to the public. Far from it. But he commanded a business empire, he owned great fleets of ships, convoys of trucks, and acres of warehouses. And he ran the complicated system with absolute confidence and incredible efficiency. The underworld knew who was the boss when it came to bootlegging.

What made Frank Costello so exceptional? How did he move so high so fast? Where did he get his business acumen? What were the traits of character that drove him to the top?

As it happens, at the height of Frank's fame and power years later, one of the noted psychiatrists in this country attempted an analysis. The psychiatrist, Dr. Richard Hoffman, was my wife's cousin, and she introduced the two of them.

Dr. Hoffman attended a Tammany district leader's meeting at Webster Hall with my wife, myself, and Frank. We sat in a box, and the procession of dignitaries, judges, and politicians making a special trip to Frank's box and fawning over him seemed to awe Dr. Hoffman. He turned to me and said, "He's like Caesar holding court."

Dr. Hoffman and Frank became good friends, and from time to time he would speak to Mina, my wife, about Frank. "An enormously fascinating man," he said. "Egocentric—but with insecurities in several directions."

"What does that mean?" Mina asked.

"He is absolutely sure of his own ability, and his own intelligence. And he has a thirst for power that's extraordinary. But this thirst for power, conversely, springs from certain insecurities."

"He doesn't seem insecure to me," Mina said.

"He's not, in the normal sense," the Doctor said. "By that I mean he doesn't lose sleep or feel shame or lose his nerve in certain situations. But let's look at his background. He revered his father as a great soldier who fought in one of the most famous battles of all time. And yet he saw his father reduced to working with a pickaxe for slave wages, snubbed and mistreated and even robbed by the native Americans who worked by his side.

"And then the circumstance of growing up near Park Avenue. Marvelous. It could only happen in New York. The grimy slums right next to luxury apartments. He even marries one of the lovely daughters from the rich neighborhood next to his slum. A first indication of his drive—and his insecurity."

Mina said, "His drive—*and* his insecurity?"

"Don't you see, Mina. That right neighborhood so close to his slum life is always in his subconscious. Success . . . power . . . all that drive from the knowledge that he was the little outsider on East 108th Street, and the real world was on Park Avenue."

My wife's reaction to this analysis was, as always, practical. "So now that he's rich why doesn't he move there and get it over with?"

She tells me the good doctor just looked at her with pity. Mina would never make it to a psychiatrist's couch.

It was shortly after that incident that Dr. Hoffman made a mistake. A reporter somehow found out that Frank was being seen around town with a psychiatrist. Dr. Hoffman told the reporter that he had advised Frank that to satisfy his inner drive he "should associate with the better people in our society."

The newspaper report made Frank as angry as I have ever seen him. He said to me, "Tell that bum I already know *more better* people than he ever heard of."

He was still angry later when Edward Folliard, the *Washington Post* reporter, interviewed him in my presence. When Folliard mentioned the psychiatrist's remark, Frank bristled: "I introduced *him* to the better people."

I am less than an amateur psychiatrist, and I am afraid I may even have garbled Dr. Hoffman's analysis of Frank as he made it to my wife. But I fear my own analysis of the causes of Frank's swift success is too simple. In my opinion, he was a natural. By that, I mean he was able to adapt to any situation he was in, to see the possibilities, and to exploit them. He had a quick eye, a ready tongue, and a very sharp mind. And in the arsenal of success in any field, these are three very fine weapons.

Add to that these other qualities, as enumerated by his lifelong friend the Professor: "Frank was a man, all his friends said so, who was especially foreign, who exerted a great fascination, a volatile man, unattainable, enigmatic, and yet so attractive all the persons who went to see him were soon seduced by his grace of talking and giving.

"No one was able to guess his thoughts, all of them got the sensation that he concealed infinitely more than he was revealing."

All of these qualities were to be put to the test in the year 1924. Frank's drive to the top had been swift, but his bootlegging empire had not gone completely unnoticed by the government. The Coast Guard was ready to go to war at last.

9

Sometime in late 1923, Frank told me, he got a call from one of his men at 405 Lexington. The man was Mike Terranova, and he was head of Frank's intelligence department. In his job Mike spent most of his time buying beer for Coast Guard sailors and officers and trying to "get a fix" on what they had in mind for combating the bootleggers. For years he had received the same answer: nothing in the works.

But one night a sailor had handed him an All Hands bulletin that looked urgent. In fact, it looked disastrous. Mike was sitting at a little desk when Frank came in. Frank said, "What's the commotion?"

Mike handed him the bulletin, and Frank read it without taking off his coat, standing in front of the desk. What he read was that the Coast Guard was ready to wage an all-out war on the bootleggers—and to begin with was borrowing twenty-five destroyers from the Navy. Destroyers! With batteries of 4″50 and 3″50 caliber guns, plus quick-firing one-pounders, and large crews armed with machine guns, rifles, and pistols. Their speed ranged from twenty-six to thirty knots.

A whole destroyer force, and this was not all. New cutters, especially designed and armed to deal with the bootleggers, were coming down the launching ways. No less than four classes of boats, ranging in length from 36 feet to 125 feet, were already in production.

The largest of them could remain on the trail of smuggling ships, without refueling, for as long as a month. The smaller boats would patrol the secret inlets and bays where the rummy skiffs sought to land.

Mike was a guy who liked to think he never panicked. But a whole big-gunned fleet—with destroyers? They wouldn't have a chance to get through. Costello was stuck this time.

Frank took out a roll of $100 bills and tossed two over to Mike. "Give that to the kid who gave you this sheet. And tell him there are more coming."

Then he left the room, and Mike leaned back and, for the first time since the previous night, smiled. Destroyers had 4″50 guns. OK. The new cutters had guns and speed. OK. But they also had people.

If Mike knew his boss, Frank would be buying half the Coast Guard. The only reason he wouldn't be buying the other half is that Bill Dwyer deserved his share.

10

By early 1925 the war was on. The Coast Guard made its headquarters at New London, Connecticut, and flung its ships across hundreds of miles, forming an inland screen that seemed impenetrable. Rum Row, off Montauk, Long Island, was the first to suffer.

Destroyers took station day and night abaft the line of ships. By night they kept their searchlights on the ships so that no skiffs could slip alongside and start loading.

Behind the line of destroyers, closer to shore, were the various types of cutters of all speeds and weaponry. Time and again a daring skiff would try to outsmart or outrun the Guard; time and again red tracers would spear the night and set the boats aflame.

Rum Row was dead. No longer would smuggling ships steam serenely to a spot beyond the three-mile territorial limit and wait for the skiffs to come at night, because the skiffs wouldn't come. And each bootlegging ship that reached Rum Row was identified, shadowed, and kept track of on a huge map at Coast Guard headquarters.

From now on smuggling would have to be done as it was in Colonial days, when rummies eluded the king's excise officers. Freighters would arrive alone, to be met at a designated spot and unloaded in minutes. And for this new phase Frank had a surprise for the Coast Guard: his own fleet. In Nova Scotia he was building rummies of a new character. They had low free-boards to reduce visibility and were supplied with engines that could attain speeds up to seventeen knots. The new ships, 160 feet long, could carry fifteen thousand cases. All of them sailed with the most modern radio equipment.

And this equipment was used. Frank set up clandestine radio stations along the U.S. shoreline which directed the movements of the smuggling ships at all times, and kept them advised of Coast Guard activity.

These new boats were fast and highly maneuverable. But the destroyers could match them, with help. What would happen was that a destroyer, sighting a speeding rummy, would radio to a flotilla of cutters lying offshore, and dozens of boats would converge on the outlaw. When they did, Frank often had a surprise for them.

One of the Coast Guard officers involved in such a surprise, Commander Thomas Backer, told federal investigators this story, and I heard it later from Frank. It was one of his favorites.

THE GUNS

11

Dawn and the bow lookout on the Coast Guard destroyer gave a shout over his radiophones: "Speedboat on the starboard bow. Looks like a rummy, sir."

Lieutenant O'Dow was the officer of the deck. When his radio man gave him the message he took his binoculars and saw one of Costello's fast new boats about a mile ahead, racing toward shore ten miles away.

O'Dow ordered engines ahead full, then called down to wake the commander. By the time Commander Backer got up to the bridge, O'Dow was in full pursuit of the rummy, cutting off the angle to shore.

The commander had on a weather breaker and his usually salty blue cap, tilted slightly. Backer was considered one of the real gung-ho boys in the Coast Guard. So far he had had three "kills" in only two weeks on station, which the crew represented by painting small boats on the side of the bridge. Now Backer smelled his fourth.

He took over the bridge while O'Dow sent radio messages to headquarters alerting the inshore patrol cutters of the location and speed of the rummy. But Backer knew it would be up to him this morning, because at the rate that rummy was going he would reach shore before the other boats could arrive on the scene.

The destroyer was drawing closer to the rummy every minute, black smoke belching from her four stacks as every engine strained to the utmost. Backer had sounded general quarters and all hands were at gun stations. Now he passed the word to a 3"50 crew. "Fire across his bow."

The crew went to work, slamming a shell home, and then the gunner swung the 3"50 into an approximate line—and flame erupted from the muzzle. A few seconds . . . and a splash on the other side of the speeding rummy. But no change in its speed and direction.

By now Commander Backer's binoculars showed him the full story. The "hams" of liquor were right on deck, stacked for immediate unloading under the new bootlegging tactics of instant unloading and departure. He also saw the name of the boat: *Elise*. Then he moved his binoculars to the little bridge of the rummy boat—and almost dropped them. Some thug in an open white shirt was *thumbing his nose at the destroyer!*

Commander Backer was not only a loyal, indeed, an eager Coast Guardsman—he was also a man who didn't drink. To the horror of his crew he never let them enjoy one drop of the "booty" they picked up in their kills. As Backer was always quick to say to his superior officers, he hated the rummies not only as criminals but for what they were doing to his country. And now right in front of him one of these illiterate gangsters, thinking his boat was too fast for the Guard, was thumbing his nose at them! "All forward guns, commence firing!" Backer shouted to the gunner's mate on the phones. "Aim for the bow."

The destroyer had three 3"50s and two 4"50s up front. Now all crews frantically started loading and aiming as Backer heard the roar of an engine. He looked up just as a seaplane zoomed over his head. Meanwhile the rummy was beginning to zigzag in preparation for the destroyer's firing, and then—what's this?—it was turning in a wide arc and heading right back toward them! Meanwhile the seaplane made a graceful turn of its own and was coming up along their side about ten yards to windward. All hell broke loose up front as the five forward guns started firing at the oncoming rummy boat. The seaplane dropped down to a few feet above the water and then smoke billowed out of its tail. The destroyer was covered with greasy black muck and Backer was shouting to the helmsman, "Steady as she goes!"

By the time the smoke lifted, the plane was already fleeing. Through the wisps of smoke Backer angrily scanned the sea and saw that the rummy speedboat had roared right by and was circling toward their stern. Commander Backer quickly alerted Coast Guard headquarters to the rummy seaplane, swung his ship to starboard so all guns could level at the boat and blow her out of the water. Then a *submarine* emerged from the sea not fifty yards away. Planes, and now submarines! The rummy boat came tearing in behind them before his gunners could get on target and Backer heard a small explosion in the stern. "What's going on back there?" he shouted over the telephones, but the helmsman was calling up over the voice tube from the wheelhouse, "Engines stopped, sir."

"WHO STOPPED THEM? FULL SPEED AHEAD!"

"The screws are hit, sir."

Oh Jesus Christ! Backer said. This will look good on my report. The ship disabled, and here was a submarine surfacing ready to blast them out of the water for good, and the rummy going merrily to the beach, unscathed. The hatch on the submarine lifted and a fat German officer emerged, blinking in the sun.

The officer put a megaphone to his lips and shouted a word which Backer didn't catch. "What'd he say?" he asked the signalman. "I didn't get it, sir." But now the German officer tried again. Loudly, and clearly the word came over the water, "OK."

Backer screamed at Lieutenant O'Dow, "Ask him what the hell he means by OK."

"Yes, sir," O'Dow said, thoroughly rattled, and to Backer's horror he shouted through the megaphone, "What the hell do you mean by OK?"

By now the submarine had drifted close to the destroyer, which itself was floating without power. The German officer shouted, "Friends, indeed. Need help. SOS."

Meanwhile the radio man asked to speak to Backer on the voice tube from the radio shack. He had a message from headquarters. "Sending aircraft to assist you. Commandant asks to pass personal message to Commander Backer. This is the message: Pull yourself together. Positively no submarines your vicinity. Positively no aircraft your area. What's the commotion? Full report required when you return to base."

Backer read the message, shaking. Great! His commandant obviously thought he was insane, but by God there was a submarine right there, one the Coast Guard knew nothing of. Maybe it was another rummy trick. By now, totally unhinged, he shouted to the sub: "Stand clear."

But both boats, helpless without engine power, had drifted so close that the German commander could call up to them without the megaphone. Backer's men were getting ready for the inevitable collision when the German called up in guttural accents: "Greetings to Americans from Oberleutnant Hochmann, commander of French submarine."

"*French?*"

"Versailles Treaty. We train French crew on our boat. French crew *verdammt!* Engine broken."

Backer looked down at the German on the submarine and just held his head.

An hour later another destroyer was on hand, sent by New London headquarters, which now knew it had a beauty on its hands in the erstwhile eager Commander Backer—his mighty destroyer put out of action by a little speedboat, a cargo of liquor going right by his nose to land, untouched, and now babbling incoherently that it was all the fault of a German captain with a French crew.

Federal investigators who heard this story from Backer before the great bootlegging trial in 1926 could not help but laugh.

Frank Costello got a laugh out of it, too, when he heard about it that day. The radio operator on the bridge of the destroyer was his man. So was the radio operator in the radio shack below who never had passed on the original message that the *Elise* was sighted by another Coast Guard ship an hour before she got to the destroyer.

12

The smugglers faced many dangers. They were battled by the Coast Guard fleet, preyed upon by hijackers both at sea and on shore, and bedeviled, too, by the fierce cold and storms of the North Atlantic. Nevertheless, the bootleggers still managed to move liquor into the country.

Since the Coast Guard had twenty-five destroyers and hundreds of other patrol craft, U.S. officials knew there could be only one way that the bootleggers were continuing to land their liquor: bribery. This information was transmitted to General Lincoln C. Andrews, in charge of prohibition enforcement in the Treasury Department. U.S. attorneys in New York were also put on notice, and an undercover agent named A. Bruce Bielaski set out to find who was being bribed.

What he found was unsettling. Not just a few men, but entire crews were on the "take." And not only did some Coast Guard patrol boats look the other way when rummy boats roared in loaded with cargo, but, worse, *some of the Coast Guard ships themselves were used to carry the liquor to shore!*

And Costello, learning a lesson from the phony Coast Guard ship that had overwhelmed one of his boats, even had camouflaged some ships to look like Coast Guard cutters for his own use. Furthermore, his crews would masquerade in Coast Guard uniforms. In fact, the incident that broke the case wide open occurred when two Coast Guard ships passed each other and the crew of one noticed that the crew of the other did not wave, breaking with the tradition of their little fleet.

The reason they did not wave was discovered when the real Coast Guard ship hove alongside. The fake Coast Guard crew consisted of a burly group of bootleggers trying to look "salty" but not quite making it. The reason was that half of them were drunk! This crew was arrested and the "captain" was soon telling all he knew to the authorities.

The result was a host of leads which led to other bribed Guardsmen who talked, and on December 4, 1925, the announcement that the biggest ring of liquor smugglers had been cracked. Big Bill Dwyer, termed a "racetrack owner," was described as the "head of the international group." A total of fifty-two people, including the Costello brothers and my client Joe Millstein, whom I mentioned earlier, also were caught in the net.

U.S. Attorney Herman T. Stichman told Judge Henry W. Goddard that the group for whom warrants had been issued, which was headed by Dwyer, was responsible for the smuggling of the greater part of the liquor that reached New York, that they had bribed members of the Coast Guard with money and women, and maintained an intelligence service which rivaled that of the government. He said the 405 Lexington Avenue office was the headquarters of the ring. Branch offices were elsewhere in Manhattan.

Bill Dwyer was a large, jovial individual who was viewed as a man-about-town. Despite the fact that Costello's office was described as the headquarters of the ring, Dwyer was the man who fascinated the authorities. A half owner of a racetrack on Long Island and the Coney Island track in Cincinnati, he was a free-spending member of Café Society. Costello was hardly known at all. So Stichman aimed all his verbal guns at Dwyer: "This man is the leading figure against whom the energies of the prohibition department in this case have been directed." Dwyer meanwhile appeared for his arraignment smiling broadly. He wore several large diamonds.

Stichman said that the Costello brothers were on the "purchasing end" of the business. They also had bribed various members of the Coast Guard.

Frank knew that many of the facts and witnesses the government would present against Dwyer actually had to do with him. He was amused when time and again at the trial Dwyer's defense counsel objected: "How does the prosecution know *whose* whiskey was being smuggled?"

In fact, much of it was Costello's whiskey, but the prosecution —blinded by the opulent Bill Dwyer—sailed right on. Costello had his men at the trial, watching. Somehow, he might be able to wriggle out of it if he could find a weakness in the government's case. I can testify that no one was better at finding such weaknesses than Frank, something that I learned after I became his lawyer in 1943.

Big Bill Dwyer's trial began July 7, 1926. The parade of witnesses against him included some of his captains, who testified, among other things, that New York City policemen were present at several of the unloadings.

But the most damaging witnesses were the Coast Guard crewmen that Dwyer had bribed. One of them, Paul Lewis Crim, of CG 203, said that all but two of the men on his ship were bribed, and that the 203 actually took liquor into shore itself.

He and other Coast Guard crewmen testified that they had turned state's evidence after being contacted by Bruce Bielaski, the undercover agent who had been assigned by Brigadier General Andrews, the Assistant Secretary of the Treasury in charge of prohibition enforcement. Bielaski admitted that some of the witnesses against Dwyer were on his payroll. Costello took note.

In the judge's charge to the jury, he stressed the fact that prohibition, the Treasury Department, and Bielaski were not on trial here—and he warned the jurors that their personal views on the wisdom of the prohibition law must not figure in the case.

The jury deliberated for twelve hours. Near midnight it returned to announce that all the defendants except Bill Dwyer and E. C. Cochran, his alleged "payoff" man, were acquitted. Big Bill and his associates were sentenced to two years in jail, plus fines.

But Frank Costello had found the weakness.

13

Frank Costello hailed a taxi at the corner of 60th and Central Park West, and went over to the Apollo Club to meet Joe Millstein, one of his bootlegging associates. Joe had called and said he was in trouble.

Well, Frank had worries of his own now. He had spotted the fact at Dwyer's trial that most of the witnesses were on the government payroll as undercover agents, and when he had brought this to the attention of his attorneys, they became excited. If the government produced the same kinds of witnesses against Frank, his attorneys would be ready to impeach their testimony as biased—and paid for.

At this time, two months before Frank's trial, the government still had not showed its hand. Frank hoped it hadn't dug deep enough to find those big names he had bribed. Even Dwyer didn't know—this high-level kind of bribery was Frank's thing.

The doorman at the Apollo was properly deferential. A big bluff man with a birthmark that discolored part of his lower jaw, he treasured the first thing Frank had ever said to him. "Who hit you, buddy?" The doorman had told Frank it was a birth-mark, and Frank had said, "We can't take out your mother."

The bright sun glinted off the doorman's cap as he opened the door for Frank and said, "Don't touch my old lady." Frank smiled and went into the club through swinging doors, and there on the right, sitting at a table with a red-checked cloth, was Millstein.

Joe stood up when Frank got there, and sat down again as Frank eased into the wall seat so he could case the room. The Apollo served no drinks, not even illegally, but the feds were always poking around, anyway.

"How's it going for you?" Joe asked respectfully.

"They ain't got the body yet," Frank said.

"You think you can . . . take care of things?"

"Yeah, I bought the jury and the judge last night," Frank said. Joe stared at him. With Frank, you never knew for sure whether he was joking, especially when it came to bribes. But Frank was looking over Joe's shoulder. "Look who's here," he said. Joe turned and saw coming into the room the famous Johnny Broderick, known in New York as "the toughest detective that ever lived."

Broderick quickly surveyed the room, saw Frank, and then just glared at him. Frank looked back, and smiled. If Broderick only knew that he had given orders to his boys never to touch the detective, even when he went into his famous act of punching and mauling them on the street. But Broderick didn't know. Instead, Frank knew Broderick called him "scum" like all the others.

Broderick suddenly turned on his heel and went out the door, apparently on his usual rounds. Millstein said, "Some day he's going to get it."

"Not from me," Frank said. "Now what's your problem?"

Joe said, "I was on the boat yesterday shooting the machine gun."

Frank sat up straight. "At what?"

"Relax, Frank," Millstein said. "Some guy was throwing up tin cans and I was shooting them. Target practice."

Frank sat back. Millstein was just crazy. There was no helping him. He said, "So you're having a nice quiet little time at target practice so every fed boat in five miles can hear you. And you're already waiting for trial on the bootlegging business. Smart."

"Well," Millstein said defensively, "the other boys were shooting machine guns too. At albatrosses."

"Alba—what?" Frank said.

"Them big birds that hang around the boat."

"What the hell was this—Fourth of July?"

Millstein said, "I didn't like them knocking off those birds. I kind of liked them albatrosses. So I turned my machine gun on those guys and told them to stop."

"Jesus!" Frank said.

"So one of them throws a knife and it bounces off the iron mast and comes right back into his leg. He's bleeding all over the place and yelling."

Frank was still trying to be mad but it was getting more and more difficult. He said, "Let me get this straight. You turn a machine gun on a guy shooting alba-somethings, he throws the knife at you, and hits himself with the knife. I got it. Very clear."

"So anyway, Frank, the guy wants to press charges against me. It won't look too good."

Frank didn't say anything for a minute, smiling. Then he said, "The only charge you got to be afraid of is murder."

"Murder? Why?"

"The stupid judge will die laughing."

Frank did take care of it. For some reason the wounded man refused to press charges. But the government did charge Joe with carrying a concealed weapon.

Joe Millstein's attorney was a young man named George Wolf. I did not miss the opportunity to recite a few verses of *The Rime of the Ancient Mariner* to a bemused judge. And when Frank Costello's trial for bootlegging began, I also did not miss the chance to watch in action the man who had helped my client. I soon saw the law had quite a man to deal with.

14

Bill Dwyer's trial made all the front pages. Costello's trial, with his brother and sixteen others, rated little attention. This was just what Frank wanted, of course.

But almost immediately sensations occurred in court, and a criminal reporter who knew what to look for would have noticed the subtle difference between the operations of Costello and Dwyer. The very first day, for example, the use of seaplanes was brought out to the astonishment of the courtroom audience. In those days, before Lindbergh flew across the Atlantic, the airplane was thought of as a toy for air fairs and crazy people. Here it was being used by a criminal as a routine part of his operation.

The incident brought out in court was not the use of a smoke screen in the attack on the destroyer, but the search for a lost rummy ship. The witness was William R. Newman, a member of the crew of one of Frank's boats, and his testimony also shed light on Frank Costello's methods as contrasted to Dwyer's. He told of the elaborate bookkeeping done on board his ship, the *Vincent White,* and the businesslike techniques followed. For instance, to foil hijackers with false papers, he said that the "contact" boats into which the liquor was transshipped from the schooner were identified by means of the numbers on dollar bills. The "home office" in New York gave him a list of numbers. When the "contact" boat came alongside, the captain of the smaller boat presented a dollar bill. If it bore a serial number on Newman's list the identification was considered good and the liquor delivered.

It was the next day that Costello exploited the weakness he had discovered in the prosecution's case during the Dwyer trial.

Witness Newman was forced to reveal he was a spy for Bielaski, the Treasury undercover agent who had testified at Dwyer's trial. Newman's pay: $250 a week. Why had he become an undercover agent? He had had an argument with Ernest and Frank Kelly, two associates of Costello, over his fee as a rumrunner, and had finally tried to blackmail them with a letter to General Lincoln C. Andrews, the Treasury Department's chief of Prohibition Enforcement.

A witness on the government's payroll who had attempted blackmail. The point was well taken by the jury.

The pattern was to be repeated when the prosecution brought two Coast Guardsmen to the stand, William R. Hughes, a machinist aboard the CG 126, and Nicholas Brown, the captain of the same ship, who had been bribed by Costello's paymaster Philip Coffey. But first, Brown would shed light on the whole operation, some of it showing the headaches a bootlegging boss had to face even *with* the bribery.

Hughes gave routine testimony concerning the 126's activities, protecting and sometimes unloading rumrunners. But Brown, the skipper, was, well, something else. For one thing he must have found the job of his dreams, smuggling liquor. How any shipment of liquor got ashore after he finished drinking was in itself amazing. Hughes testified that their good captain was always tipsy, and Brown himself gave some colorful details.

On one occasion, he testified, he carried 350 cases of liquor ashore for the rumrunners. "I drank a great deal that day. I got drunk but I didn't pass out until I reached the buoy at Montauk Point. Next morning I woke up at nine-thirty and Coffey came to the boat and told me I was a fool to bring in the liquor because if I was going to get drunk when I did that sort of thing I would spoil the whole game."

But when the laughter subsided, Brown gave one more peek into the methods of Costello as distinct from Dwyer. And it was what Frank had been fearing. The feds had found the "big names" Frank had reached. Brown testified that he had received $1,180 from Coffey to take care of a man "higher up" in the Coast Guard. The man named was Samuel Briggs, the executive officer at New London headquarters. Brown paid $1,000 to Briggs in two payments.

So the government knew that Costello's techniques of bribery had not stopped with seamen, or captains, or even whole crews of Coast Guard ships. He had reached the men at headquarters directing the whole operation against the bootleggers. No wonder the Coast Guard, destroyers and all, had been unable to stop the flow of illegal liquor into the country.

Other bribed Coast Guardsmen testified, but then on January 13th the real bombshell exploded. The driving force behind the whole effort against the smugglers was General Andrews, Assistant Secretary of the Treasury and head of the Prohibition Enforcement Division. An imposing title, an imposing man, but Costello—with his flair for reaching for the top—had gotten to the general himself, according to the testimony of Samuel Briggs.

Briggs, a slight, sandy-haired young man, wearing glasses, testified that on November 16, 1925, he had received a telephone call from a man named John Davis, and as a result of this conversation he called up a certain room in the Mohican Hotel in New London. He identified "John Davis" as Philip Coffey, Costello's paymaster. On the following day, by arrangement, he went to the Mohican Hotel and had lunch with Coffey.

"What took place at that luncheon?"

"During the discussion at the luncheon Coffey told me . . . that the schooner *Athenia* and its cargo was owned jointly by his people—the Coffey people—and General Andrews and explained that after all expenses, overhead, etc., had been paid, General Andrews' share of the transaction would amount to approximately $2,000."

"They were going to give General Andrews $2,000?"

"Yes. But he told me that after they once got started they planned to make a trip each week, and where there were fifty-two weeks a year it would be approximately $100,000 that General Andrews would be receiving."

"This was a proposition they were going to put up to General Andrews?"

"No sir—as I understand it, the proposition had already been *made*."

The general was immediately contacted after this testimony, and laughingly denied the story. "My only connection with the rum rings is to put them all in jail," he said.

If that was so, his headquarters in New London wasn't much help. Briggs, the executive officer, made certain that the Coast Guard ships bribed by Costello were assigned to secret locations to give the rumrunners a friendly welcome on their arrival from St. Pierre, while the unbribed Coast Guard cutters were dispatched to locations far away from the area.

As a result of this testimony, Frank was a worried man. The prosecution had uncovered *everything*. All he had going for him was the weakness he had discovered in the government's case. On cross-examination, each of the government witnesses was asked whether he was now—and had been—paid as an undercover agent by the Treasury Department's Bielaski. All but one were forced to admit it was so.

And with the bibulous Captain Nicholas Brown, Frank got a windfall. On cross-examination, Brown said that he had been chained in irons in the brig of the Coast Guard ship *Seneca* until he agreed to testify for the government.

Juries are always suspicious of witnesses who are in the pay of the prosecution, as well they should be. Here Frank engineered a master stroke to emphasize this point, one, I believe, only Frank would have thought of. Into court the next day came one of the defendants, Frederick J. Lewis, with a scarred and swollen face, a blackened eye, and a severely cut lip. His attorney told Judge Winslow that his client had been assaulted by three men he recognized as members of the staff of Bruce Bielaski, head of the undercover agents.

No motive for the beating was offered, but there sat Lewis, battered and scarred, as the attorneys for the prosecution and the defense made their summations to the jury. The defense counsel did not fail to label Bielaski a "mysterious and invisible power who employs as agents hijackers, pirates, crooks, and bribe takers." He pointed out that almost without exception the witnesses had admitted they were on Bielaski's undercover staff. Dropping his voice almost to a whisper, the defense counsel told the jury:

"The depraved character of the witnesses and the foul use of money in this case by the government makes it an insult to your intelligence to have to pass judgment upon it."

Twenty-four hours later the jury was back with its decision. Eight of the fourteen defendants, including Ed Costello, were acquitted. The jury "could not agree" on Frank and the others.

The government attorneys were furious. They announced they would bring Costello to trial again.

But funny things happened. Delay followed delay. The witnesses against Frank somehow disappeared. And when the government some years later finally announced itself ready to proceed to trial, it was discovered that the entire file on the case, with all the evidence, had vanished.

A day in December, 1943. I sat with Frank in the Waldorf Grill, enjoying broiled bluefish and white wine. Whether it was the seafood or the wine, I don't know, but I suddenly remembered Joe Millstein, the albatross defender.

"You ever hear from Joe Millstein?" I asked.

"Yeah, he's around," Frank said.

"Give him my regards. I was his lawyer on that albatross case."

Frank looked at me, and started laughing. "I almost choked when he told me. How did the judge hold up?"

"He let him off with a hundred-dollar fine. What did you expect after that crazy story? The judge told me he thought he should condemn Joe to read *The Rime of the Ancient Mariner* a thousand times."

"Who the hell was that?" Frank asked.

"A man in a poem who says albatrosses bring bad luck."

"I got to read it," Frank said, and gave me a wink. Frank never stayed up too many nights reading books. I smiled, but I was remembering something else, too.

"What happened on your trial?" I asked him (as if I didn't know!). "It was a hung jury, wasn't it?"

"Yeah," Frank said rather proudly. "I hung it."

Frank told me the jury voted eleven to one for conviction "but I owned the one."

"What's taken the government so long to retry the case?"

"The witnesses ain't in the telephone book these days, and the file kind of got lost."

I didn't bring up the matter of the judge in the case, the Honorable Francis A. Winslow. Whether Frank got to him also, I don't know, but it is a fact that two years later Judge Winslow was forced to resign after a House Judiciary Committee had charged him with "general corruption, collusion, favoritism, oppression and judicial misconduct."

Frank's case was cited.

15

Frank's success in beating the rap when everyone in the underworld knew he was guilty was a turning point in his career. The mystique of Frank Costello grew. By then he was a millionaire, with business booming. His businesslike methods of operation made many Mafia and other underworld associates rich, too. "Everybody gets his share," was Frank's often-quoted motto.

But prosperity was wreaking havoc in the Mafia at the same time. Too much money was at stake; ambitious underworld chiefs quarreled and then assassinated and then quarreled again. Frank would have preferred to ignore this strange and fruitless warring. But he knew that the violence, if it kept escalating, would eventually bring a public reaction far different from his popular support at the bootlegging trial.

Bodies were falling all over Chicago as Al Capone battled Dion O'Banion. In New York the Mafia chieftains were engaged in a mortal battle for supremacy. Frank knew he could only save his own business, and his own skin, by trying to mediate their violent quarrels, and bring the same efficient techniques he had used in bootlegging to the rest of the criminal world.

At the moment none of the underworld chiefs wanted to listen. They were too busy plotting against each other's lives.

16

The first big-time criminal I ever had any dealings with was Johnny Torrio, whose case brought me a great deal of publicity. Torrio sought to obtain the legal services of Max D. Steuer, who was secretary of Tammany Hall and a noted trial lawyer of both civil and criminal cases.

This was in 1939, and Steuer, not wishing to get mixed up in Torrio's case, recommended me to Torrio. I was not in Mr. Steuer's income tax bracket, and readily accepted the assignment.

But as I was to do with all defendants I represented—including Costello—I urged Torrio to tell the truth, and, what was worse from his standpoint, pointed out the truth to *him!* The charge was income tax evasion, and Torrio wanted to plead not guilty. I told him that the evidence in the case against him was overwhelming, and he should plead guilty and hope for a lesser sentence.

After we had both consulted with Steuer, Torrio did as I told him and received a reduced sentence, serving, as I remember, about three years. He then permanently retired to Brooklyn to live a quiet life with his wife.

But from 1920 until 1939 Johnny Torrio had had quite a life, a career that merged with Costello's, and reached its summit in a boardwalk hotel in Atlantic City in 1929. It has been suggested in the press that Frank Costello is "the real godfather" of the Mafia. If that is the case then Johnny Torrio, the Brooklyn boy who went to Chicago in 1920, was "the great-godfather." In fact, when Costello called together the great peace conference in Atlantic City's President Hotel in May, 1929, Torrio was at his side as the conference's elder statesman.

It was a conference that came at the end of a decade filled with blood, ironically much of it Torrio's fault. For he was the man who brought Al Capone to Chicago as his "muscle." The "muscle" soon grew too strong for the "brain" that was supposed to control it.

In fact, "Scarface" Al Capone was the symbol of what has been called the lawless decade. All through the Twenties it was Capone's name that frightened ordinary citizens. And it was his city, Chicago, that got the name of Mobtown, a city so violent that even Lucky Luciano called it "a real goddam crazy place. Nobody's safe in the streets."

Because of Capone, Torrio would be a "man without a city" before the decade was out. And when Torrio returned to New York, it would be Frank Costello who saw that the violence in Chicago would ruin the underworld in New York. Enraged officials and the citizenry at large made no nice distinctions between Chicago and New York gangsters. After Capone started killing, they wanted all "gangsters" put away.

And so it was Chicago which eventually forced Costello to abandon his hoped-for behind-the-scenes role and come to the forefront in underworld leadership. He was smart enough to know it was a question of survival, and when things reached that point, Costello would show what a man, and what a diplomat, he was.

It is a strange story that begins with a phone call from the Chicago crime boss, Big Jim Colosimo, sometimes known as Diamond Jim. The call was to Johnny Torrio in Brooklyn, and the message was that Big Jim needed help.

Big Jim Colosimo was having trouble with an outfit called the Black Hand. The members of this group were extortionists, preying on Italian citizens with threats of kidnapping and murder. No one was sacred, not even the boss of crime.

Torrio went to Chicago and within a few months had the situation under control. A few well-placed informers, some shots in the night, some bodies disappearing into Lake Michigan, and the Black Hand stopped troubling anybody.

Big Jim was impressed with this eastern talent, and he gave Johnny the go-ahead to import some more of his boys. One of the first men Johnny thought of was Al Capone, then a bouncer at Frankie Yale's Harvard Inn on Long Island.

He brought Al to Chicago as his lieutenant and bodyguard. For special jobs, where out-of-town talent was needed, Torrio would use Frankie Yale.

In those days Yale was regarded as a "comer." Only twenty-five years old, he already was head of the Unione Siciliano, a charitable organization that included many Italian gangsters. For profit Frankie provided thugs with baseball bats to either side of a labor dispute, acted as a prizefight manager, and owned a stable of racehorses.

But all of Yale's business from racehorses to nightclubs was secondary to the real reason for his success: violence. Frankie even owned his own funeral parlor to take care of the bodies.

In May, 1920, Frankie Yale got a message from his old Brooklyn buddy, Johnny Torrio. The bloody underworld wars of the Twenties were about to begin and Frank Costello, fighting to stay out, would be in the middle of the climactic violence.

THE GUNS

17

As his bride later told the story, on May 11, 1922, Big Jim Colosimo, Chicago's Boss of all Bosses, woke up between crisp cool sheets. The smell of bacon and eggs being cooked in the kitchen told him once again that he was on his honeymoon.

Big Jim and his new bride had been back in Chicago a few days, but his wife felt they were still on their honeymoon.

A large, hulking man in his pajamas, Jim got out of his bed and went straight through the living room into the kitchen, where his wife, Dale Winter, was making breakfast.

Dale had been a singer in a church choir, and when she had come into Big Jim's club, the famous Colosimo's Restaurant, looking for a job, Jim had been fascinated. She was so young, so . . . untouched. Dale had been hired immediately, and soon the town was alive with the news that the boss had flipped over a little "choir kid." Jim heard the talk later on and he heard the complaints that he wasn't paying enough attention to the business, that he had gone "soft." But, as he told his wife, he would show them who was soft.

Dale looked up in surprise as he came into the kitchen. She was a natural blonde with lovely green eyes, and a pert way about her that drove Big Jim up the wall. And she was nice. Now she said, "You big hunkie. I wanted to serve you breakfast in bed."

"I want *you* in bed," Jim said. "Coffee I can get at the office."

Dale laughed and started to put some scrambled eggs on a dish, and then dropped the dish when Big Jim suddenly gave her a bear hug, kissing her on the back of her neck. The dish broke and eggs went all over the place. "Look what you've done," Dale said, but she had to smile. Big Jim, the ferocious gangster, feared by everyone, acted like a teen-ager with her. He couldn't get *enough*.

She had turned around and they were kissing when the telephone rang in the living room. "Forget it," Jim said, but Dale couldn't stand the continued ringing. She broke away and went to answer it, Jim padding along after her. It was Johnny Torrio, Jim's lieutenant, on the phone. She recognized right away the coldness in his voice. Torrio didn't like her. In fact, when Jim had mentioned his plans to marry Dale, all that terrible little man had said was, "It's your funeral."

And now after she handed the phone to her new husband she knew Torrio was bugging Jim. She could tell by the way the muscles in Jim's cheeks were twitching, as they always did when he was irritated. He hung up. "Got a delivery of two truckloads at the club at four o'clock," he said.

"Why can't Torrio take the delivery?" Dale asked.

"It's a special shipment of whiskey from Canada, and the boys will only deal with me," Jim said.

Colosimo's Restaurant was the most famous nightclub in the city. Movie stars, politicians, athletes, and celebrities from everywhere made it a point to stop there when they were in Chicago. The illegal booze was the best; beautiful girls aplenty came from Big Jim's far-flung panoply of whorehouses; and the prospect of rubbing shoulders with real gangsters was alluring.

At night Jim reigned as the king, a giant of a man dressed in the height of fashion, with diamonds glinting from his fingers. Stopping at tables occupied by elegantly gowned ladies and tuxedoed men who were on a slumming tour, he would call for champagne on the house, while afar off on the stage his chorus girls kicked their pretty legs, and laughter rang through the club.

But now on a gray afternoon the café was practically deserted. Big Jim got there precisely at four, wearing a homburg and a bright red rose in his lapel. He found no trucks. Tired of waiting in the lobby, he went back into the club and found the assistant manager scurrying around while some cleaning ladies got ready for the evening's rush. He talked to the manager, but his ear was listening for the phone. Surely Torrio would have called him if the shipment had been delayed for some reason.

By four twenty-five he was obviously furious. He left the employees, telling them he was going home. He walked past the deserted little tables of the club until he reached the door to the vestibule, then pushed the door open, and strode through the lobby toward the street exit.

Frankie Yale came out of the cloakroom behind Jim with a .38 pistol in his hand. He fired once, twice. The first bullet entered just beneath Big Jim's right ear, tearing through his brain. His big body lurched sideways, and then forward, and Big Jim plunged to his death on the porcelain tiles of the nightclub lobby, blood running gently from beneath his ear.

A few hours later the Chicago police apprehended Frankie Yale about to board a train bound for New York. Frank said he was in Chicago on a friendly visit, and the authorities, with no evidence, had to let him go.

The boss was dead, and it was a death that would affect the career of Frank Costello, hundreds of miles away. For the new boss, Johnny Torrio, would have trouble in the ranks—and in the end it would be Costello he turned to.

18

Big Jim Colosimo's demise brought Johnny Torrio, who wept at his funeral, to power. Johnny, a dandy little fellow with dainty hands and feet, had hired stocky, muscular Al Capone for the "heavy" work.

Frank told me he liked Torrio. "He's reasonable," he always said. But Capone was another matter. Even though all of his life Frank, the diplomat, managed to stay on good terms with the Chicago killer, he disapproved of Capone completely.

"We were all raking it in in the Twenties," he said to me once, "and Capone's got the feds excited. For what? Stay quiet, do your business, and everything's set."

Capone's first move as Torrio's deputy was to take care of the leader of Chicago's rival syndicate, an Irishman named Dion O'Banion. O'Banion had an unusual "front"—a florist shop from which he regularly sent out wreaths to demolished rivals, complete with cards stamped "Deepest regrets."

But the next wreath from that shop would be for his own funeral. On November 10, 1924, O'Banion was trimming some roses, humming softly, when a Cadillac sedan drew up to the curb outside. Out of it stepped an old friend, Frankie Yale, back in Chicago for another visit. He was accompanied by two heavyset men.

O'Banion went to the door to greet them. "Hey, Frankie," he said. "Long time no see."

A clerk in the florist shop was straightening up some ferns. They had a big order for a wedding on the North Side that afternoon. O'Banion told his employee to go in the back room while he talked to his friends, surrounded by roses and peonies and chrysanthemums.

O'Banion held out his hand to shake Frankie's. The next thing he knew his hand was gripped like iron and his arm jerked forward, and he stumbled into Yale's arms while the two other thugs had pistols out blazing bullets into his head. Dion O'Banion crashed among vases of white peonies, spraying them with droplets of blood.

This hit against the rival chief of crime in Chicago was not Johnny Torrio's idea—but Al Capone's. It was Capone's signal that he was in charge. Torrio tried to make peace across the city, but he was powerless. The war that broke out on Chicago's streets claimed more than five hundred lives before it was finished. Torrio himself lasted only two and a half months. Then, on January 24, 1925, he made what he said to me years later was "a small mistake." He helped his wife with some packages.

THE GUNS

19

Mrs. Ann Torrio said to her husband, "Take the two long boxes, John. Michael will be able to handle the rest."

They were standing in front of their apartment house,

Michael, the chauffeur, reaching inside the limousine to get the things Mrs. Torrio had bought that afternoon on a shopping trip. She and the chauffeur had picked Johnny up on the way home.

Johnny encouraged his wife to make these shopping trips because she deserved the best things in life. Everyone in Chicago knew she was devoted to her husband, whom she always called "the greatest husband in the world," despite the fact that Johnny owned the largest string of whorehouses in the Windy City.

Now Johnny said, "You strong enough, Mike?" Mike came out of the car with four huge boxes. He said to his employer, "She bought half the fifth floor."

"I did not." Ann laughed, as Johnny reached in and got the two remaining boxes. He cradled them in his arms, sideways, and the three of them in single file started walking toward the apartment house door. That was when the Cadillac limousine drew up.

Two men jumped out with machine guns, and a firestorm of bullets jerked Johnny's body off his feet. The packages went flying. Bullets poured into his face, his chest, his groin, his arms. His wife screamed and began pulling him by the arms on his stomach toward the house. The two gunmen saw him inert, blood spurting from several wounds, and they turned and ran to the car where two getaway men waited. The wheels of the car spun on loose gravel, and the car roared off. Johnny, lying on the pavement, kept repeating, "Mamma mia, mamma mia."

Johnny Torrio was wounded in so many places that three surgeons had to operate on three areas at once. Incredibly the little man lived. Johnny managed to get two ideas across: One, he knew who had shot him but he would never tell. And two, he was retiring.

Johnny Torrio left Chicago to Capone and came home to Brooklyn, a premature elder statesman. One of the first men he contacted in New York was Frank Costello. Frank set him up in a little bootlegging business.

He could afford to be generous. With his far-flung bootlegging organization funneling millions into his pockets, Frank was already esteemed as the shrewdest—and the richest—gangster in New York. He was above those far-off Chicago feuds and the

New York Mafia rivalries. But events were to catch him up in their swirl.

20

In the mid-Twenties the New York underworld was chaotic. It was a time when the Mafia was a small organization, and independent Jewish and Irish operators dominated the scene.

Frank was then one of the sub-capos in Joe Masseria's family in Manhattan, the branch of the Mafia that was the largest and best organized. Others in the family were Salvatore Lucania (Lucky Luciano), Vito Genovese, Albert Anastasia, Joe Adonis, Anthony Anastasia, Carlo Gambino, and Willie Moretti. Ciro Terranova, the "Artichoke King," ruled the Bronx. Frank Yale held sway in Brooklyn.

But in those days Arnold Rothstein, Dutch Schultz, Legs Diamond, Owney Madden, and Bill Dwyer were the names the public knew as criminal leaders. The small, tightly knit Mafia was virtually unknown to the public. Joe Masseria, "the Boss of all Bosses," lived most of his career in the shadow of these more glamorous names, and was probably happy to do so.

In 1922 Joe Masseria thought his position was in danger from a rival, Umberto Valenti. For a year they exchanged assassination attempts which bordered on comic opera—until Valenti eventually went down.

To emphasize how small an operation the Mafia was in those years, compared to its emergence into big-time crime less than a decade later, it is only necessary to point out that on the first assassination try at Valenti, Joe, "the boss" himself, was in on the gunplay, stationing himself in a doorway with two associates at 194 Grand Street, not far from police headquarters. When Valenti and one of his men, Silva Tagliagamba, came down the street the Masseria people fired. Valenti and Tagliagamba returned the fire as citizens dove for cover behind parked cars and bullets zinged across the crowded street. Only Tagliagamba was wounded. Masseria, with little dignity, raced down the street, ditching his revolver. He ran straight into the arms of a policeman who hit him over the head with a nightstick.

Tagliagamba died, but somehow Masseria was never brought to trial for the murder, despite the many witnesses. Who was paid off we will never know, but Umberto Valenti understood what was happening. Masseria was going to go free. Well, he would pay for it.

THE GUNS

21

August 9, 1922, was a hot day in New York. Joe Masseria looked at his new straw hat before putting it on in the vestibule of his home at 80 Second Avenue.

He surveyed himself in the mirror, tipped the hat to the proper jaunty angle, and strolled outside, turning north toward Fifth Street.

He was walking into a trap! Two of Valenti's killers waited in a coffee shop on his route. Two other thugs were in a limousine parked up the street.

Swinging happily down the street, Joe suddenly saw two men leap out of the limousine and come running toward him with drawn guns. He turned to flee, and saw two other killers behind him emerging from a coffee shop with pistols in their hands.

One of the men in front of him was already firing; Joe saw a millinery shop next to him and plunged into it. One of the gunmen came inside to finish the job. The proprietor of the shop, Fritz Heiney, froze in horror.

"The man with the revolver came close to the other fellow and aimed," Heiney said later. "Just as he fired the man jumped to one side. The bullet smashed the window of my store. Then the man fired again and the fellow he aimed at ducked his head forward. This shot went into the wall. The man fired again, the other fellow ducked his head to the side, and the bullet made another hole in my window."

Twice again the killer fired at the bobbing head of Joe Masseria, unable to hit him from a few feet away. The killer was unnerved! It couldn't be happening! But a final click told him his gun was empty. People were racing toward the scene, and he had to run out of the store leaving an unharmed Joe Masseria.

The killers were so mad that when the getaway car was stopped by the crowd they fired into the unarmed people, wounding five, one of whom died.

By the time police found Masseria he was in his apartment, sitting forlornly on the side of his bed, his aching feet in a pan of warm water, and on his head a straw hat with two bullet holes through its crown.

After this experience, he might perhaps be excused for thinking he was God's anointed man. It was not to be for many years that this role of his was challenged—by Frank Costello and Lucky Luciano, a very unlikely team.

22

Lucky Luciano, No. 2 man in the Mafia under Joe Masseria, had a lot in common with Frank Costello—at least on the surface. In his heyday I remember he kept a suite in the Waldorf and, although he didn't frequent the East Side spots that Frank did or make such an effort to be accepted by the "best" people, he did dress sharply, and looked neat and well turned out. This despite a disfiguring scar that ran from the corner of his right eye down to his chin.

Frank once told me, "I never heard nobody call him Lucky, not even behind his back." And to the end of his days Luciano would snarl at newspapermen who called him that. He despised the name Lucky because, in his opinion, there was no luck at all in the incident which inspired the name. It was pure *omertà,* the code of silence of the Mafia.

Many romantic legends have sprung up about that event. What happened for certain was that Luciano was taken for the sort of "ride" from which few people ever return, and that he somehow escaped alive in the night at a lonely spot on Staten Island. But not before, according to reports, he was hung by his thumbs, his face slashed by a knife, his feet burned with cigarettes, and an ice pick plunged into his body several times. An escape after this would surely merit the name Lucky.

The question of who took Luciano for the ride was answered in several ways—romantic revenge for the rape of someone's daughter, mob rivalry, gangsters looking for narcotics, among others.

Years later when I was preparing to represent Luciano in the successful effort to get him freed from prison, I asked Frank some questions about the general character of my potential client, anything that would impress a skeptical judge. Frank gave me what he could, including the fact that Luciano "almost got himself killed on Staten Island just to protect a jerk he didn't even like." I didn't think this loyalty, praiseworthy as it was, would affect a judge, so I didn't use it.

Frank told me what really happened on that famous ride. The boys who picked up Luciano were not gangsters but cops. The way he got his wounds was simple. They threw him in the back of the car and proceeded to grind their heels into his face. They were looking for Legs Diamond, who was on the loose, and they knew Luciano could tell them where he was. As it happened, Legs Diamond wasn't exactly a favorite of Luciano's—his independent killings and hijackings had caused trouble for years—but nevertheless Luciano wasn't about to tell the police that the killer was hiding in his own house.

Hours later Luciano was found wandering in the dark on a deserted road in Staten Island, bleeding and battered. The legend grew until the wounds from a policeman's heel became fantasized into ice pick perforations, hanging by the thumbs, and other tortures.

Of the men at the top in the Mafia in those early days, it was apparent that Luciano and Costello had the brains. But Lucky was a killer, Costello was not. Lucky dealt in narcotics, Frank wouldn't touch them. Lucky had a string of whorehouses (more a hobby than a vital source of income), Frank didn't fool with such trivialities.

What brought these two different types of men together was necessity. Joe Masseria, the boss, was the very prototype of "greaser," a man who still clung to the traditions of Sicily and would someday launch a foolish and bloody war with a rival Sicilian sect.

But even more immediate was the fantastic orgy of killings in Chicago by Johnny Torrio's successor, Al Capone. Capone was on a rampage, killing everyone from Italian and Irish rivals to assistant district attorneys. The public outcry was growing. Young J. Edgar Hoover called him Public Enemy No. 1.

And still the killings went on. On one memorable occasion Capone invited three Sicilian leaders to a banquet at his Hawthorne Inn in Cicero, the Chicago suburb. After the banquet, complete with good red wine, Capone's henchmen grabbed the three men and tied them to their chairs. Then Capone took a baseball bat and methodically chopped and smashed at them until their bodies were pulp. The corpses were found with hardly a bone unbroken.

Such was the savagery of Al Capone. But now Capone was reaching even farther, right into New York. His eastern representative was the ubiquitous Frankie Yale, whose job was to make certain Capone's bootlegging trucks got through from New York to Chicago. But, for some reason, in the late 1920's fewer and fewer trucks seemed to be arriving in Chicago. Capone blamed it on Frankie—and Frankie did not exactly get a chance to defend himself, even at a kangaroo court. One Sunday, he took his car out for a drive in a pleasant residential section of Brooklyn. He did not notice a sedan moving up alongside him until it was too late. A machine gun poked out of the open window. The resulting fire not only killed Frankie, but sent his body sagging over the loose steering wheel.

Up ahead on the right was a lovely garden party, with women in flowered hats sipping tea. Frankie Yale's car plowed into the house behind them, careened off the stone steps, and Frankie's dead body came flying out into the middle of the screaming women.

Costello told the Professor some years later about the effect the killing of Frankie Yale had on the New York boys. "It was the last straw for Capone," he said. "We sent some of our boys out to talk to Al in a nice way. He chased them. So we waited."

Less than eight months later, things came to a head in a warehouse on Chicago's North Side. The occasion was a holiday—St. Valentine's Day, 1929. George "Bugs" Moran had inherited the O'Banion gang, and was causing Al Capone a little trouble. This time Al went for the whole ball game. Seven of Moran's henchmen were lured into a garage to await a shipment of illegal liquor. A sedan pulled up with two uniformed "policemen" and three in plain clothes. The "policemen" lined the Moran men against the wall as if it were an arrest, then the three others tore all seven apart with bullets from their tommy guns.

Bugs Moran was on his way to the garage when it happened, and thereby escaped. But his cry to reporters rang as far as New York, "Only Capone kills like that."

23

Frank Costello was worried. He waited nervously in the cardroom of the Neapolitan Club in Greenwich Village. He was doing something he often did in moments of crisis, playing solitaire. Right now he couldn't get one goddam ace.

Lucky Luciano came in the door. "Hey podner," he said, and took off his hat and skimmed it onto the couch. He grabbed a little folding chair and sat across from Frank. "The red queen, kid. You blind?"

Frank smiled and moved the red queen on the black king. Both of them saw the significance of the king. That was the man Lucky had just been to see, Joe "the Boss" Masseria. "What'd the big man say?" asked Frank.

Lucky pulled out a cigarette, lighted it, then puffed smoke a minute. His swarthy face, with its vertical white scar, was impassive. He said, "No deal."

"Big surprise," Frank said. He found an ace in the deck, and placed it at the head of the table.

"I think Al scares him," Lucky said.

"I say we move without him."

Lucky looked surprised. "Get everybody in the country to come to New York, and the boss ain't invited? Come on, Frank."

"I got an idea," Frank said. "What we all need is a vacation in Atlantic City."

Frank once told me about that "vacation."

24

Atlantic City in the Twenties was the summer playground of New York. The great hotels on the famous boardwalk were fronted with dazzling white beaches on which girls paraded in bathing suits ending daringly above the knee while prosperous men smoked big cigars and thought indecent thoughts.

Frank Costello sat on a bench on the boardwalk in front of the Traymore Hotel, the sun shining brightly on this spring morning in 1929. Beside him, paunchy little Johnny Torrio was consulting a penciled list of names.

"They're all in," he said to Frank. "Al brought Nitti and Guzik."

He handed the list to Frank who scanned it. Jesus, if the feds had this list! Last week he had sent invitations all over the country for this convention, and everybody was coming. Lou Rothkopf and Moe Dalitz from Cleveland, King Solomon from Boston, John Lazia from Kansas City, Joe Bernstein and others from Detroit, Sam Lazar from Philadelphia—and most important, Al Capone and his boys from Chicago.

With Frank from New York were Luciano, Joe Adonis, a Brooklyn don, Lepke, the king of the garment district rackets, and Torrio.

Frank said to Torrio, "You think Al will go for it?"

"He'll scream," Johnny said.

Frank smiled. "Anything else except scream?"

Johnny looked across the boardwalk out to sea. "That ocean is a good dumping ground."

"I heard," Frank said.

Later Frank strolled down the boardwalk and stopped in front of one of those windows where taffy was being made, the gleaming machine twisting and then cutting off chunks of the candy in front of your eyes. People inside at the counter were buying boxes of the taffy hand over fist, but Frank didn't go for it. Somebody tapped him on the shoulder, and he turned. It was Joe Adonis. Joe said, "Buy yourself a box. It may be your last meal."

"Tell me some more good news," Frank said.

The two of them walked away, Adonis with his arm around Frank's shoulder, talking softly. He said, "Capone is steamed. He thinks this whole sitdown is aimed at him."

"Yeah?"

"He's thinking of leaving."

"He'll stay," Frank said.

But in fact he wasn't sure. Capone had been Frank's big worry ever since he had gotten this idea for a peace conference to stop the wild killings which were bringing the government into the picture, and threatening everything they had built up. At this time Capone was earning $10 million a year, owned a $250,000 home in Miami, and was sitting pretty.

But Costello, too, had some credits. By 1929, at the age of thirty-eight, he was widely respected everywhere in the underworld as the epitome of what "businesslike" methods in crime, as opposed to violence, could achieve. He had made millions from bootlegging, and had even beaten the rap when brought to trial. Yet everyone knew that Costello told his men never to use guns except in self-defense.

Frank was at the height of his power—and now he must use it. He had spent many nights talking to Luciano and Torrio about what should be done. They had agreed that a nationwide meeting of all the leaders of crime should be called. The ostensible purpose would be to establish some sort of working relationship between the mobs in control of the various regions of the country. But the hidden reason would be to stop the violence —and somehow clamp down on Al Capone, without starting the bloodiest war of all.

And now Capone smelled what was happening! But he was too late. Frank, Torrio, and Luciano had been busy with the visiting delegations and they found that all of them were agreed that Capone should be stopped.

Adonis and Frank were walking back toward their hotel when a chunky, smiling man surrounded by very tough guys came up to them. "Frank, I've been looking for you."

It was Enoch "Nucky" Johnson, Atlantic City's crime boss and unofficial host of the crime convention.

"What's up?" Frank asked.

"I'm going to make you famous," Nucky said.

"I get famous with one more jury I've had it," Frank said. But he was smiling with Nucky a few minutes later when a newspaper photographer took a picture of the two of them. The picture, printed in the Atlantic City newspaper the next day, was as good a signal as any to Al Capone that Frank *was* the *real* host here.

A large conference room had been provided by the President Hotel, and it was quite picturesque. A crystal chandelier dangled above the rich mahogany table and chairs, which gleamed from recent polishing.

Now the great criminal chiefs from around the nation sat uneasily, wondering what was going to happen. Near one end of the table the Chicago delegation sat, menacingly. Frank "the Enforcer" Nitti, Jake "Greasy Thumb" Guzik, and a bodyguard named Frank Rio flanked the glowering Al Capone.

The New York delegation sat at the other end, Frank at the head, Torrio on his right. But Torrio, as the "elder statesman," was the first one on his feet. Cigar smoke curled to the ceiling as the gang leaders looked at the little man. Torrio said, "The reason we called this meeting is we have to get organized. Everybody's working on his own, we got independent guys muscling in, and that's got to stop. What we need is a combination around the country where everybody in charge of his city is the boss, but we all work with each other."

With this preface, he introduced Costello. Frank stood up and carefully kept his eyes away from Capone's. He said, "The reason we got to organize is that we got to put ourselves on a business basis. That's what we're in, a business. We got to stop the kind of thing that's going on in Chicago right now."

Not a murmur in the room as Frank turned impassively.

Frank said, "You guys are shooting at each other in the streets and innocent people are getting killed, and they're starting to squawk. If they squawk loud enough the feds get off their tails and start cracking down. And you know what that means. We got a thing where millions of dollars can be made just getting people what they want. When I was on trial three years ago on the whiskey deal, all the people were behind me. And I was able to stay in business.

"But if you make the people afraid of you, then they're going to turn the other way and start yelling at the government to clean us out. That means the Internal Revenue boys, the FBI, the narcos, and every DA in the country. It ain't worth it."

He paused. Everyone was half listening to him and half watching Al Capone's reaction. Frank said, "From now on nobody gets killed without a commission's saying so. Johnny and I have got a little piece of paper we want to show you. We're going to have a national commission with every family represented, twenty-four by our count. No boss will be attacked unless the commission says he has to go. And no button man gets hit without a hearing from his own boss.

"The old way—killing a guy who bugs you, or who's in your way—is no good any longer. If we run our thing like a business, we'll get respect and all the dough in the world. If we keep the fireworks going we'll all be out of business in a year."

He sat down. Frank could see the other gangsters were impressed. Capone was waiting for his chance to speak. But before he could, Frank nudged Torrio, and Capone's former mentor got to his feet. He looked down the length of the table at Al. "You're going to jail, Al."

"To what?" Capone was smiling.

"To jail. We have to smooth this thing over right now. You go back to Chicago after that Valentine Day shoot-out, and O'Banion's boys will be at war—and the heat will go higher and higher. We think you need a vacation, Al."

Unthinkable. Capone looked around the table at these men, none of them big enough to shine his shoes. And they were saying he should go to jail!

Nitti was leaning close to him, and whispering, "Stall them and let's blow."

Instead, Capone said to Torrio, "Tell me when I'm supposed to laugh."

But the answer came from Frank Costello. "This ain't a joke, Al. We got too much invested for you to ruin the gravy train. Make it easy on yourself. Think of a way. But we need you off at 'college' until things cool down."

Al said, angrily, "I'll let you know," and he and his boys moved out of the room, slamming the door behind them.

Al spent the night checking out things with the various delegations. Apparently what he found frightened him. He could fight O'Banion's boys—but the whole world?

And so, two days later in Philadelphia, a remarkable event occurred. Al Capone, the untouchable, who had ordered the murders of more than a hundred men, Capone who had never been arrested, was picked up in Philadelphia for "carrying a gun." He and Frank Rio were taken into custody as they walked out of a movie theater at 19th and Market streets. The arresting officers were Detective James (Shooey) Malone and John Creedon.

The inexplicable arrest brought Philadelphia's Mayor Harry A. Mackey running to headquarters to see the famous figure for himself. Later, Mackey told reporters, "He looked to me like he was running away from something."

Capone and Rio were sentenced to serve a year's imprisonment for carrying concealed weapons. The legendary "Scarface" became number 90725 in the Holmesburg County Jail.

The "inexplicable" arrest became more explicable a few weeks later when it was learned that the arresting officers, Malone and Creedon, had been guests at Al Capone's luxurious home in Florida the year before.

Not that the "arrest" was prearranged. It was just by chance, they said, that they had spotted the gangsters leaving the theater.

The fresh salt air blowing across the Atlantic City boardwalk must have seemed refreshing to Frank and those of his friends who stayed behind to enjoy a few days of sun after the conference was over. Capone had been defeated. The war in Chicago could finally be brought to a halt. A national crime commission, with rules, had been formed.

The future looked promising to the young Turks such as Costello and Luciano. But they did not reckon with the man who wasn't there. Their boss, Joe Masseria, was about to break their own New York City wide open. All because of a Sicilian feud, exactly the kind of feud they had just ruled out in solemn conference in Atlantic City.

Al Capone, doing a bit of gardening at the Holmesburg jail when the first shots rang out, must have had himself a laugh.

25

In New York everybody in crime was "going to the mattress." Joe Masseria had decided he didn't like Sicilians born in the area of Castellammare del Golfo. Therefore they must be executed.

Unfortunately for Masseria, the underworld leaders from that region were some very tough characters: Salvatore Maranzano, Joe Profaci, Thomas ("Three-Finger Brown") Lucchese, Joseph ("Joe Bananas") Bonanno, and Stefano Magaddino, among others.

Joe Masseria, "the Boss," began the war by having Tommy Reina, a Castellammarese family leader, cut down on February 26, 1930. Both sides took shelter in hideaways, sleeping on mats, unable to go out on the street without risking their lives.

Frank, a most unwilling participant, told me he had to stay away from his office and let others run his flourishing bootlegging operations. The whole situation was insane, he said. He and Luciano and Vito Genovese, another rising Mafioso, were in a bind; they weren't Castellammarese so they couldn't be accepted by that group. At the same time they were against Masseria's pointless war.

One night the three of them met in Luciano's hideaway on Broome Street in lower Manhattan, and made the decision. Masseria must go. Luciano was the superior of the other two. He would have to arrange the killing.

Masseria treated Luciano almost like a son; he had elevated the dapper young man to the rank of sub-*capo de regime,* over Vito Genovese, a man who was always ambitious. Lucky had earned his "bones" many times since then, and Joe had complete confidence in him.

Masseria told Luciano that one thing bothered him. Lucky had not stopped Costello at the meeting in Atlantic City when Frank had invited everyone, no matter where they came from, into the organization. He had even included Jewish mobs. Of course, Costello wasn't from Sicily—and that probably explained it. The only reason Masseria himself had not talked to Costello was that he knew it would eventually make no difference. No matter what Frank said in Atlantic City, Sicilian blood was all that mattered, Masseria told Lucky. And the *right* Sicilian blood! The Castellammarese were trying to take over some of Masseria's rackets, but Joe Masseria would deal with them.

But the boss was beginning to feel the strain. So he was delighted when Luciano suggested they have a long lunch at Scarpata's, a great seafood resturant in Coney Island.

The luncheon took place on April 15, 1931. It included linguini with red clam sauce, fresh lobster, rich Chianti wine. The trouble was the food was too good; Joe ate too fast. It was two-thirty and Lucky Luciano had to stall Masseria for an hour.

Joe stretched and said, "OK, great, kid. Let's get back to the city."

Lucky began signaling to the bartender, who came to their table. Lucky said, "Got a deck of cards?"

If that bartender had said no, the history of the Mafia in New York might have turned out differently. As it was, the bartender brought the cards and Luciano managed to persuade the boss that a pleasant game of rummy was just what he needed to relax after the tension of the last three months.

At precisely three-thirty Lucky excused himself and went to the men's room in the back of the restaurant. He was scrubbing his hands when he heard a chain of explosions in the front room. Four men had come in with pistols and found Joe "the boss" sitting with his back to them. Before Joe Masseria could turn they fired twenty shots, all of them into his head. This time Joe couldn't duck.

26

Frank, Lucky, and Vito Genovese, the displaced Italians, were now welcomed by the Castellammarese group headed by Don Salvatore Maranzano. There were spectacular celebrations: huge rallies in a convention hall on Washington Avenue in the Bronx, with hundreds of the faithful attending, and banquets with many toasts to the new order.

But, as Frank once said to me, "A greaseball is a greaseball." What he meant by that was that Maranzano, despite his polished appearance, was of the same ilk as Masseria. In fact, he was even more pompous. His first announcement was that the organization needed a "Boss of all Bosses, which is myself."

Maranzano announced the other family bosses. His own family he divided into two wings, one under Joe Bonanno, the other under Joe Profaci. Tom Gagliano took over the original Reina family. Philip and Vincent Mangano would rule Brooklyn (but uneasily, Joe Adonis and Albert Anastasia were in the wings). Luciano took over the Masseria family, with Genovese as his underboss.

Everything was organized at last, Frank felt, but then he heard a disturbing rumor. He was on a "kill" list—and he was in good company. Capone, Luciano, Genovese, Dutch Schultz, and fifty others were scheduled to be executed. The man who told Frank about the list risked his life in doing so. But Frank could only laugh. He could not believe such a fantastic massacre was actually being planned.

But when he saw Luciano, he was convinced that Maranzano, the new Boss of all Bosses, indeed intended to kill many of the top Mafia leaders. Maranzano's list was apparently one of the worst-kept secrets in the history of the *omertà* society. It seemed that, even with their tradition of silence, mobsters who got a glimpse of a "hit" list with such famous names on it could not resist talking about it.

Frank and Luciano discussed how they would deal with Maranzano. They knew that Maranzano could not be lured to a deserted restaurant—and, especially, not by Lucky.

It was at this time that Frank and Lucky both benefited from an association they had begun years ago—with the Jewish gangs headed by Bugsy Siegel. They got in touch with Bugsy just in time. That very day a call came from Maranzano who said that he wanted to meet Luciano at two o'clock the next afternoon, September 10, 1931, in his office at 230 Park Avenue.

Unknown to Lucky, one of the most ferocious killers in the history of crime, Vincent "Mad Dog" Coll, was scheduled to arrive at two-ten. Maranzano had hired the best.

Instead of Luciano's scheduled two o'clock arrival, a delegation of "city detectives" entered Maranzano's office, all Jewish. Two of them whipped out guns and started firing. Maranzano staggered back under the impact of the bullets, desperately pulled open a desk drawer and tried to grab a gun, but two other "detectives" were on him, plunging knives again and again into his stomach.

The killers ran outside and down the stairs, where they met a most surprised young man, Mad Dog Coll, who was on his way up. "Get lost, Vincent," said one of the men.

27

I believe it is fair to say that without Lucky Luciano, there would have been no modern-day Mafia. A vital change had to take place for Costello to rise eventually to the top. Frank would never have engaged in the violence necessary to eliminate the "mustaches" and "greasers" from Sicily, and bring the Mafia into the twentieth century.

Without someone like Luciano to order in cold blood the murder of dozens of these old chiefs around the country, as he did, the Mafia might have gone on feuding indefinitely. And Frank would have continued as an independent. The life-span of an "independent" was usually brief.

The new Boss of all Bosses was Luciano, and he became the founder of the modern Mafia, with its regional families, its rules against indiscriminate assassinations—all the principles Frank had announced in the face of Al Capone's skepticism at Atlantic City. It was during this period that Frank earned the title of "Prime Minister of the Underworld," a role which he liked and for which he was ideally suited. Let others become the boss of bosses. Frank would show the boys how to make money and how to stay out of jail, the two most important factors of underworld life, next to sheer survival.

With Luciano's fearsome reputation taking care of any possible rebellion from the criminal ranks, Frank turned to the other threat to underworld riches: the legal authorities. He had learned as a kid at crap games in East Harlem that police could be bought. He had discovered at his bootlegging trial that jurors could be reached. Money he had in abundance, and money could pave the way right up the line, from precinct detectives to district attorneys to judges.

All of these officials were either elected or appointed. Frank's money could arrange either. And so he began his invasion of the democratic process.

The Democratic Party ruled New York; Tammany Hall ruled the party. Frank started inviting Tammany Hall leaders to breakfasts at his new apartment on Central Park West. Within one year he would be so successful that he would accompany Jimmy Hines, the leader of Tammany Hall, to Chicago to work for the nomination of the Democratic candidate for President of the United States. From 1931 on everyone in the underworld, including Luciano, knew that Costello was the only man to see when the legal authorities were involved.

28

June 28, 1932. Frank Costello stood in the window of an Edwardian suite in the Drake Hotel and looked out over the skyline of Chicago. He had a hangover that was a beaut! Two days in Chicago and they hadn't been to bed before dawn. What a way to elect a President.

When you were a kid you thought a political convention was a gathering of statesmen and politicians to pick the best man to run for President. And here in Chicago, what did it turn out to be? Guys running up and down hotel corridors day and night trading votes and offering jobs and threatening political revenge just like little old Tammany Hall.

And then at night the delegates poured out into every bar and saloon in the city to celebrate what they had done during the day.

Frank smiled, thinking of that pretty cancan girl who had danced on Jimmy Hines's table last night. Hines, the Tammany leader, had forgotten politics for a moment and grabbed her foot, and the girl—garter belt glinting in the lights—had toppled onto the head of a passing waiter carrying dinners aloft on two trays. Wherever those trays had landed, they had lost votes.

Frank loved Hines. He was so dumb. For two days he and Jimmy had entertained delegates and twisted arms for Franklin Roosevelt. And Jimmy had been pleased—though not officially—with Frank's support. In fact, he probably couldn't understand why one of the top New York underworld figures was working so hard for Roosevelt, who had never promised any of them anything, and never would.

What Hines didn't know was that Lucky Luciano was with Al Marinelli, the leader of the New York supporters for Roosevelt's rival, Al Smith, in another hotel room. Luciano was putting on just as much of an effort for Smith. The boys were covering both flanks.

The door to the suite opened and Hines came in, a tall, florid man of easy disposition. But now he was angry. He said, "You're playing games with me, Frank."

Frank had known it was coming. Even Hines was bound to wake up sooner or later. He said, "I couldn't stop Lucky. He likes Smith. It's personal."

Hines sat down heavily, and looked up at Frank. "You guys will never learn. You play it on both sides of the fence, you end up with your pants split."

"Luciano says it's a free country," Frank said.

"As long as you pay the right people," Hines said.

"I never heard you complain about your salary," Frank said, and Hines thought it smart to drop the subject right there.

29

By 1932, Frank had survived the legal attack on his bootlegging operations, resurrected his organization, and was making more money than ever. But Costello could not sit still. One secret of his success was that he was never satisfied to start an operation and just watch the money roll in. He knew he must look ahead; he must plan. The great depression, which began in late 1929, hadn't hurt him much. People now drank even more of his liquor to forget the pain.

But Franklin Roosevelt was about to repeal prohibition. The very fount of the enormous profits that had changed the criminal syndicate from a small-time, gang-ridden subculture to a great nationwide business was going to vanish. What would happen to the leaders of crime families when the money stopped? What would happen to Frank?

I don't mean to imply that Frank sat down one day with a pencil and paper and wrote out what he was going to do, with "options," as they say in bureaucratese. But, as he told me once, he "had to go where the action was." And this could have been narcotics or prostitution. But, to Frank's credit, it wasn't. He turned, instead, to his own great love: gambling.

As I once said at a trial, of all victimless crimes, this is the "most victimless." It wasn't good English, but the jury got the point. In my opinion the starving widows and poor people who have been "ruined" by gambling can be counted on the fingers of one hand. The current government lotteries being run in various states today support that point of view. Instead of "ruining" poor people, it gives each of them one shot at riches or at least a happy windfall.

If I am diverging from my story here for an opinion of my own, I apologize. But knowing that most of Frank's so-called "criminal" career was in two phases, importing whiskey (whiskey was later legalized) and gambling (gambling was later legalized), I must pose a favorite lawyer's question: Is a crime a crime if later it is not a crime?

In the narrow legal view, yes. But in a broader view, in my opinion, no.

And this may be why years later, when Frank sought to become recognized as "legitimate," when he attempted to join yacht and country clubs and was rebuffed, he was so hurt. There was no time in Frank's life that he publicly characterized himself as anything other than "a gambler." August Belmont *owned* a racetrack. August Belmont banned Frank Costello from the track. I know. I was the one whom an angry Frank sent to confront Belmont when it happened.

But in the early Thirties that was all in the future. Frank began his gambling career in three phases: as a "bookie"—or as he put it, a "commission broker"—as the owner of hundreds of slot machines, and as the proprietor or part owner of gambling casinos around the country.

As a commission broker he had first become allied with his old mentor Arnold Rothstein. But Arnold ran into a little trouble. He was killed in 1928, for reasons unknown.

Unfortunately for Frank, when Rothstein's papers were searched after his death, four important items involving Costello were found.

One was a little black memorandum book, several pages of which were filled with closely written records of financial dealings between Rothstein and Costello. Alexander Mayper, the lawyer who found the book and later negotiated with me final settlement of the estate's claim for $6,500 against Costello, said at the time that only Rothstein could have explained all the entries. Costello, of course, wasn't talking.

The other three items found among Rothstein's papers were two notes and a check. All signed and delivered to Rothstein by Costello. One note for $25,000 was made payable to Rothstein's operation company, the Rothmere Corporation. It was dated September 4, 1928. The other note for $10,000 was made payable to Costello's order at the Chelsea Exchange Bank in New York, and was endorsed by Costello. It was dated September 26, 1928. The check, also for $10,000, was made out to Rothstein, signed by Costello, and drawn on the Chelsea Exchange Bank. It was dated October 28, 1928, one week before Rothstein was killed.

With his political clout in New York legal channels, Frank was able to hold off all of these matters until I appeared in 1943, and finally talked him into settling.

Immensely more important to Frank was what Rothstein's death meant: his whole "bookie" operation was ripe for a take-over by ex-partner Costello. And Frank knew just the man he needed for a front, Frank Erickson.

30

Frank Erickson was a big, jowly man who had started on his own as a commission broker, and made quite a good thing of it. Frank liked him. Later, when they both lived on Long Island, they were constant golf companions.

In 1951 Senator Kefauver estimated that about $15 billion was bet illegally on horse races in the United States every year. By that time Erickson, with Costello's backing, had become the most famous bookie in New York, earning about fifteen million of that illegal money a year.

But Erickson was more than a "bookie," of course. He was in reality a banker. The small-time bookie joints needed a man of huge finances to "lay off" their bets. For this service, Erickson charged a flat 10 percent off the top of the winnings.

I use Erickson's name throughout, but it must always be remembered, as Frank Rizzo, Frank's friend, said to me, "Costello *was* Erickson." The two of them began taking over Rothstein's operation in New York and then, with Costello's genius, expanded nationwide, making arrangements with operators in every major city. In the end a gigantic bookmaking empire was established, its tentacles reaching into every area of the United States.

And the Costello rule was always followed. Everyone gets his fair share. And it was because of this rule that the bookmaking network throughout the nation suffered no harmful publicity for so long, and managed to stay in operation for two decades. In those twenty years, millions flowed into Costello's pockets.

It was during this time that Frank became quite a figure at the fashionable racetracks. The season at Saratoga was a must. In those days the upstate New York town was a prime resort for wealthy New Yorkers; great wooden hotels with large shady porches and lovely tree-lined streets made a pleasant background for the excitement of the racetrack. Frank had a part ownership in the Piping Rock Club, one of the gambling casinos that took the tourist's money at night after the horses stopped running.

A marvelous mixture of gangsters and New York's aristocracy —that was the charm of Saratoga until the publicity spawned by the Kefauver hearings closed the casinos and the New York tracks brought racing closer to home.

Frank and his friends would take a train up from New York, and after checking in at one of the hotels would stroll around the town, greeting fellow New Yorkers. Lunch at a sidewalk café with good red wine, surrounded by dandies and their beautiful girls, and then off to the track to try their luck.

Many times they had inside information, but that did not happen as often as you might assume. I know because I frequently accompanied Frank to the track—to my own misfortune —and watched him lose race after race, betting a thousand dollars a throw. I say to my own misfortune because *I* assumed Frank did have inside knowledge and my own little tens flowed hopelessly into space with his grands.

The mention of Frank at the races reminds me of a later day when I was present with Frank at a New York track. August Belmont, the New York socialite who owned the track, had not yet ruled Frank *persona non grata*. In fact, Frank and he had what I would call a "joshing" acquaintance. The chilly aristocratic Belmont had a sense of humor.

But his sense of humor failed him when the following event occurred. Frank stopped Belmont, in my presence, and said he had a sure thing in the sixth race. Belmont said the horse didn't have a chance. Frank offered to wager with Belmont personally, even up, that the horse would win, even though Frank's horse was a long shot. Belmont enthusiastically agreed.

But the amount of the wager hadn't been fixed by the time the race was about to begin. Frank, peering around, saw Belmont in his box about thirty feet behind him. Frank held up two fingers, and Belmont nodded.

The race started, and to Belmont's dismay Frank's horse romped in ahead of the field. Frank was elated, because he had bested Belmont one on one. I joined Frank as he went to Belmont's box and watched the millionaire ruefully pull two one-dollar bills out of his wallet and hand them to Frank.

"What's this?" Frank asked.

"Two dollars. I lost," Belmont said.

"Two *thousand* was the bet," Frank said. "What are you trying to pull?"

This was where Belmont's sense of humor disappeared. Two thousand dollars was *money*. "You raised two fingers and I nodded," he said, heatedly. "I agreed to a two-dollar bet."

Frank looked at him in what I could see was real astonishment. Two *dollars?* Nobody bet two dollars. "You know what you are?" he said angrily. I was starting to pull his elbow, hoping to get him away. All of the other men and women in Belmont's box were watching the contretemps. But nothing could stop Frank. "You're a *welsher!*"

The word "welsher" has an almost deadly significance in the underworld. Next to an informer, a man who welshes on money is the lowest type of human being with the shortest life-span ahead. But it did not have that significance to Belmont. He just looked at Frank and laughed. And Frank had enough sense to turn away before he said anything else. But he was sore as hell.

Personally, I was on Belmont's side. Who, I asked Frank, would think two fingers meant two thousand dollars? Nobody, I said.

But Frank's idea was different. In *his* set, *everybody* would know.

31

How Frank Costello managed to stay behind the scenes in the Erickson operation is still a wonder to me. When Erickson was arrested years later, he was proclaimed the "King of Bookmakers" as if he alone were the brains of the operation.

Erickson would go to jail eventually. He would testify before two senatorial committees and still never once admit his relationship with Costello.

Instead, he respectfully took the Fifth Amendment in a shy, whispery voice which eventually got on Senator Charles Tobey's nerves. The "fire-and-brimstone" member of the committee angrily said:

"If you were out in the woods and the shades of night were falling fast, and the owls began to hoot, the eerie tones of night gathered around you, and you wanted a helping hand, would you speak no louder than that, or would you holler as loud as you could?"

Erickson, for once, topped the Senator with his answer, "The last time I spoke to you, Senator, I spoke too loud."

Laughter filled the hearing room, for it was known that Erickson had previously testified to a Senate commerce subcommittee. On the basis of that testimony he was arrested in New York and jailed for bookmaking.

At that earlier hearing Senator Ernest W. McFarland of Arizona had become angry at Erickson's denials that he belonged to any crime syndicate and his insistence that he operated all alone.

"You're your *own* crime syndicate, aren't you?"

"I don't know what you call it."

And this triggered Tobey, who was on that committee, too, to shout, "How do you reconcile your lawlessness? In your soul, don't you ever think this is a hellish business, that it isn't worthy of a man?"

People at the trial thought this furious statement got under Erickson's skin, because he dropped his head and muttered, "I have felt that way."

In reality, as Erickson told Frank, he dropped his head to keep from laughing.

32

Frank told me he met Dandy Phil Kastel, his partner in slot machine operations, through Arnold Rothstein.

Dandy Phil had quite a background. Before the first World War he had managed a nightclub in Montreal. Later he came to New York and became, along with Frank, one of Arnold Rothstein's protégés. Arnold tutored him—and soon he was one of New York's virtuoso stock swindlers, a career cut short when he was arrested on extortion charges and sentenced to two years on a securities swindle and for using the mails to defraud.

But Costello had seen enough of Phil's operations to appreciate his business talents, and now wanted to use him in more legitimate business. Frank had conceived a slot machine that dispensed candy mints along with slugs which could be redeemed for money. They could arguably be called candy machines. At least arguably enough to give him several years' worth of the law's delay.

Frank traveled to Chicago and made the necessary arrangements with the Mills Novelty Company to manufacture the machines, and then returned to New York to organize the Tru-Mint Company, with branches throughout the city.

Once again, as in rumrunning, Frank was faced with opposition from two sides: the law and the underworld. Once again, he prevailed—until New York elected a dynamic little leader named Fiorello La Guardia as mayor. And even then Frank was able to shift his operations smoothly to another territory and keep rolling up profits.

By 1931, Frank's company had installed more than 5,000 machines in speakeasies, stationery stores, candy stores, and other locations in New York. Frank was even benevolent to children. He thoughtfully provided little ladders so the toddlers could climb up high enough to feed their nickels to the machines.

His take was almost impossible to calculate, but he once told me it wasn't as great as the reporters thought. For one thing, there were numerous expenses and he wasn't talking about maintenance, or the cost of the machines. He needed political protection, and he bought it from the avalanche of silver that poured through the machines. He even got an injunction from a federal judge against seizure of the machines, which kept him in business in New York long after the police would have closed him down.

And to protect himself against underworld raiders he organized a private police force which won grudging praise for its efficiency from the authorities. A report from his company's files shows the thoroughness of Frank's little FBI:

Date 12-4-33
Machine No. 295632

1544 Second Avenue
Beer Garden
     Broken into between 3 a.m. and 6 a.m. Took machine, $18 from register, wines and cigars.
     Found Andy in cellar of 246 East 80th Street. This is hangout of gang. Recovered, Dec. 4.

Whether the words "Recovered, Dec. 4" should have been written in blood, we will never know.

By 1934, Frank was doing quite well. The law, in the form of the federal injunction, was protecting him from police harassment, and his private police force was fending off underworld rivals. The country, gripped in a paralyzing depression, was starving—and Frank was receiving millions in cash. Small wonder

New York's political candidates and hopefuls turned to Frank for help—such help always coming with "conditions." It is understandable that district attorneys and judges could not bring themselves to crush his slot machine empire. No explanation of how Frank became such a political power in New York can be complete without taking into account the depression, which cut off most private sources of campaign funds and forced politicians to go to the man who had the cash.

Frank, who had soared in the prohibition era, was doing even better in the depression, when an event occurred that depressed *him*. Mayor La Guardia came into office. A sparky, vibrant, opinionated man, he hated "crooks." His very first public announcement was that he was going to send Lucky Luciano to jail. Very soon after, he was announcing to 200 ranking police officers:

"I have been told that Fulton Street is considered the deadline for crooks. That deadline is now removed. It is replaced by the Hudson River on the west, the Atlantic Ocean on the south, the Westchester County line on the north and the Nassau County boundary line on the east. The crooks and the racketeers must be kept out. That is your job."

Privately, the Little Flower happily ordered his police commissioner to adopt a "muss 'em up" policy toward criminals.

There is a legend that Frank and La Guardia once had been friends but fell out, and in the argument which ensued Frank had spat in La Guardia's eye. Frank denied this to me. "The guy was a hustler," he said. "He comes in after Jimmy Walker so naturally he gets his Brownie points jumping all over me."

33

A cold wind blew along the East River wharf. Mayor La Guardia handed his light gray homburg to one of his aides and started taking off his overcoat.

They were standing on a police tugboat half loaded with slot machines. The aide said to La Guardia, "If you take that coat off, you'll catch pneumonia."

La Guardia handed him the coat. "I can't hurt my swing."

Above them the assembled reporters and photographers were jostling for position on the dock. They laughed when the mayor picked up a long, heavy sledgehammer and almost dropped it, the aide skipping awkwardly aside as the hammer thudded onto the deck next to his toe. Then there was the roar of a motor and a two-ton truck came alongside, loaded with more seized machines.

City workmen started transferring the slot machines from the truck to the dock, and soon the pudgy mayor in a pinstripe double-breasted suit was hefting the sledgehammer above his right shoulder while the photographers pleaded, "Hold it right there, Mr. Mayor." Cameras were clicking, newsreel film was rolling, and the mayor was starting to perspire, holding the hammer aloft. Then he swung it down, viciously, and heard a satisfying crunch. Again he swung. Then he handed his hammer to one of his aides who took a whack himself.

The machines were hardly dented, but the symbolism was recorded for New York's citizens. La Guardia turned to one of his men. "A picture like this is worth a thousand indictments."

A few minutes later he was on the dock facing a battery of microphones. The tugboat was heading out to sea to dump the machines overboard. One of the newsmen said, "I hate to say this, Mayor La Guardia, but what you're doing is illegal, isn't it?"

"That makes it more fun," said the mayor with a smile.

But it would not be illegal long. Mayor La Guardia's fusion administration fought the federal slot machine ruling to the United States Supreme Court and obtained a dismissal of the injunction against seizure of the machines. By May 7, 1934, it obtained an amendment to the state penal code which gave it clear authority to seize and destroy gambling machines.

But by that time Frank Costello, never a man to sit still, was in New Orleans together with the one politician in America who might be considered even more colorful than La Guardia: Huey P. Long, Governor of Louisiana.

34

There are many legends surrounding the strange relationship between Louisiana's governor and Frank. Of these legends the most picturesque was the story that Long, while spending his weekends in New York, had become involved with a woman. Some underworld characters attempted to blackmail the Kingfish, and he went to Frank for help. Frank supposedly called in the blackmailers and ordered them to lay off. In return, Long invited Frank to bring his slot machines to Louisiana.

Frank scoffed at this story, and told his version many times before different grand juries and eventually to the Kefauver committee. I was alongside him at the time. Always those who heard Frank's version were understandably skeptical. Because, Frank said, it was all for charity.

As he testified at one hearing:

"I got Philip Kastel, which is my associate, to go down there and work the thing out. He went down and he incorporated . . . [Huey Long] wanted to get himself about 25 to 30 thousand dollars per year to donate toward some fund . . . There was supposed to be a tax to the state and that tax was going to some relief of some kind."

I questioned Frank myself about this deal before he appeared at the Kefauver hearings. At the risk of being termed naive I must say I fully believed his story, even though on the surface it sounds "Kingfishy" (a pun someone used at the time). Frank was always anxious to work within the law whenever he could, and this was a heaven-sent opportunity, just when he needed it most. It was of no concern to him what happened to the percentage off the top. If it went to legitimate charity, fine. If it went to a politician's private pocket, OK too. That was the way "business" was conducted in the world in which he lived.

Unfortunately, almost as soon as Frank's machines were being set up around New Orleans, the Kingfish was assassinated, on

September 8, 1935. That was a traumatic moment for Frank. The new mayor of New Orleans, Robert S. Maestri, promptly announced that Frank's slot machines would not be permitted to operate in his city.

But two days later Mayor Maestri made a mysterious trip to Hot Springs, Arkansas, where a friend of Frank's from prohibition days, Owney Madden, held sway. The mayor vacationed there for two weeks, and when he returned he found all of Frank's machines in their old locations, and most surprisingly, he didn't object. What happened in Hot Springs to change his mind we do not know. Perhaps the mayor, like Bernadette at Lourdes, saw a vision.

By 1945 there would be more than 8,000 slot machines in New Orleans and in the Jefferson and St. Bernard parishes. The Beverly Club, a posh gambling casino operated personally by Dandy Phil Kastel, Frank's partner, was the place to go in the bayou city.

Built at a cost of a million dollars at a location not more than fifteen minutes from downtown New Orleans, the Beverly Club catered only to the upper class. Dinners ran from $15 to $20, and no gambler could approach a table with less than a $5 bet. The club was an instant moneymaker.

Somehow, Frank had survived both La Guardia's election and Long's assassination. Between the racetrack commissions rolling in from his silent partnership with Frank Erickson and the take from his slot machines and gambling club in New Orleans, he was in very good financial shape indeed.

But trouble was brewing in his own backyard, Manhattan. A young lawyer with a silly mustache was tearing up the underworld. Despite all the publicity he received, La Guardia's jurisdiction extended merely to the metropolitan police and therefore his power was somewhat limited. But Thomas E. Dewey came in with all the might of the federal government and later the state government and an unparalleled ambition for convictions. There was panic in the underworld. Dutch Schultz, the numbers king of the Bronx, was the first to break.

35

Louis "Lepke" Buchalter controlled the rackets in the garment industry. A thin, wiry, sleek man, he strolled into the lobby of the Waldorf Hotel, his shoes sinking deeply into the rich pile carpet. Luciano kept a room on the twenty-ninth floor of the Waldorf, which didn't seem to Lepke to be the kind of place for the talk they were going to have with Dutch Schultz. The Dutchman might pull a revolver and smash some million-dollar chandeliers.

In the elevator he was pressed between florid businessmen and touristy wives, all chattering. At Lucky's floor Lepke got off and walked down the quiet corridor to the room and knocked. The door opened a crack, and there was Frank Costello.

"He ain't here yet," Frank said.

Lepke came into the large, airy room with its view overlooking the East River. He sat down in one of the chairs and said, "Where's Luciano?"

Frank was sitting across from him, lighting an English Oval. After he took a puff he said, "He can't make it. It's you and me."

Lepke stood up as if he'd been jolted. "What?"

"Relax. Nothing's going to happen."

"That goddam Dutchman is flipping out—and we got to handle it. Listen, I—"

But a knock on the door silenced him. Arthur Flegenheimer Dutch Schultz came into the room. A pale, chunky, muscular fellow, he didn't waste time making his feelings known. "I hear Charlie ain't coming. So what's new?"

"He's got a problem," Frank said, in his raspy growl, which always seemed to quiet people down. "Let's have a sitdown and hear what you have to say and then Charlie will talk to you himself."

"I talk to him or nobody."

"OK," Frank said. "Forget it."

He stood up and faced the Dutchman who had never left his position in front of the door. The Dutchman said, "I got to know whether Charlie agrees."

"On what?" Frank said, facing him.

"Dewey goes," Dutch said.

Lepke came over but said nothing. Costello was as calm as ever. "That's the message?" Frank asked.

"One more thing," Dutch said. "Tell Luciano my boys saw a little list in Dewey's office. He's right at the top himself."

"I'll tell him," Frank said.

The Dutchman looked at him. "So ain't you got a message for me?"

"Charlie calls the turn," Frank said. "He'll get in touch with you."

The Dutchman paused as if he wanted to say more. Finally he said, "What do you think Charlie's going to say?"

"I tell you what *I'm* going to say," Frank replied. "Don't make a move against anybody until you hear from Charlie. This is too big for one guy, Dutch. Charlie has to see what all the others think."

The Dutchman made one last attempt. "You guys don't *understand!* Dewey is different. By the time he's finished we'll all be up the river. Total. Everybody!"

"Yeah," Frank said. "OK, Dutch. Calm down. Charlie will get to you tonight."

The Dutchman left and Lepke was looking at Frank admiringly. "Jesus, you could handle anybody."

"Big deal," Frank said. "Let's get out of here. I'll buy you a drink downstairs."

Lepke said, "Frank, what's going on?"

"Nothing, kid. Charlie tells Dutch tonight to lay off or he gets his head handed to him."

"But what if the Dutchman goes ahead anyway?"

"Charlie will think of something," Frank said with a smile.

An hour later they were in the Waldorf's Norse Grill drinking whiskey sours when an assistant DA from Brooklyn spotted them, walked over, and shook Frank's hand. "What's new, Frank?"

"Nothing," Frank said.

36

In the early 1930s, Tom Dewey came to me with a problem on which he wanted my advice. He was just starting private practice after having served as chief assistant to George Z. Medalie, a federal prosecutor and a friend of mine. Dewey was worried about his ability to pay the rent on a new apartment he wanted to lease. "It's $150 a month," he said. "I'll have to do pretty well to afford that."

I said, "Tom, you're going to do so well in a few months you'll have more clients than you can handle—and you'll be asking me to help with the overflow."

Which is exactly what happened. The reason I knew Tom would be a success was not only his spectacular, if brief, tenure as assistant federal prosecutor, but because he was the greatest preparer of cases I have ever known. No attorney ever went into a courtroom more fully briefed on every detail of a case than Tom. He was not a great trial lawyer, that is to say a lawyer who can persuade the judge and jury through eloquence, but he always had the evidence, the testimony, the legal precedents before him. That preparation accounted for his astounding number of convictions later in his career when he returned to his role as a government prosecutor, this time for the state.

Throughout his career I was to remain a friend of Tom's. Events would dictate that I was personally involved in the only legal matter which ever clouded his name, and I will show later that this was a false cloud, as I know the facts.

But that would be in 1943; now in the early Thirties, Dewey was just getting his start. He had met Medalie, a former assistant attorney general of the state, on one of his cases as a private practitioner. Tom Dewey had only recently graduated from Columbia Law School. Medalie had been impressed with the dynamic young lawyer and when he, Medalie, was named United States Attorney for the Southern District of New York, he appointed Dewey to the post of chief assistant, with sixty lawyers working under him. Dewey was twenty-eight years old; no one as young as he had ever held the post of chief assistant U.S. attorney in New York.

"I dropped him in cold water and let him swim out," Medalie said later, in describing what happened during the first few months after Dewey's appointment.

Dewey swam faster than any prosecutor before or since. Indictments came left and right against swindlers, crooked contractors, and underworld characters who up to then had led charmed lives. First to go was the infamous Jack "Legs" Diamond, the independent operator who had survived so many bullets from so many assassins that he earned the title of "Clay Pigeon of the Underworld." Dewey shot him down for good with a four-year sentence for operating a still.

Then Dewey reached higher. He found that a numbers king had been sending gifts to James J. Hines, the Tammany district leader who controlled much of Harlem. He also learned that J. Richard "Dixie" Davis, known as "the Kid Mouthpiece," a friend of Hines and counsel for the policy rackets operators, might also be involved.

With lightning speed Dewey began to probe not only the political racketeers, but the underworld chiefs themselves. His first two targets were Dutch Schultz and Waxey Gordon. Dutch departed hastily from the New York area and went into hiding until Dewey left the U.S. attorney's office. But Waxey Gordon was caught.

Waxey was a swarthy, pudgy, unimpressive man, but he had brains. He owned breweries, two hotels on Broadway, and nightclubs. His financial accounts were a maze. Dewey went after him on income tax evasion, persuaded frightened witnesses to talk, and nailed Waxey Gordon for ten years.

At this point a Democratic victory ousted Republican officeholders, and Dewey found himself back in private practice, and worrying about his ability to pay the rent. But not for long. The district attorney of New York County was a man named William Copeland Dodge, a political creature of Hines, the Tammany district leader. A grand jury was hearing evidence on the policy rackets when the members realized something wasn't right. Dodge assigned the greenest young man on his staff, Lyon

Boston, to present the evidence. The grand jury was disgusted. Its foreman, Lee Thompson Smith, led a revolt—and demanded a new prosecutor.

Governor Herbert H. Lehman stalled, but finally submitted four names from which the jury would choose a special rackets prosecutor. The jury jumped at the chance to name Dewey.

One of Dewey's first announcements was that he would track down the missing Dutch Schultz and this time put him away for good. (Dutch had managed to get himself acquitted in the interval when Dewey was away.)

Schultz by now knew his man. Dewey would send him away for thirty years if he could lay his hands on him. The Dutchman therefore took steps of his own. He posted a man across from Dewey's apartment on Fifth Avenue, and watched him emerge every morning to meet two aides and stroll around the block to a coffee shop before driving downtown. No problem, reported the lookout. Dewey could be taken.

THE GUNS

37

October 23, 1935. The Palace Chop House and Tavern on East Street in Newark was having a bad night. So far only four guests. And they sat quietly at a round table in the back of the room, so busy with accounting papers that they hardly had time to drink.

Dutch Schultz was going over his accounts. He had gathered three of his most trusted associates, Bernard (Lulu) Rosenkrantz, Abe Landau, and the immortal Abbadabba Berman to talk them over.

Abbadabba was to live forever—in literature—as the horseplayer Regret in Damon Runyon's stories. Runyon named him after the filly that scored an astounding upset in the 1915 Kentucky Derby. Regret was a horseplayer who never seemed to get a win in Runyon's stories.

But Abbadabba Berman was more colorful in real life than in fiction. He was an authentic mathematical wizard and the job Dutch had given to him proved it. At this point he was earning $10,000 a week to rig the pari-mutuel figures at select racetracks with last-minute bets so that the poor people of Harlem wouldn't take too much money out of Schultz's policy banks. Only the lightning speed of Abbadabba's brain could accomplish such a feat.

According to papers found at the scene, Abbadabba had figures which must have cheered the Dutchman. In the preceding six weeks, with his split-second calculations shutting out the most heavily played numbers on any given day, the banks had taken down bets of more than $800,000 and paid out only slightly more than $200,000.

But the papers on the table showed that the other figures Rosenkrantz brought Dutch were not good. Dewey's campaign against him was obviously hurting him financially, too.

The Dutchman was sitting against the wall, as he always did, watching the door. But—as Lucky Luciano had once done himself on a similar occasion, but for different reasons—he got up and made his way to the bathroom. The rest room door closed behind him just as the front door of the Palace Chop House opened and two men came in wearing overcoats. The man in front, heavy-set, with curly black hair and brown eyes, held a .38. The man behind him, with a sawed-off shotgun, was slightly taller, obviously older.

Guns out, they aimed at the Dutchman's table. The Dutchman was not there. His seat was empty. But members of the party at the table were pulling their guns, and the two killers started firing, raking the men at the table. Seven slugs ripped into Lulu Rosenkrantz, going from his chest and abdomen down to his right foot. Abbadabba, who was not armed, took six bullets in his left side; the man Runyon named Regret tumbled to the tile floor in a pool of blood. He lay there, moaning.

Abe Landau was hit three times but had his .45 out and blazing. The door to the men's room opened and the Dutchman came out. A rusty steel-jacketed .45 bullet crashed into his body just below the chest on his left side and tore through the abdominal wall into the large intestine, gall bladder, and liver.

The .45 bullet, ironically, came from the gun of his assistant Landau who was wildly firing at the killers.

The assassins fled with Landau in pursuit. Meanwhile, the bartender, Friedman, saw the Dutchman still on his feet. "The first thing I noticed was Schultz," Friedman later told the police. "He came reeling out like he was intoxicated. He had a hard time staying on his pins and he was hanging on to his side. He didn't say a cockeyed thing. He just went over to a table and put his left hand on it kind of to steady him and then he plopped into a chair just like a souse would. His head bounced on the table and I thought that was the end of him but pretty soon he moved. He said, 'Get a doctor, quick,' but when he said it another guy gets off the floor. He had blood all over his clothes but he gets up and he comes over to me and he looked like he was going to cry. He throws a quarter on the bar and he says, 'Give me change for that,' and I did."

The man who wanted change was Rosenkrantz, and it says something for his financial training under the Dutchman that—in that moment of all moments—he didn't stake the telephone company to an extra twenty cents even for a life-and-death call.

The police came. The Dutchman, raving incoherently, lived for hours before he died.

The underworld had decided that the assassination of Dewey would bring heat from the government such as had never been seen before. So the impulsive Dutch Schultz must go.

Tom Dewey now could take that walk to the coffee shop each morning safely. But Lucky Luciano, the man who "saved" him, would soon have second thoughts. Dewey was going after the Boss of all Bosses, Luciano himself. And this time Frank Costello would have to make the hard decisions.

38

A bitter, wintry evening in New York, January 31, 1936. Policemen in prowl cars nosed down snowy streets and drew up in front of brownstones, apartment houses, and hotels. Tom Dewey was launching a raid on the "prostitution racket."

Soon the girls were coming out, laughing or cursing, girls with names like Jennie the Factory, Sadie the Chink, Frisco Jean, Nigger Ruth, and Gashouse Lil. Some were madams, others just "working" girls. They were taken to the House of Detention as material witnesses and held on $10,000 bail apiece.

Some of them mentioned, under prodding, a man named Charlie. Others, under even tougher prodding, gave his full name, Charlie Lucky Luciano.

Frank once told me it was a bum rap; witnesses were being "persuaded" to link Luciano with so-called "organized prostitution." "It was about as organized as a flea circus," Frank said.

Whether this was true or not, Dewey's purpose was apparent in his appeal to Judge Philip J. McCook for high bail.

"His business [Luciano's] is far-flung, and brings in, to my certain knowledge, a colossal revenue. He is one of the largest beneficiaries of the policy racket. His henchmen operate a number of industrial rackets as well as drug importing and bookmaking. He is one of the biggest illegal importers of drugs in the country. He is head of a large syndicate with sources and amounts of income far in excess of any bail you might set."

Then Dewey probed further into the problem of nailing a man like Luciano. "Today crime is syndicated and organized. A new type of criminal exists who leaves to his hirelings and front men the actual offenses and rarely commits an overt act himself. The only way in which the major criminal can be punished is by connecting to him those various layers of subordinates and the related but separate crimes on his behalf."

The trial began May 11, 1936. Three pimps and some madams, including one Cokey Flo, had turned state's evidence. In truth, the parade of witnesses Dewey had to place on the stand brought that upstanding young man some horrors of conscience. He told the jury:

"Frankly my witnesses are prostitutes, madams, heels, pimps and ex-convicts . . . I wish to call to your attention that these are the only witnesses we could possibly have brought here. We can't get bishops to testify in a case involving prostitution. And this combination was not run under the arc lights in Madison Square Garden. We have to use the testimony of bad men to convict other bad men."

When Luciano took the stand there was one amusing moment.

The witness admitted that he had obtained pistol permits under false pretenses. He also said he carried two pistols, a shotgun, and forty-five rounds of ammunition in an automobile "to shoot birds with."

"What kinds of birds?" Dewey asked.

"Peasants," Luciano said.

Luciano's sentence for "pimping" was a shocker: thirty to fifty years. Some, like Mayor La Guardia, were jubilant. He said that Luciano could never have run his rackets without the knowledge of "some of the very people entrusted with law enforcement. I recommend," said the jaunty little mayor, "that at least six public officials commit hara-kiri."

But, on the other side, some prominent legal authorities took issue with Dewey's handling of the trial, from the joining of prostitution with other charges that were unproved in one indictment (called a "joiner indictment"), thereby subjecting Luciano to a much harsher sentence than he might have had on prostitution, to the use of prostitutes and pimps whose testimony was hardly reliable.

But Luciano went to jail, and a nervous tremor ran through the underworld. As Joe Valachi told author Peter Maas, "I was stunned. Charlie Lucky wasn't no pimp. He was a boss."

Luciano was sent to "Siberia," which is what convicts call Dannemora, an isolated fortress of a prison near the Canadian border. There he would remain until the early Forties when I was called to his aid.

39

After Luciano was sentenced in 1936 the Dewey steamroller surged forward. Many high-ranking underworld chiefs moved to New Jersey to escape Dewey's jurisdiction. And Vito Genovese, next in line to be Boss of all Bosses, was another casualty of the ambitious prosecutor. When Ernie "the Hawk" Rupolo started

to link Genovese with the killing of the small-time hoodlum
Ferdinand "the Shadow" Boccia in 1934, Genovese was indicted
by Dewey and promptly sailed to Italy, bringing enough cash to
launder all of Benito Mussolini's black shirts.

It was 1937. Frank Costello stood alone. How did he survive,
while others fled or went to prison? Why didn't Dewey turn on
him, as next in line?

As Frank said, "He couldn't touch me because I was legit."
And what Frank meant by that was "legitimate" in underworld
terms. He wasn't in narcotics. He wasn't in numbers. His source
of income, so far as the authorities knew at that time, was the
slot machines in Louisiana, an activity outside of Dewey's jurisdiction.

And so Frank moved quietly into position as Boss of all Bosses
of the Mafia, with no fanfare, no banquets such as Maranzano
had given himself.

New York at that time had five Mafia families, including
Frank's. From now on all major decisions that crossed family
lines would be brought to Frank for a ruling. In practice, Frank
never would act without the consent of all family bosses on the
national commission in a sitdown. Other Mafia families across
the nation would be coequal, yet in practice they would defer to
Frank, as the head of the mightiest family, in underworld matters affecting national interests.

Frank was head of the Manhattan family. I don't know how
many members were in that family, but it certainly didn't number more than a few hundred who were, as Frank would say,
"connected." Of course, his family cooperated with many other
independents or with Jewish and other non-Mafia groups on
various deals which were profitable.

Frank's closest advisers during these years were Joe Adonis, a
gangster who operated out of Brooklyn, and Meyer Lansky, a
financial wizard whose preference, like Frank's, was for "legitimate" deals, that is, gambling clubs, et cetera, and not narcotics,
murder, or mayhem. I believe Adonis was Lansky's official liaison
man with the Mafia, and that is why I saw so much of Joe with
Frank. Lansky spent much of his time in Florida, where he was
opening gambling and night clubs.

Albert Anastasia, who controlled the Brooklyn docks, was the other arm of Costello. Frank used Lansky and Adonis for advice on business; he used Anastasia for security purposes. Anastasia was a killer, the ex-chief of Murder Incorporated, and he was loyal to Frank. These two men, so unlike in their views, were friends all their lives. Perhaps each saw in the other something that he admired—perhaps to be cynical, Frank only used Anastasia for his own purposes. But I believe it was the former, because when Anastasia was killed I saw genuine grief in Frank's eyes when he called me to him right after the shooting.

So Frank was set up with brains to advise him on one side, and muscle to keep everyone in line on the other. And he began his reign as Boss of all Bosses in typical fashion. By saying nothing, and lying low.

The technique worked. Dewey gradually cooled off on his rampage through the underworld. He had trumped two kings, Luciano and Genovese, and figured the rest were small-time cards.

Almost immediately upon Frank's accession, the underworld became quiet. Valachi has said, "Frank was a peaceful guy. A diplomat."

Frank's skill as a diplomat was to be proven during the events which overtook Louis "Lepke" Buchalter in 1939.

40

August 24, 1939. The columnist and radio newscaster Walter Winchell, battered brown fedora cocked on the back of his head, hand trembling above a Morse code key from which he emitted various staccato bursts, sat in a radio studio and shouted across America:

"Are you listening, Lepke? Are you listening? Come out, come out, wherever you are!"

Louis Lepke Buchalter was in deep trouble. The indefatigable Dewey wanted him on a New York State murder charge. The Federal Bureau of Narcotics wanted him on drug charges. Lepke was hiding out—and the pressure from both sides was growing.

"A confidential informant" of the FBI made an appointment with Frank one day. His message from J. Edgar Hoover was direct and personal: If Lepke doesn't surrender, the FBI will make it very unpleasant for a lot of people.

Frank was faced with a tough decision, and he had to rule for the benefit of all. But, as a born compromiser, he made it as easy as possible on Lepke, too. He would arrange to have Lepke surrender to the FBI and thereby face the lesser charge of narcotics dealing, rather than the New York State charge of murder.

And so occurred this drama on a darkened street corner in Manhattan. J. Edgar Hoover himself was in a car, waiting. Alongside him sat Walter Winchell, who afterward would claim credit for the "surrender." A man walked across the street and peered into the window. "I'm Lepke," he said.

A car full of FBI agents was parked behind and came roaring up, but all was peaceful. Lepke climbed into the back seat between the FBI director and the gossip columnist and was peacefully taken to jail.

The headlines for J. Edgar Hoover, and the purple prose of Winchell, were enough to turn back the threat of increased FBI pressure for a while. Frank had quietly seen his people through a crisis.

But Dewey was furious. His target had been snatched away by the federal government. A bitter internecine war broke out between the state and federal legal authorities. Dewey, as a state district attorney, won. He was allowed to take jurisdiction over Lepke, and proceeded to try to convict him on the murder charge.

Lepke, incidentally, is the only top gangland leader ever to be executed. It was not an honor he appreciated. And from his death cell the night before his execution he gave his version of what had happened to a New York *World Telegram* reporter. He charged that it was Frank Costello who had betrayed him, that Costello had ordered Lepke to give himself up "or else," and thus had started him on the road to death. A "personal deal" had been made between Costello and J. Edgar Hoover, Lepke swore.

I once heard Frank talk about this with one of his associates. Did he suggest to Lepke that he surrender? "I told Lepke the story. The heat was on. Everybody was suffering. But I didn't tell him 'or else.' I told him his chances on the narcotics deal were good. And they were. The trouble was, the guy with the mustache was looking to run for President. He would have gotten Lepke sooner or later anyway."

As it happened, Frank himself had to surrender a year later on another charge: income tax evasion. The federal government, well aware of those slot machines in Louisiana, was moving against Frank. You might say the evasion was total. Frank had never filed any tax returns.

41

In late 1939 I received a call from my friend Morris Ernst. His law firm, Greenbaum, Wolff and Ernst, was representing Frank Costello in his income tax case in Louisiana. He wanted me to assist at the trial.

I traveled to New Orleans, where I found Frank, his partner Dandy Phil Kastel, and other associates in their Bayou Novelty Company in real trouble. They were subject to both criminal and civil actions by the government for tax evasion.

My participation in the trial on tax evasion was in the selection of the jurors and in cross-examination of some of the witnesses. It became apparent that the government had not prepared its trial well—or was unable to get the witnesses it needed. Most of the evidence in the criminal trial was circumstantial, and on May 15, 1940, the judge ordered a verdict of acquittal.

In the civil action, however, Frank was ordered to pay taxes plus penalties for a number of years to the federal government. And New York State sought its missing state taxes. At hearings held later, in 1943, Frank would testify he had to pay $550,000 in back taxes. How I managed to put a portion of that to good use will be detailed in a later chapter.

But for now, in 1940, Frank wasn't worried about money. The

country was agog with revelations about an organization in Brooklyn named Murder Incorporated. Thousands of people had been assassinated by killers for hire.

And Abe Reles was singing.

Abe Reles was a tough little man with a tough nickname: Kid Twist. This nickname evolved from his favorite manner of murder by strangulation, which he did under contract. Reles was leader of a Brownsville group that operated under Albert Anastasia.

After one of these murders, he was arrested, and started to talk about his organization. According to his confession, Murder Incorporated operated very much like any efficient business organization. Its members received contracts to murder people, and they executed the contracts—along with the people, of course.

Most of the time they didn't even know their victims. They would receive a contract to murder a man in Cleveland, for example, and would go to Cleveland and kill him. The cold-bloodedness of this operation almost defied belief, and when Reles testified that his organization had accomplished more than a thousand murders coast to coast, the public was revolted.

Was Frank connected to this organization in any way? As Boss of all Bosses he surely knew of its existence, but Reles reportedly testified that his immediate boss was Anastasia, and above Anastasia, the man connected to the syndicate—the combine of the Italian Mafia and the Jewish gangs—was Joe Adonis.

And when Reles told authorities the names of the top men who would kill him if they could get their hands on him it was said he mentioned Willie Moretti, Meyer Lansky, Bugsy Siegel, and Longie Zwillman along with Adonis and Anastasia, but not Costello.

Reles was right in his fears. William O'Dwyer, the Brooklyn DA who was handling his case, placed him in a hotel room under guard, five policemen in the corridor, one in the suite. And Reles knew this was strange right off. He should have been in a special isolation cell in a jail.

What happened next has never been fully revealed. This is the story I heard at the time. Whether "the boys in blue"—as Frank called them—were real policemen or gangsters masquerading in uniform, I do not know.

THE GUNS

42

A cold November night. Wind swept down the deserted board-walk at Coney Island. On the sixth floor of the Half Moon Hotel a man was trying to sleep but he was having difficulty.

Abe Reles, lying in bed, must have been thinking—where did that goddam guard go? He was supposed to be sitting in the living room of the suite, guarding the famous prisoner, and now he was gone. Just like that.

Two policemen came into the room, neither of them the guard who had been stationed in the suite; Abe said, "What's up?" and then he was rolling on the bed as both cops grabbed him, striking out at the faces above him. Then a chloroformed cloth was smothering him, his arms held back, and he was blacking out, and going limp.

The cops went into the front room and got to work. One of them started to twist two sheets together. The other attached a wire to the radiator, tied the wire to the sheets, and then cut the wire in two with a razor. What they didn't know was that Abe was not unconscious; he was watching them. Then one of the cops saw him. "Christ, he's awake," he said to his partner, who had already drawn his gun. "Easy does it, Abe. We're going to give you a break."

Abe was obviously too frightened to talk. The cops came over, got him out of bed, and half carried him to the window. One of them said, "We're going to let you escape, with the sheets."

But Abe had seen the cut wire. "You son of a bitch!" he shouted, swinging wildly at the face nearest him. The cop ducked, and then strong arms were squeezing him, and one of the cops grabbed him around the legs like a football tackle, lifting, lifting. Abe saw beneath him six floors of empty space, and death, and he screamed in terror but too late. Thrown forward from the window, the air hurtling up at him as his head rushed toward the cement below, he smashed and died in a black instant.

Above him in the framed window one of the cops was angry. "You idiot," he said to his partner. "You threw him *too far!* He's supposed to fall from the building, not fly."

The man who strangely put Abe Reles in a hotel room instead of a jail cell was William O'Dwyer, the Brooklyn district attorney. One year later O'Dwyer would come to Frank Costello's apartment, and get his approval to run for Mayor of New York City.

43

At the Kefauver hearings in 1951, former Mayor O'Dwyer was asked why, in his investigation of Murder Incorporated in the early Forties, as Brooklyn's Kings County DA, he had never gone after Frank Costello. O'Dwyer said, "Frankly, in all the evidence his name never came up."

In fact, while I can't print the epithets Frank threw at the informer Abe Reles, it's my opinion that Frank had nothing to do with that crew of killers.

What Frank did do, typically, was try to smooth things over. I have no knowledge of what influence, if any, he brought to bear in any way on O'Dwyer. But O'Dwyer's strange actions— including the placing of Reles in a hotel room instead of jail— and the subsequent "disappearance" of certain files, lead one to wonder. Especially in light of the fact that in the middle of the war O'Dwyer, then an army major with hopes of eventually becoming mayor, by his own admission paid a visit to Frank's apartment where he got Frank's approval to run.

Also, for some reason O'Dwyer refused to send Reles to California to testify in a murder case where Frank's old friend, Bugsy Siegel, was on trial. Bugsy was acquitted.

But if you take the viewpoint of the underworld, anything

Frank or any of his associates did to stop Reles was beneficial. For never in crime was one informant so dangerous. Reles knew enough to send the entire Mafia hierarchy to prison, with the exception of Frank.

For example, Reles had much to say about Joe Adonis, but Albert Anastasia was in even worse shape. Reles directly connected him to a garment center killing. O'Dwyer stated to the press that he had the "perfect" murder case against Anastasia, who promptly went into hiding.

But something was going on behind the scenes. Although Reles was in O'Dwyer's custody for nineteen months before he died, O'Dwyer never took him before a grand jury to testify about Anastasia, never tried to get a murder indictment against Anastasia.

Small-time killers went to jail, but Anastasia remained free. When Reles went out the window, Assistant District Attorney Burton Turkus, in a confidential memorandum to O'Dwyer dated April 8, 1942, declared in the strongest possible language that "should Anastasia frustrate justice, it would be a calamity to society. Somewhere, somehow, corroborative evidence must be available." He urged "redoubled effort" to overcome the loss of Reles and build a strong case.

What happened next was instructive. Just twenty-six days after Turkus called for "redoubled effort" the slate against Albert Anastasia was wiped clean. The "wanted cards" that showed he was being hunted for murder were spirited right out of police files! The DA's staff that took over after O'Dwyer and Turkus left never bothered Anastasia again because he wasn't "wanted."

44

When the Japanese bombed Pearl Harbor on December 7, 1941, they indirectly brought peace and prosperity to the underworld. New opportunities opened on every side: stolen ration cards and black market products—sugar, meat, gas—were in great demand. The underworld supplied them.

With Frank at the top everything was peaceful. Assassinations in the street were a thing of the past; underworld rivalries were settled at sitdowns. The "diplomat" was in charge.

I myself was busier than I had ever been in my life. In addition to my legal practice, I had volunteered to hear army draft appeals for the government. This was a time-consuming business, but I did it gladly.

Then in late 1942 I received word that Moses Polakoff, Luciano's attorney, wanted to see me. The scenario Moe unfolded to me was incredible. And yet it rang true. It seemed that—legitimately—the U. S. Navy needed Lucky Luciano's help.

In 1942, Naval Intelligence was greatly concerned about the possibility of sabotage and espionage along the sprawling New York waterfront. The great French liner *Normandie,* converted to a troop ship capable of carrying an entire division, had burned and sunk at her Manhattan pier in a mysterious disaster; German submarines seemed to be supplied with uncannily accurate information about sailing dates of convoys bound for England. Naval Intelligence felt a counterforce was needed along the waterfront and it was suggested that perhaps the underworld mobs could help. Some of the more scrupulous officers at Navy headquarters at 90 Church Street reacted with horror, but wartime exigencies overrode all ethical sensibilities.

The late Commander Charles Haffenden (USNR) was placed in charge of Operation Underworld Counter Espionage. Haffenden contacted District Attorney Hogan, and Hogan assigned Murray Gurfein, then in charge of his rackets bureau, to work with the Navy. With Gurfein's help, an approach was made to Joseph "Socks" Lanza, czar of extortion in the huge Fulton Fish Market and the Lower East Side docks. Lanza was then under indictment and about to go to trial and Gurfein made it clear to him he could expect no deal. Socks decided to cooperate anyway, but shortly afterward he told Haffenden "certain elements" wouldn't help unless they got the word from Charlie Lucky.

One of these "certain elements"—unnamed, of course—was Frank Costello, who wanted Luciano back in charge so he could resume his own businesses without the responsibility that came with the title Boss of all Bosses.

Socks's statement to the Navy brought Moses Polakoff, Luciano's brilliant attorney, into the act. And soon the word went to the government that Luciano was willing to be patriotic, but he wanted some consideration in return. For one thing, he was unhappy in the bleak Dannemora prison in upstate New York; he felt he would be much more comfortable in Great Meadow Prison, just north of Albany, known as the "country club" of New York State penal institutions. This was a small favor, and his transfer was obligingly arranged.

There followed an extraordinary series of pilgrimages from New York to Albany. Polakoff and Lanza made the first trip, explaining the proposition to Charlie Lucky. Luciano is reported to have appeared surprised, but agreed to do whatever he could to help. As a result, during the next three years Polakoff made some two dozen similar visits to Great Meadow, one of them with Frank Costello. Others were with various underworld chiefs such as Meyer Lansky and Willie Moretti.

I find it hard to believe, myself, that the conferences these visitors had with the former boss were devoted *exclusively* to German espionage. But one fact is indisputably on record. There was no sabotage in the vital Port of New York during the remainder of the war.

There was one other item. When American forces invaded Sicily in the summer of 1943 an American combat plane dropped a packet containing a yellow flag with the letter "L" near the church. This "L" flag was passed along to the head of the Sicilian Mafia, Don Calogero Vizzini, and when American troops arrived they found the countryside crowded with Sicilians ready to help the free world's crusade against the hated dictator, Mussolini. The American military was so impressed with the zeal and assistance of these "patriots" that they supplied them with arms, and turned the machinery of the government over to Don Vizzini.

It was in that same year, 1943, that I was to be drawn into the middle of the controversial affair, indeed as the key man, the attorney who represented Luciano.

Luciano's trial had been bitter and acrimonious. Now Polakoff, Luciano's attorney, visited Governor Dewey in Albany and told him he was going to make a motion to reduce Luciano's long sentence. But this motion would come up before the same judge, McCook, who had presided at the former trial.

Dewey suggested that an attorney unconnected with the previous case make the motion, and suggested his old friend, me.

The first news of this came to me when Polakoff called at my office with a court reporter's transcript of the trial, consisting of a number of volumes, and asked me to represent Luciano on a motion for modification of his sentence. I told Polakoff that I did not like the smell of the case.

When he told me that I was specially recommended to him by the governor I told him that I wanted assurance from the governor himself.

We both visited Governor Dewey's office, and in Polakoff's presence I informed Dewey of my misgivings about appearing for Luciano in this odd case. Dewey asked Polakoff to step into an adjoining room so that he could speak to me alone. He then said, "George, I will see to it that no reflection will be cast upon you in representing Luciano on this motion."

I said, "Tom, under those circumstances I will make the motion."

And I did. At the hearing before Judge McCook, one of the witnesses I put on the stand was Murray Gurfein, who later served with distinction as a U.S. district court judge for the southern district of New York. I elicited from Gurfein the facts that on behalf of Military Intelligence he had enlisted Luciano's aid in preventing sabotage, and also obtaining information in Sicily that was helpful to our armed forces.

During the hearings Judge McCook interrogated Gurfein alone in his chambers to learn precisely what Luciano's services included.

When I made my motion to reduce the sentence the judge remarked, "I am thoroughly satisfied after my conversation with Mr. Gurfein in chambers, and from what Mr. Wolf has described in his argument, that the defendant did make an effort toward helping the government."

He then said, with a smile at me, "Taking into consideration these facts—and with all due respect to your eloquent plea, Mr. Wolf—I have decided to presently deny the motion." But then came the turning point decision. "However," said the judge, "if you will get Governor Dewey to commute his sentence and arrange for his deportation—because we don't want men of his caliber in this country—we can get around the matter that way."

It was a clear signal to Governor Dewey, to which he responded as soon as the war was over. I will describe later the controversy which raged then, but for the moment I must concentrate on a personal turning point in my own career. Before I represented Luciano, I had assisted at the trial of Frank Costello for income tax evasion, and had advised Johnny Torrio on another matter.

But now I had stepped across an invisible boundary line. I had represented the former Boss of all Bosses in the climactic case of his career and scored what the underworld considered a brilliant success. Now the reigning boss, Frank Costello, would call me in to assist him on another matter, and soon ask me to be his personal attorney.

I did not know that the roller coaster of triumph and heartbreak for Costello was reaching its final phase. I was to be along for the ride.

BOOK III

The Boss of
All Bosses

1

In July 1943 New York District Attorney Frank Hogan obtained a court order to place a wiretap on Frank Costello's telephone at 115 Central Park West. The tap was only for a two-month period, but that was time enough for a record of conversations which revealed to the public for the first time the fantastic range and scope of Frank Costello's power—in Mafia circles, in New York politics, in nationwide illegal rackets of all sorts.

For among the calls from men identified as Mafia leaders such as Willie (Moretti) Moore, and gambling concessionaires such as Costello's partner Dandy Phil Kastel, was a call from a man who had just received the Democratic nomination as a New York State supreme court justice, Magistrate Thomas A. Aurelio.

To put it as mildly as possible, the call seemed to imply that underworld leader Frank Costello had more than a little to do with Aurelio's nomination.

Aurelio: "Good morning, Francesco, how are you and thanks for everything."

Costello: "Congratulations. It went over perfect. When I tell you something is in the bag you can rest assured."

Aurelio: "It was perfect. It was fine."

Costello: "Well, we will all have to get together, you, your missus, and have dinner some night real soon."

Aurelio: "That would be fine, but right now I want to assure you of my loyalty for all you have done. It's undying."

Costello: "I know . . ."

2

In 1943, when Frank was fifty-two, all seemed quiet on the crime front in New York. Fiorello La Guardia, the slot-machine-smashing mayor, was driving the criminals he called "bums" out of town. Lewis J. Valentine, perhaps the finest police commissioner New York has ever had, was keeping a close eye on the wartime city. And in Albany was the "racket-buster" himself, Governor Thomas E. Dewey, the man who had sent Lucky Luciano to prison for thirty years.

Surely New York had never been more unsafe for criminals. Surely none could operate there.

Then, on August 29, 1943, the headlines in *The New York Times* burst upon the city:

GANGSTER BACKED
AURELIO FOR BENCH,
PROSECUTOR AVERS

New York County District Attorney Frank S. Hogan had issued a formal statement which charged that "Frank Costello, exconvict and underworld leader . . . brought about the nomination of Magistrate Thomas A. Aurelio as a candidate for Justice of the Supreme Court."

The New York Times said, "The District Attorney's accusation that a man he characterized as a 'racketeer and gangster' had brought about the nomination of a candidate for Supreme Court Justice fell like a bomb in political circles."

Suddenly, Frank Costello's name was on everyone's lips. Everyone knew Lucky Luciano, but he was in prison. Who was Costello? Time and again over the last two decades his name had been in the press, but always subordinate to someone else. In the Twenties he came to trial for bootlegging, but the headlines all spoke of his partner Big Bill Dwyer. In the Thirties when Mayor La Guardia gleefully smashed his slot machines with a sledgehammer and pushed them over the side of a boat into the bay, Costello was reported as a "gambler and slot machine operator," but a minor figure when compared to Frank Erickson, the reputed king of the gambling interests.

Now, suddenly, Frank Costello was the man who was selecting and no doubt controlling supreme court judges. The *Times* said, "of Frank Costello little is definitely known." It called him "a shadowy figure."

Until the Aurelio story broke, New York voters had been completely oblivious of Costello's power. Now they were shocked into awareness. It was one thing for corrupt Irish politicians like the charming Mayor Jimmy Walker to take a little graft. But the *Italian underworld* choosing the city's judges and district attorneys? The whole system of justice would break down. No businessman, no citizen, would be safe!

Few political scandals before or since caused the same feeling of terror in New York. More and more questions were asked by worried newspapers. Were the stories of his influence true? And how could Costello have such power in a city where La Guardia was mayor and a state where Dewey was governor?

The man who in open court exposed Costello's real secret power was the last man Frank would have expected to do so: himself. And the lawyer responsible for the testimony that shocked New York was me.

3

Frank Hogan's announcement of the Aurelio wiretap was made on August 29th. On September 11th I received a call from Morris Ernst, who had represented Frank on some cases, once in New Orleans with my assistance. Morris told me that Costello would be needing some "help" on the Aurelio case, and that he had recommended me.

Like all New Yorkers, I had kept up with the fast-breaking Aurelio story, which amounted to the agonized struggles of both parties to remove the offending candidate from the ticket. So far they had been unsuccessful.

Strangely enough, Aurelio's background was a model of judicial rectitude. In 1943, Aurelio was forty-eight years old and had spent twenty years in public life. He was appointed an assistant district attorney on May 1, 1922. In 1931 Mayor Jimmy Walker appointed him a magistrate and on May 1, 1935, Mayor La Guardia reappointed him, saying, "I know of your record and have known you as a boy and a law student. You are the kind of career man I want on the bench."

Even more ironic, Aurelio's entire record on the bench reflected his vigorous support of the police when their duties brought them into conflict with criminals. As to Costello, it was Aurelio who, when required under an injunction to free slot machine operators, urged enactment of a law making the mere possession of slot machines a crime "to enable the courts to cooperate with the police in their drive against gamblers."

On the surface, it didn't seem plausible that Costello would back a man like Aurelio. But there was the intercepted phone call. And there were the words "undying loyalty." Why had Aurelio said *that?*

4

As I always did in important cases, I began a diary the next morning. I still have that diary. The opening words showed no hint that my own career was turning a corner; that from now on I would be forever known as "Frank Costello's lawyer," no matter how many other legal matters I tried, or how many other community or public services I rendered.

> *September 12, 1943*
> Received a telephone call from Frank Costello at about 9 A.M. today, asking me to call at his home at 10 o'clock. When there, Costello told me that he wanted to retain me to represent him in the Aurelio situation and explained the facts.

I went to Costello's apartment at 115 Central Park West and saw immediately that Frank lived in style. His apartment was a seven-room penthouse on the eighteenth floor, obviously furnished in extremely good taste by a fine decorator. The living room was enormous, with antique gold hangings with scalloped valances, lamp tables of beautiful mahogany, antique lamps, and a wood-burning fireplace with a Howard Chandler Christy oil portrait above it.

Costello was dressed in a conservative dark suit. I saw a swarthy man, with black hair brushed straight back from his forehead, brown eyes, and creases around his thin lips. His nose was sharp and gave him a sort of Cyrano de Bergerac profile.

His voice was husky and rasping, the result of an operation to remove a tumor from his vocal cords performed by Dr. Douglas Quick, who later gave us so much trouble at the Kefauver hearings.

In addition to the Aurelio matter, Frank had another thing on his mind to discuss with me: a note found when the famous gambler Arnold Rothstein died saying that Costello owed Rothstein $10,000. The estate wanted Costello to pay it.

According to my diary, this was the basis for Costello's role in the Aurelio matter, as he explained it:

> COSTELLO told me that the principal aid which he rendered to AURELIO was discussions in which he advised him to get the support of certain Italian organizations and have them speak to KENNEDY [Note: Michael Kennedy, Tammany Hall leader] about his candidacy. Also to obtain MAYOR LA GUARDIA'S support, and for LA GUARDIA to speak to KENNEDY. COSTELLO was also to speak to KENNEDY, which he did. AURELIO reported to COSTELLO that he saw the Mayor twice . . . The Mayor told AURELIO that his case was hopeless.

Costello told me that Aurelio's name had been suggested to him by Dr. Vincent Sarubbi, a Tammany Hall district leader. Aurelio had approached Sarubbi.

"And Sarubbi came to *you?*" I said to Frank. "Why?"

Costello took a pair of horn-rimmed glasses out of his pocket and put them on, as if to get a closer look at this man who was to be his attorney. "What kind of a question is that?" he asked roughly.

"The whole thrust of the matter, so far as Hogan will be concerned, is what influence *you* have. Why must *you*—a private citizen—speak to Kennedy? Why didn't Dr. Sarubbi?"

"Well, Kennedy is a friend of mine."

"He's more than that," I said.

Costello said nothing, and I went on, "How many other Tammany leaders are 'friends' of yours?"

I was surprised at Costello's prompt answer. "Five," he said. "But they're all at the top."

"Would it be fair to say that through your five friends, including Mike Kennedy, the leader, you control Tammany Hall? And that you control every candidate the Democratic Party nominates?"

"Are you making a case?" Costello asked. He was becoming angry. But it's always been my experience that it's best to get your client angry at you before he testifies and gets angry in front of a judge.

Besides, I have to confess I was curious. Until now I had no idea how much power and influence this man had in the Democratic Party. An occasional judge, yes. But the whole party? Including the party's candidates for mayor? And there he sat, now pulling out a package of English Ovals and lighting one up, after I refused one myself. He was obviously stalling for time.

"Look, Mr. Wolf, I told you enough. You want to find out more, go talk to Abe Rosenthal, Clarence Neal, Dr. Sarubbi."

I said I would talk to those Tammany leaders and was about to leave when he asked me again about the Rothstein note. "I advise you to settle with the estate," I said. "Make an offer of $5,000."

"But I don't owe it!" Frank said, angrily. "I paid him the money and he just forgot to tear up the slip."

Knowing the way those men operated I was sure this was absolutely true, but I said, "You can't afford to open up matters like that. You're not out of trouble with the Louisiana tax case yet and if the Rothstein matter gets sticky, they'll be into your net worth question again."

But Frank was far from persuaded. He said, "He forgets to rip up a piece of paper and I get hit for $10,000 I don't owe. There ain't no justice in this town."

I laughed, and after a while Frank laughed with me. How the reporters swarming around the Aurelio case would have loved to hear Frank say that!

As a historical note, Frank allowed me to settle for $6,500 with the Rothstein estate. "It's the first time I paid off a corpse," Frank said.

Three weeks later the New York Bar Association brought disbarment proceedings against Aurelio before the state appellate court. On October 4th Frank Hogan called me to arrange for Costello to be at my office the next day to accept a subpoena as a witness before the grand jury.

By then I knew enough of the outlines of the Aurelio case—and Costello's influence at Tammany—to advise my client about his legal position. I took a cab from my office in Wall Street and joined him at a table in the Waldorf Grill. Not exactly private, but in light of what I wanted to tell him it didn't matter.

Frank was alone at a corner table, nursing a Scotch. He seemed in a good mood, especially when I told him about the grand jury subpoena. This was the first time I was exposed to a Costello characteristic that few people knew: he *loved* to testify. It was a characteristic that was to cause me some anguish in the years to come.

But if he was in a good mood, that soon changed with my first words. "Frank, I want you to tell the truth to the grand jury."

I doubt that Frank had ever heard such advice before. He was absolutely startled. "The truth as to what?" he asked. I said, "The truth about your relations with Tammany Hall and anything else that Mr. Hogan asks you."

He was staring at me, his eyes seeming to flicker. I believe he couldn't understand whether I had lost my mind or just misplaced it. I said, "You've committed no crime, Frank. Helping to get Aurelio a place on the ticket is not a felony or even a misdemeanor. Thousands of people use influence every election year to get certain nominees on the ticket." I paused, and then went on. "The only crime you can be convicted for out of this affair is *perjury!* Tell a few lies, and Frank Hogan might pull out evidence in those wiretaps to show you're lying, and you're in trouble."

"Hell," Frank said, "I have to think about that."

I found out later that he not only thought about it, but he asked such friends as Meyer Lansky, whose judgment Frank always respected. Lansky not only told him to listen to me, but added a compliment: "You've got yourself a smart lawyer."

So that is how it came to be that Frank Costello told the truth —or, to be precise, *some* of the truth. But even that portion was enough to change him overnight from an unknown "mystery man" to one of the most feared criminals in America. For he had some story to tell.

5

On October 14, 1943, Frank Costello picked me up in a cab, and we went down to the supreme court building. Frank was dressed in a light blue suit, light overcoat, and gray felt hat. He seemed amused when he saw a crowd had gathered to await his arrival. I told the reporters that Frank had prepared a statement and would release it after the grand jury proceedings.

Attorneys are not allowed to sit alongside witnesses at grand jury proceedings. Therefore I remained outside the hearing room while Frank went through his ordeal. It took two and a half hours, and when he came out he said to me in a low voice, "The guy done his homework."

That meant DA Frank Hogan, as I had feared, had done enough research and had enough wiretaps to trip Frank up if he told any lies. I had been right to urge Frank to tell the truth. I said, "You *did* tell the truth, I hope."

"Yeah, with a little salt," Frank said. But he was in a good mood, and this mood was heightened when we tried to slip out of the building via the DA's entrance at 155 Leonard Street, and found the reporters had anticipated us. But to all of their shouted questions, Frank said, pleasantly, "No comment, but my lawyer's right here."

The attempt to disbar Aurelio was a proceeding before the Appellate Division of the New York State Supreme Court. Charles B. Sears, a noted attorney, was the referee. It began on October 25, 1943.

To the evident pleasure of the packed crowd in the courtroom, Hogan called Frank Costello as his first witness. The crowd saw a stocky, broad-shouldered man, faultlessly groomed, face tanned from sun lamp treatments, take the stand. They watched as he crossed his well-pressed trousers, revealing highly polished shoes —and began to fiddle nervously with his horn-rimmed eyeglasses under Hogan's blistering attack.

The district attorney quickly brought out Costello's background. Frank testified that he was fifty years old (he was fifty-two), born in Lauropoli, Italy, naturalized as a United States citizen in 1921 (actually 1925), and lived at 115 Central Park West. He had never held an official position in a political party and for that matter never had registered to vote.

"What business or employment do you now have?"

"Candy machines," Frank said. "When you put in a nickel and pull the handle, a pack of mints drops out."

Hogan smiled. "Isn't it true that once in a while two or four slugs drop out with the package?"

"Yes."

"Then isn't it also true that this 'candy' machine is commonly called a slot machine?"

"I guess that's right," Frank said.

But now came the startling disclosure that Michael Kennedy himself, the all-powerful leader of Tammany Hall, had been placed in office by this swarthy criminal testifying from the stand. The implications were quickly grasped. If the *leader* was beholden to Costello, the whole Tammany Hall organization must be under his control, too.

Frank, of course, put it on a "just friendship" basis. But the true facts were obvious. Frank testified that he had known Kennedy for ten or twelve years and that they were such good friends they always called each other "Mike" and "Frank." He said that he often saw Kennedy at racetracks, bars, restaurants, and at Madison Square Garden.

Frank recalled that Kennedy was elected the Tammany leader after he "discussed" the problem with Tammany district leaders.

"What instructions did you give those leaders with respect to Kennedy?" Hogan asked.

"I told Kelly, Sarubbi, and Rosenthal that I would consider it a nice thing if they would go along."

The words "consider it a nice thing" hung in the court. Especially after it was revealed that, for some strange reason, Jim Fay, the favorite, had abruptly withdrawn from the race, and Kennedy was elected. Frank admitted that after the election Kennedy thanked him for his help.

As to Aurelio, Frank said that he heard from time to time that his chances looked good. But unknown to Costello, President Roosevelt was taking an active interest in this election—he had a candidate of his own, an Irish Catholic Congressman named Joseph A. Gavagan.

The President talked to Kennedy about it, and Kennedy must have felt he was a man between two giants, either of whom could crush him. Somehow he couldn't find it in his heart to inform Costello of Roosevelt's candidate. Frank, of course, heard of it soon enough—and hit the ceiling. According to his own testimony, he went storming over to Kennedy's office and told the Tammany leader, "Now you've got to be either a man or a mouse! Come out with it. Declare yourself! You're the leader of Tammany Hall. Are you going to be the boss or not?"

After this conversation, Frank testified blandly, "Kennedy told me he was definitely going to have Judge Aurelio on the ticket."

And so the President of the United States got his comeuppance. Aurelio, who had been undercut by President Roosevelt, had his nomination anyway, because of a man more powerful in New York politics than either of them.

In the courtroom, Hogan drove the point home, bringing out Frank's criminal background with a series of questions that elicited a roll call of names as famous as were to be found in crime, some almost legendary.

It is my belief that it was this testimony of Frank's which led to the first public realization in this country that there was a nationwide criminal network—not just vague and separated gangs and individual racketeers, as had been believed. Certainly when the first great investigation of nationwide organized crime was made by the Kefauver committee, this testimony was cited over and over again. For in it Frank stated that he knew criminals from all over the country, and powerful men they were, too.

"Do you know Benjamin Siegel, also known as Bugsy Siegel?" Hogan asked.

"I've known him about ten years," Frank said.

"Do you know Abe Zwillman of Newark, also known as 'Longie'?"

"Yes," Frank said. Longie, too, was an acquaintance of seven or eight years.

On and on the names went. "Little Augie" Pisano, "Socks" Lanza, Al Capone. On that name the audience murmured. Frank said he had known Al for twenty years. Frank Nitti, another Chicagoan? Sure. Joey Rao of Harlem? Yeah. Johnny Torrio, the Chicago mobster who gave Al Capone his start? "No," Frank said. (I never asked why he lied on that one name.)

But the truth began again with the next list: "Trigger Mike" Coppola, Louis "Lepke" Buchalter, Lucky Luciano, Dutch Schultz, Dutch Goldberg, Owney Madden, "Little Ziggy," Vito Genovese.

The names rocketed through the court and later through the nation's newspaper headlines. And perhaps Frank was aware of the sensation he was causing because he suddenly spoke up from the witness stand. "I want you to understand, Mr. Hogan, that I never had any dealing with any of these people. I had bundles of real important friends of mine, too. I don't want to mention their names."

Hogan merely smiled, apparently satisfied with the spectacular testimony he had drawn forth that day. It would alert both government and civic leaders that a criminal with nationwide underworld connections controlled the Democratic Party at every level in New York.

But when Aurelio's attorney, Thomas Sheridan, took over the cross-examination he eagerly pursued Frank's testimony about his legitimate friends. And Frank had his first happy moments.

"Do you meet people of refinement?" inquired the lawyer.

"The best—they are personal friends of mine," Frank answered, smiling for the first time.

"Has it been your idea for the last eight or ten years to meet with the better people?"

"Yes," Frank said, "but I want to make a statement. I do know some of the finest, biggest businessmen in the country. But I wouldn't want to embarrass them by giving their names."

Sheridan was obviously hoping that Frank's acquaintance—which was real—with "decent" people would influence the referee, and just before the court adjourned for the day he arranged to have Frank give the names the next day *in camera*—that is, off the record.

But that would be tomorrow, today had been a nerve-racking experience for Frank—relating even "a portion of the truth" had so obviously startled the court that, as he told me later, he had felt the audience reeling back from him in alarm and fear.

But for this day at least, Frank had the last laugh. Defense attorney Sheridan's final question brought out that it was Costello who had originally telephoned Aurelio and left a message.

Sheridan asked who answered Costello's telephone call to Aurelio's home. "Was it Mrs. Aurelio?"

Frank growled in his inimitable raspy voice, "It wasn't Mrs. Aurelio; it was a *lady*."

Laughter went through the room and the referee decided it was time to adjourn until the next day.

6

Frank and I went uptown to the Madison Hotel cocktail lounge. This was one of Frank's favorite watering places, which became famous in New York in testimony at later hearings. Not because of anything that happened there, but because of the fact that the leader of the Mafia spent his day in elegant East Side hotels, bars, and restaurants. The public was fascinated. Later I would always be conscious of a stirring when, for example, we sat in the St.

Regis King Cole Room. People would be whispering to their companions *"That's Frank Costello!"* And the companions would glance over, trying not to be noticed, and see a swarthy business-man dressed in conservative clothes having a quiet drink with a friend, exactly like the Madison Avenue account executives and businessmen nearby.

But this was the Boss of all Bosses of the Mafia! Where were the steely-eyed bodyguards? Where was the suspicious bulge indicating a shoulder holster? How could the head of the crime syndicate go so unconcernedly around town without bodyguards or protection of any kind?

The truth was that Frank not only had courage (I only saw him frightened once in his life—after Anastasia was shot) but that he had sense. "If someone wants to score," he always told me, "the bodyguards are the first ones they buy off." But what protected Frank even more was the knowledge he had learned on the streets. He preached nonviolence and he would live as if nonviolence was to be expected. And disputes would be settled only by negotiation and the negotiation would always be fair. Everybody trusted Frank Costello's word.

But now in 1943 these days of public recognition were far ahead, and although Frank's testimony would alert and alarm everyone in tomorrow's newspapers, at this moment he was just one more "businessman" in the Madison Hotel lounge, conferring with an associate. I told him I was disturbed about one thing.

"What?" he asked.

"You shouldn't have brought in that testimony about the 'decent' people you know. We made the point in the press release, but there's no reason to bring these people's *names* in."

"Well, hell, I know that. I didn't tell names, did I?"

"Still, you have to testify *in camera* tomorrow. My advice is to refuse to testify, and let me speak to the referee. I have the feeling he's not going to be so eager to get those names revealed either."

Frank was lighting a cigarette. When he finished, he growled, "Whatever you say." He paused like an actor after opening night. "Why don't you tell me how I did up there?"

"You handled yourself well," I said. "It was rough, but the

information would have come out sooner or later anyway. Those wiretaps gave them all the leads they needed. This way, you came forth with the information, and that fact's bound to take some of the sting out of their reaction."

But Frank was peeved at something. "Hogan had to bring in Capone and those guys. What did Capone know from Aurelio? He wouldn't know Aurelio if he dropped through the toilet."

I smiled. "He wanted to prove that you're the big boss of crime, Frank—and that Aurelio was bound to know it after all those years as an assistant DA and a magistrate."

Frank was looking at me. "What kind of crap is that?" he said. "Boss of all crime! I'm a gambler, period. I'm a businessman. Just because I run into those guys at the track and the Copa, Hogan makes a federal case out of it."

"Who is the boss?" I asked (as if I didn't know by now!). But Frank surprised me with his answer. "Hell, you know better than anybody else. Charlie Lucky. You're the guy getting him out of 'college.' "

Throughout my long relationship with Frank I felt he viewed the Mafia leadership as a burden he had to bear, and would have loved to disavow. He always thought of himself as a "business-man" in businesses which were currently illegal but would some-day be legal, as alcohol had become. (The establishment of state lotteries and off-track betting shops brought many a wry com-ment from Frank in his last years.)

After this chat with my client, I was not surprised the next day on our way to the *in camera* session to discover that Frank had changed his mind again and very much wanted to testify as to his "important" friends in "civilian life."

"Can't I tell just a couple names?" he asked. "Just to shake them up a little."

"No names," I said. "It might hurt them—and it might hurt you later."

And so he went into the session and declined to name them. I spoke to Sears, the referee, and he agreed not to press the matter. As I had suspected, he really didn't *want* the names.

And this incident brings to mind another closed hearing years later before the New York State Liquor Commission, which al-lows me once and for all to put to rest a certain statement that has been publicized recently in the press—the statement Frank Costello made to best-selling author Peter Maas in an interview shortly before he died. Maas is an excellent investigative reporter and I have absolutely no doubt he obtained the statement correctly as Frank told it to him.

The statement was dynamite. Costello told Maas that Joseph Kennedy, father of the late President, had been Costello's partner in a liquor importing business.

The full story of the Alliance Distribution deal I'll tell in its proper place, but for now I'll just say that over the course of thirty years I had to sit with Frank through dozens of hearings and investigations and trials. I spent most of my time restraining Frank from blurting out some big legitimate name to "shake them up a little."

As it happened, this particular statement about Mr. Kennedy was not strange to me. I had been through the mill with it before. In a closed State Liquor Commission hearing in the late Forties the staff counsel was questioning Frank about his connection with the House of Lords Scotch distribution. The fact is that Frank's partners in that deal were Irving Haim and Phil Kastel. All of the financial details of that company are on record, including all names of partners, so imagine my surprise when this dialogue took place.

> Q. "Who were your partners in this deal?"
> A. "Phil Kastel, Irving Haim, and," he paused, ". . . Joe Kennedy."
> Q. "WHO?"

The staff counsel was stunned. I jumped in to clarify things, knowing that Frank had done it again. He always reached for the biggest name to "shake them up"—and he knew Joe Kennedy had made a legitimate Scotch distribution deal with another brand, which was on the record. I said, "Excuse me, but as counsel I want to ask my client a question. Are you referring to the ex-Ambassador to England?"

> Frank: "What?"
> Wolf: "Are you referring to Joseph Kennedy, the ex-Ambassador to England?"

Frank: "Hell, no."

Wolf: "Then which Joe Kennedy are you speaking of?"

Frank: "Joe Kennedy, the old bootlegger in Toronto. I known him twenty-five years."

The staffer dropped that hot potato in a hurry and Mr. Kennedy's name was, rightfully, never brought up in the open sessions of the hearings. When I got Frank outside that afternoon, I was furious. "Now you just have to stop dragging people in like that. If that had been in an open hearing, you'd have been *sued!*"

Frank just smiled and said, "The kid jumped a mile, didn't he?"

So it is my personal belief, based on this incident and my longtime knowledge of Frank's habits, that the mention of Joe Kennedy's name was yet another indication of Frank's long yearning for legitimacy, to be "associated with the right people." A Scotch distribution deal with Irving Haim? What was that? Nothing. But with Joe Kennedy? That was class, that was the "right people."

7

Judge Aurelio took the stand and said yes, he had been told that Costello had influence with Kennedy, the Tammany leader, and he had asked for his help. But as to the statement of "undying loyalty" he was indignant. "That's just the fulsome way Italians express things," he said.

And so it was to prove, much to Frank's anger. Aurelio was allowed to stay on the ballot as the result of the hearing, the referee saying the charge had not been proved. And as he was the only name on the ballot he easily defeated write-in candidates. Ironically, he went on to become one of the finest judges New York City has ever had. He served his fourteen-year term as a supreme court justice and then was elevated to the appellate bench. Not once in all those years were his actions and judgments in any way suspect; on the contrary, he became known as one of the toughest judges a defendant could face. It is a hopeful comment on the human condition that Aurelio could win the respect of lawyers and fellow judges after such a disastrous start.

Frank, as might be expected, did not share my enthusiasm. In fact, early in Aurelio's career as a supreme court justice he sent an intermediary to "feel the judge out" concerning the forthcoming trial of a friend of his. The intermediary reported to Frank that the defendant was "cooked" if he was tried before Aurelio, especially as the good judge now knew that his old "friend" Costello was interested in the case.

That didn't stop Frank. Through another intermediary he tried again on a later case. Again he was icily rebuffed and this time he was sore. "A lousy ingrate" was one of the lesser terms he used. To newspapers he coined a more gentle phrase which became famous, "I can't even get a parking ticket fixed with him."

But Frank, God bless him, was not a man to give up easily. For certainly he knew that it was Aurelio's call which had sprung him from the comfortable life of a rich unknown racketeer into the blinding spotlight of publicity that now followed his every move. Overnight, he became the No. 1 criminal in New York, and he blamed the little judge. Now the judge was treating him like dirt.

And maybe there was one more point, too, one never uncovered by the press, and never revealed until this time. After Aurelio had been on the bench for many years, his reputation now secure, Frank called me to his apartment. I was shaken by what he showed me: a note to Costello for $7,500 signed by Aurelio in 1943.

If the note was real, Aurelio's testimony at the trial that he merely asked Costello to put in a good word for him was false; instead he had taken money from Frank—and the debt had remained active throughout his long term on the bench. Now Frank was mad and wanted me to go to the judge's chambers and ask for the money back!

I said, "My advice to you is to tear that note up and forget it ever existed."

But Frank had his back up. "Dammit, he owes me $7,500 and he's going to pay it. I'm getting nothing else out of him."

I was angry myself. I said, hotly, "Haven't you caused that man enough trouble!"

But this only sent Frank into greater fury. "Dammit, you're taking this note to Aurelio and tell that little mouse he better pay up or I'm exposing this whole deal."

In moments like that I never argued with Frank, for I knew there were other ways to get around him. Tempers, Italian style, are all the same: violent, but brief.

I took the note and went to Justice Aurelio's office. This was one of the most painful errands of my life because as a lawyer I respected, and still do respect, the integrity of the late judge. I showed the judge the note, and Aurelio went off like a fire-cracker, "Tell that gangster if he ever gets near my court I'll have him thrown in jail and buried there. I paid that money back years ago."

When I took the note back to Frank and told him what Aurelio had said, he became very angry, but he did not object when I ceremoniously tore the note up into little pieces in front of him, and burned them in an ashtray.

Frank wouldn't tell me what the money was for. I do know it never got him anything. I can say with authority, based on my long relationship with Frank Costello, that Aurelio never did Frank one favor of any kind on the bench as long as he lived.

But he did do one *social* favor—and it took some courage. In 1949 when Frank was asked by the Salvation Army to assist in their annual charity banquet, he sent personal invitations to the entire power elite in New York, including Aurelio. My wife and I were the official hosts and I remember my surprise when the judge and his wife showed up, even though the judge was certain to know what the newspapers would say if his appearance was noted.

And it was indeed noted, along with that of all the other politicians. That dinner at the Copa was the scandal of the year in New York—my, how many "friends" Frank Costello had in Congress, on the bench, and in City Hall, just aching to help the Salvation Army!

But by then events had taken an ironic turn. Aurelio was just a small name in Frank Costello's past. For Frank had made it big, much bigger than he wanted. *Time* and *Newsweek* and *Col-*

lier's ran cover stories on him; newspapers published five-part series exploring every detail of his life and career. He had become, more than any other Mafia leader before or since, a legend. Almost plaintively, it seemed, his words ran beneath his picture on *Time*'s cover: "Who do they think I am? Superman?"

That was in 1949. From 1943 on, I had been trying to change his image. It was like trying to rechisel a marble statue with a soft sliver of soap. The statue might be cleaner, but the monument remained as it was, menacing.

8

After the Aurelio hearings, Frank was never again out of the public spotlight. The old days of the silent power-behind-the-scenes were gone. I knew he would have to learn to live in the public eye, not the most desirable position for a man whose income came from gambling, then considered a crime by the authorities.

I told Frank my intention was to legitimize him to the extent that this could be done. He loved the idea. From now on he would file income and state taxes, as required. (He didn't like that as much.) And he would invest in truly legitimate businesses.

I remember one conversation that delighted him. It took place in 1943 in the St. Regis King Cole Room.

"Frank," I said, "what do you think of Wall Street?"

"The biggest thieves in the world," he said. "They break more widows and orphans every minute than any of us boys ever thought of."

"I'm going to put you on Wall Street," I said.

Frank turned to me, his eyes glittering with suppressed amusement. "What's it going to be, Hornblower and Costello?"

"Not a brokerage firm. I want you to buy a building on Wall Street."

"You mean, own a building, one of them skyscrapers? What the hell are you driving at, George?"

But I could see he was enjoying the idea. "Actually it's three buildings," I said. "One thirteen-story and one fourteen-story building together right on Wall Street, and a little four-story building around the corner on Water Street. We'll put the whole package together, set up your headquarters there, and call it the 79 Wall Street Corporation."

Frank ordered us two more drinks. He was obviously figuring the angle. "What's up your sleeve, George? Me on Wall Street? Who's that going to fool? They'll say it's a front, a way to avoid taxes. They'll be all over that building."

"Two things, Frank. One, it's a good investment. The owners are hard up and for about $50,000 cash against a mortgage you can get the whole deal. Second, we'll rent out the offices in the buildings, and you'll contribute all your rental income above expenses to charity." I paused. "And the reporters will find that out, too. We'll make sure. All legitimate from beginning to end."

Frank was sipping his drink. Then he said, "You know, George, you got some good ideas. If it checks out the way you say, I'll go for it."

He looked around the restaurant, filled with businessmen discussing deals over martinis. Then he turned to me and smiled. "You done it, George. Wait till those creeps in Sands Point hear that their shady neighbor is the president of a Wall Street corporation. I like it, George. Beautiful."

Frank had just purchased a home in Sands Point, Long Island, to the displeasure of some of the residents.

After an investigation, Frank bought the Wall Street buildings, paying $55,000 above the mortgage of $249,483.31. The buildings were assessed by the city at $510,000, so it was a good financial deal.

But the boost to Frank's morale was even more valuable. From then on all business mail addressed to Frank went to his company, "The 79 Wall Street Corporation," no less.

It was a move F. Scott Fitzgerald's Gatsby never thought of. But then, Gatsby never made it to the rich section of Long Island's North Shore, either, as Frank did. In fact it was a town like Sands Point, called by Fitzgerald East Egg, toward which Gatsby looked with such longing across the bay.

Frank made it for him.

9

But of course the 79 Wall Street Corporation didn't deter Mayor La Guardia—or the press. They knew by the revelations at the Aurelio hearing that Costello was the reigning mobster in New York, and considered the Wall Street operation, as Frank had predicted, only as a tax shelter. It was in 1944 that an embarrassing incident occurred which showed me how tough it would be to make Frank "legitimate." The most amusing part of the incident, which captivated New Yorkers, was Frank's reaction to the whole business.

In brief, a taxicab driver named Edward Waters dropped Frank at the Sherry-Netherland Hotel. A few minutes later, while cruising, the cabbie happened to glance into the back seat and saw that his passenger had left two envelopes.

He pulled over to the curb, reached for the envelopes, and found they contained $27,200. On one of the envelopes he found written in hand the various denominations of the bills, and the initials F.C.

It has always been my opinion that that cabbie must have had quite a shock and not because of the amount of money. I just *know* he knew who F.C. was! And how dangerous it was to have $27,200 of F.C.'s money. Be that as it may, he lost no time turning the money over to the New York City police property clerk.

Meanwhile, Frank was quite upset himself. He called the doormen at the Hotel New Yorker, where the cab had picked him up, and at the Sherry-Netherland, where he had been dropped, but neither one could identify the taxi or the driver. He then called me.

I met Frank at his apartment late at night, and found him pacing the room. It wasn't, of course, the money that concerned him—but the legal complications that would be created if the envelopes were turned over to the police.

"Don't you want the money back?" I asked.

"Hell, no. Forget it," he said.

"You can't forget it, Frank."

"Why the hell not?"

"Because if it turns up, or word gets around," I said, "you'll look like you're hiding something. You've got to be forthright."

And while he was staring at me, I called the police property clerk and was told the money had been delivered to the police station on East 67th Street.

I turned to Frank after I hung up. "You see, I was right. Now you come with me down to the clerk's office, and put your claim in."

"Put a claim in!" Frank shouted. "Can't we just forget the whole damn thing?"

"Absolutely not. You left your handwriting all over the envelope. The police will trace it, anyway."

It was at this point that Frank was so sore he made me laugh. "Damn that stupid cabbie!" he said. "Why didn't he *keep* the money?"

It was after midnight when we took a taxi to the property clerk's office. The clerk, a man named Maurice Simmons, was very cooperative. We explained what had happened, that it was Frank's handwriting on the envelope, and that the cabbie could identify Frank. But the conversation went no further because just then the clerk's phone rang. It was Mayor La Guardia, who somehow had been tipped off. The Little Flower yelled so loud I could hear him myself, "Don't you turn that money over to that tinhorn bum. If you do, you're fired!"

At the end of *that* conversation, the clerk was shaking. "Orders from the mayor," he said. "I can't turn it over to you. It's against the law."

In the cab going home Frank was furious. "What do we do now?" he asked.

"You have to sue."

"Goddamit to hell—"

"You've got to sue and get it back, Frank. Play it straight, or it will mean even more trouble."

Six months before the incident, the New York City Council and Board of Estimate had passed an ordinance which required a claimant to lost property to prove not only that the item had been lost, but that the claimant had a clear and legal right to it. The new law further provided that a claimant could have no legal right to lost property if it was the proceeds of, or intended to be used in connection with, any illegal activity.

Acting under this statute, the police—at the mayor's insistence —refused to surrender the money to Costello; they said it was clearly the proceeds of gambling or racketeering and suggested that $12,000 of it may have represented Costello's weekly take from a roadhouse and gambling joint in New Jersey. Mayor La Guardia characterized the $27,200 as "outlaw money," adding: "What I'm interested in is where did the bum get it and where was he taking it."

The police department was determined to turn the money over to the police pension fund. And I must say it looked as if that might happen. Because Frank would not reveal—in public— where the money came from. He did say—and it was true—that $15,000 of it was intended for use in the purchase of the 79 Wall Street Corporation, a perfectly legal real estate enterprise.

Meanwhile, New Yorkers were enchanted with the story. Almost all of them at one time or another had left something in the back of a cab. But $27,200? How rich *was* Frank Costello if he carried so much cash around?

This was exactly the kind of speculation that I, as Frank's attorney, wanted to stop. If Frank made a determined effort to get his money back, it might end such talk. So I went into court to recover the money.

Furthermore, I did so with unique legal assistance. I knew that the money Frank lost in the cab was almost the exact amount he still owed the federal government as the result of his New Orleans tax case. At the hearing on my action to recover the money, I moved to interplead the Bureau of Internal Revenue on our side, as an interested party. The extraordinary spectacle of a government lawyer appearing side by side with Frank Costello resulted.

As I expected, State Supreme Court Justice Carroll G. Walter held that the $27,200 belonged to Costello and should be returned to him, but that Costello must then satisfy the government tax liens.

Incidentally, at the trial before Judge Walter, Frank finally admitted where the money came from. He testified that $15,450 of the money had been sent to him by his slot machine partner, Dandy Phil Kastel, and that he had borrowed the remaining $11,750 from his brother-in-law Dudley Geigerman, who worked for the slot machine corporation in Louisiana. Geigerman, according to Frank, had handed him both envelopes at the Hotel New Yorker a little while before he got into the cab.

The city was unable to prove that these sources were illegal, and the jury ruled in Frank's favor. It was not exactly a financial triumph. Of the total amount, $24,286.90 went to the government for tax liens, and court costs were $166.45. Frank had already given the taxicab driver $2,625.

The grand sum Frank kept, after that costly slip in the back of a cab, was $121.65.

But my strategy paid off in one way. As Frank was leaving the courtroom he said to the reporters, "Give me a break for a change and write a nice story about me."

They did.

10

Frank Costello was a marked man, no question about it. The taxicab incident only made New Yorkers even more aware of the underworld leader in their midst. And the authorities never stopped bedeviling him.

A nightclub's license was about to be renewed; sure enough, the licensing bureau dragged Costello's name into it—and proposed to refuse the club's license on the basis that Frank, a former convict, owned a piece of the club. I went down to court time and again on behalf of my client, demanding that they show proof that Frank owned any part of the club. None was forthcoming.

The matter was finally resolved when the city offered a compromise which said that Frank Costello had "terminated" any interest he had in the nightclub, so that the license could be renewed. This was done in spite of the fact, which I believe is true, that Frank never did own any interest in the club.

At another point Frank made the front pages of the newspapers for absolutely no reason at all. A rumor was printed that DA Frank Hogan was investigating Frank in connection with some crime. The story played three days before the DA officially announced that no such investigation was taking place.

Meanwhile, Frank's new "celebrity" had both its hazardous and its humorous consequences. Letters from pregnant women poured into my office claiming that Frank somehow had sired their children, and a generous amount of money would certainly be a help. Then, of all things, a crudely written note in block letters threatened Frank with death unless he turned over a certain amount of money.

In the days following, the letters continued, each one more threatening, and Frank became curious. "Let's see who these jerks are," he said.

"They may be mentally unbalanced," I said. "Just forget the whole thing."

The last letter said Frank must bring the money to the lobby of the Palace movie theater on Broadway at eight o'clock that night—or else. Frank read the letter again and looked up at me with a smile. *"You* come with me, George."

"Me?"

"I'm going to make a citizen's arrest. You can handle the legal stuff."

But I was thinking of a sudden knife in the back, a shot—who knew what these people, who would be insane enough to write threatening notes to a powerful ganglord, would do. "If it's all right with you, Frank," I said, "I'll pass."

"You're coming," Frank said. He was smiling. Frank got a shopping bag and stuffed it with paper, placing a few dollars on top. Then the No. 1 man in the Mafia and myself cabbed over to the Palace.

I don't mind saying I was nervous. Both of us were unarmed. Maybe we would be kidnapped. Maybe I would be killed because I was a witness!

Frank, however, was cool as ice. With me trailing behind, Frank lugged his shopping bag into the cavernous lobby, stopped and looked around. No one was there. The movie was on, and everyone was beyond the partition, watching the show. Then a nervous youth in a tattered brown sweater and green slacks came out from beyond the partition, walked over to Frank and me, and said, "I got a gun, so no squawks. Is that the money?"

"Right here," Frank said with a smile. Then he grabbed the youth's wrist. "There are ten cops out front and five at the side door," he growled. "So what do you do now?"

Another youth had appeared, saw what was happening, and ran out the front door as fast as he could. The young man whose wrist Frank held said, "I need the money."

To my surprise, Frank let go of his wrist. He dug into his pocket and came up with two hundred-dollar bills. "Here, kid, stay out of trouble."

"But the cops—"

"There ain't any—and you don't have a gun either, right?"

The kid didn't answer at first. Then he said, "Right, Mr. Costello. I'm sorry I . . . bothered you."

Recalling the death threats in those notes the boy sent, I thought the word "bothered" was rather mild. But Frank laughed and slapped the youngster on the back. "Take the shopping bag, kid. There are a few more green ones there. And get lost quick."

The boy did, and Frank was still laughing as we emerged from the movie into the swelling Broadway crowd. I was stunned. "Why in the world did you give him money?" I asked. "He threatened you with death!"

"I'll tell you the truth, George," Frank said. "I saw that kid—and what I saw was me, thirty years ago. Maybe if some guy had given me a break like that I might have changed myself." He punched me lightly on the shoulder. "And you wouldn't have me as a client. So tell Mina I did it for her."

11

Nineteen forty-five was a tumultuous year. In many important ways, it would prove a landmark for Frank. These are some of the events which loomed ahead as the year began.

Mayor La Guardia was at last retiring from office. Frank's candidate was Bill O'Dwyer, who had visited him during the war to get his approval.

But La Guardia didn't like his administration being turned over to O'Dwyer, whose performance in the Abe Reles fiasco had rendered him suspect. La Guardia would field a candidate of his own. And to complicate matters, the official Republican candidate would be a Democrat! As John Gunther once said about the 1945 mayoralty election, "Of all crazy elections in the history of New York City, this was one of the craziest."

Next in importance to Costello would be Luciano's future. The hearing in 1943 to free Luciano had resulted in Justice McCook in effect turning the problem over to Governor Dewey. At the end of World War II Dewey would rule on whether Lucky was to be freed. Frank was confident the New York governor would approve the release of Luciano because he had been able to end sabotage against the Navy and because it was Luciano who helped get Sicilians to aid Allied troops when they landed. If that happened, Luciano would come back to power and Costello would be free of the burden of overseeing the affairs of the Mafia.

Third, in 1945 a new mayor would be elected in New Orleans. DeLesseps Morrison would not only ban all of Frank's slot machines, but he would make certain charges against Frank that would eventually ignite into the Kefauver hearings.

As New York City's mayoralty election got under way, it was apparent that O'Dwyer's two opponents were running not against him but against Costello.

Jonah J. Goldstein was the Democrat turned Republican—and his blasts against Frank echoed throughout the city.

The fact is Goldstein, a candidate who could attract the city's Jewish vote, was running on both the Republican and the Liberal Party tickets. He might well have had a chance against O'Dwyer. But this time the Little Flower blundered. Perhaps La Guardia's most famous statement was: "I don't often make mistakes, but when I do it's a beaut."

I don't recall when this statement was made, but it certainly could have applied to this election, because now La Guardia decided to field his own candidate, Newbold Morris, then president of the City Council and a monument to civic purity. Morris, an able man, was a millionaire who devoted much of his life to bettering urban life, but as a candidate he had his failings. The saying at the time was that "he was born with a silver foot in his mouth."

La Guardia enthusiastically backed Morris as a "No Deal" candidate—and Morris was soon inveighing against everybody's favorite target: Frank Costello.

Despite the Aurelio case and the subsequent publicity, Frank still controlled Tammany with an iron hand—and he delivered. Morris' candidacy split the anti-O'Dwyer vote, and Bill O'Dwyer, the erstwhile Brooklyn prosecutor, won the election handily.

Frank breathed a sigh of relief. After years of harassment from the Little Flower, his own man was in office.

It was shortly after the election that Frank handed me copies of the signed resignations of all the Tammany leaders, with a few judges thrown in.

"If anything happens to me, you know what to do with these," he said.

I didn't tell him that I *didn't* know, because to me the whole thing was irrelevant. It was not until some years later when I read that Tammany leader Judge Francis X. Mancuso had suddenly resigned from the leadership—and was claiming he didn't *know* he had resigned—that I realized these were not meaningless pieces of paper. If Frank decided any official he controlled got out of line, that official suddenly found himself out of office, his resignation on his superior's desk.

I will now describe what happened to Mancuso, as one example. I am happy to report that Mancuso lived to a fine old age and died a natural death. For a while there, both he and I were worried.

12

The public facts were these. During Bill O'Dwyer's reign as mayor he would periodically announce "wars" against Tammany Hall, but somehow the key men always remained in power.

When they rebelled, as did Francis X. Mancuso, strange things happened. As I mentioned in the previous chapter, like other leaders, Mancuso had been forced to leave his signed, undated resignation with Frank before taking office at Tammany. But, apparently, as a good citizen he was never happy about Frank's influence, and began in a guarded fashion to criticize Frank— and O'Dwyer—in public.

In 1949 O'Dwyer was going to be opposed by Vincent Impellitteri in the election for mayor. One day Mancuso went to Impellitteri and promised him his support. It turned out to be a very dangerous move.

Both Frank Rizzo, Costello's long-time friend, and I had roles in what happened next. In a letter to me about the incident, the Professor writes in a mixture of broken, yet literate, English:

> I think it is important to write something about former Judge Francis X. Mancuso, who by order of Frank was forced to leave the leadership just because he doublecrossed Frank by secretly working for Impellitteri. Of course you must know something about it, but not what I know as I was the person who gave the ultimatum to Mancuso in his own home on Park Avenue.
>
> It was an early Sunday morning when my telephone rang. It was Frank's low voice, "Professor, please come to my house as soon as you can. I got a letter from the bishop of my town and I want you to read it for me, as it is written in Italian."

I thought the call was for the preparation to welcome Bishop Barbieri at the Waldorf Astoria, which I had almost established. Bishop Barbieri was ready to leave Italy to meet Frank for the completion of financing for the Lauropoli Boys Town. So I rushed to get all the papers about the welcome and in a half hour I was at his house on Central Park West.

"Professor," Frank said, "write to the Bishop to postpone his departure. You know that *pidocchioso* [lousy] Judge Mancuso is a dishonest man. He let me believe he was helping us, instead he was helping Impellitteri, telling him secrets about me and Carmine DeSapio [Tammany Hall's leader]. Go to his house at once, tell him not to come to my house anymore, and tell him to resign or otherwise ask him to give you back the $5,000 that I gave him twenty days ago."

While he was talking I was thinking to myself, why is he sending *me* there.

I called Mancuso. It was nine o'clock. "Good morning, Judge. I'm Frank Rizzo. I'm sorry to call you so early in the morning, but it is important for some matter of myself."

Mancuso: "Yes, yes, but why can't you tell me the matter on the phone?"

"It is too long and very important. It is better to come to your house."

I rang the bell. He met me at the door. "Good morning, Judge, how are you?"

Mancuso: "Not so well, how are you? Please come in, come in and tell me your matter."

"Judge," I began, "it is not my own matter that is bringing me here, but someone else. I'm sorry, indeed very sorry, to bring you such a bad message. You have to resign from leader, otherwise you will be forced to do so in a different way. Don't permit yourself to go to Frank's house anymore. He doesn't want to see you anymore, and if you go to his house he will throw you out the window. It is his message, that's all."

He took my message, shaking, and then he said, "Professor, you know how I always like you and tried to help you on getting work. I always considered you as my best friend, and I'm begging you to do a favor for me now in exchange for what I have done for you. You have to convince Frank to receive me at his house for only once so I can explain all such misunderstanding. I'll be grateful to you."

"I can't, Judge. Frank doesn't want to see you anymore. You have to pay for what you did."

After I left Mancuso's house, I went to the other district captains giving them Frank's message which was received with a big OK.

By the evening we reached all the district captains and at 9 P.M. we had a meeting and we came to the unanimous conclusion of not recognizing Mancuso as leader.

There was a stool pigeon among us, and Mancuso was informed of the meeting in the late night. He ran to District Attorney Hogan.

What happened next was instructive. Frank simply filled in the date on Mancuso's resignation, turned it in, and the next thing New York—and Mancuso—knew the Tammany leader had resigned. It said so, right on the front page of the *Times*.

Mancuso announced to the newspapers that he had definitely *not* resigned, and angrily kept his date with DA Hogan. What he told Mr. Hogan I do not know, but I do know that by nightfall another messenger from Frank must have reached the judge, for my own telephone rang. It was Mancuso. He sounded on the verge of hysterics. "George," he said, "you know I've had some misunderstandings with Frank, but I trust you as a legitimate and honest person. I want you to know that I've always had the deepest respect for you."

I was mystified. I said, "And I respect you, Judge, but why the call? Is there something you want me to tell Frank?"

"Yes. Tell him I'm going away and I'm never coming back. I'm disappearing."

"Disappearing?"

"Yes. Tell him that message, George. Please."

And he hung up. I never saw Judge Mancuso again. I am told

he spent his last years in Florida, far from the New York political scené.

Knowing Frank's feelings about violence, and his smartness, I believe the judge's fears were exaggerated. But I do not deny that the call frightened me at the time. Frank's power in New York City was awesome. And it was obvious he used it when he was crossed.

13

The Mancuso incident happened in 1949. By then, Frank was all-powerful. This was because the Lucky Luciano situation came to a crisis on VE Day, 1945, a crisis which eventually catapulted Frank into the position of Boss of all Bosses.

It began when I filed on behalf of Lucky Luciano a petition to Governor Dewey for executive clemency in 1945. What happened next became a controversy which was to shadow Dewey throughout his career.

Dewey turned the petition over to the New York State Parole Board, and after a few months of investigation the board unanimously recommended that—on the basis of his wartime efforts—Lucky should be released.

Enraged newspaper editorials appeared across the land. Most of them said it was ridiculous to claim that Luciano had any effect on the war's outcome since he had been in prison throughout the conflict.

These charges brought back a rumor that had been circulating over the years. The rumor was that one of the major sources of the governor's campaign funds had been the underworld.

I happen to have been the man on the spot throughout, appearing for Luciano at a motion for the reduction of his sentence, and participating in numerous legal conferences about his release—and I can say the rumor involving Tom Dewey was completely untrue. One of the reasons has been made public. The other comes from my own private knowledge.

First, the public reason. There is no doubt that Luciano did assist in preventing sabotage. To say that he could not have provided war aid because he was in prison is to say that the President as Commander-in-Chief could give no orders to his troops in Europe because he was thousands of miles away. Remember that part of the deal with Luciano was that he was allowed frequent conferences with the underworld chiefs who controlled the docks. The word from Luciano then was to obey the law around the docks. At the time everyone expected him to be free and back in power after the war.

Second, from my private knowledge I know that Luciano was furious instead of satisfied with the way things turned out. While he was set free he was not allowed to remain in the United States. Instead, as a condition of his release he was deported to Italy. Luciano felt the governor had gone back on his word. But Dewey insisted on deporting him—and Luciano did go off to exile, a very bitter man, he told me.

I believe Dewey's actions were impeccable in this case. And let us recall that the original charge against Luciano—based on "organized prostitution"—was a slim charge to merit a thirty-year sentence. I believe that Dewey weighed this factor, too, in his decision.

As far as Frank was concerned, Luciano's deportation would dramatically affect his life. For years Frank had been holding what might be called a "caretaker" office. Now it appeared that the former boss was going to be exiled, and that meant Frank would at last be alone as Boss of all Bosses.

Unless Vito Genovese had other ideas.

Vito Genovese, like Frank, was born in a poor village near Naples. His birthplace was called Rosiglino, and the date was November 27, 1897. His family did not emigrate to this country until 1913.

The Genoveses settled in Little Italy on Mulberry Street and —again like Frank—Vito was soon in trouble with the law, receiving his first sentence on an identical charge—carrying a gun.

But Vito soon made an important friend in Little Italy— young Lucky Luciano. They grew up together, and Lucky came to rely on his friend for the execution of the rough jobs. As

Lucky moved higher and higher in the Mafia, he brought Genovese along as his underboss.

Frank, at the same time, came into power from a different level—business. Astute as he was, Luciano appreciated Frank's talent for making money and acquiring political influence. Different as they were, Frank a diplomat, Luciano a strong-arm type, the two of them made a good team. Vito Genovese, Lucky's underboss, could not help being nervous about the ambitions of Lucky's uptown friend when Lucky got into trouble with the law. Genovese was next in line—the mantle of power should fall to him. Would Frank put in a claim?

The matter became academic when Genovese himself tangled with the law in the Rupolo incident. The story of that incident has become a treasured underworld legend illustrating Genovese's devious mind.

Ferdinand Boccia was the manager of one of Genovese's gambling shops in Brooklyn. In 1934 Boccia was pleased to report to Genovese that he had fleeced a businessman out of a fortune, namely $100,000, which he obediently turned over to Genovese. The underworld rule of thumb in this situation was that Genovese would return one-third of the money to Boccia as his slice. Instead he hired two hoods, Ernie "the Hawk" Rupolo and Willie Gallo, to kill Boccia, thus cleverly wiping out both the debt—and Boccia.

The devious plan was that as soon as Boccia was killed, Rupolo would then murder his partner Gallo. As we have seen, Rupolo had a little bad luck. His attempt on Gallo's life failed, and Rupolo ended up in prison.

This made "the Hawk" angry enough to talk, and Genovese was indicted for murder and had to flee to Italy. There he remained throughout the war, becoming—in a twist of fate—an aide to the American occupation troops who found him an invaluable liaison man when they entered Italy. He was even more invaluable to himself, it turned out, when the Army's Criminal Investigation Division looked into the huge black market activities going on and found that their friend Vito Genovese was the kingpin.

The CID sergeant assigned to the case, Orange C. Dickey, soon discovered that Genovese was wanted for murder in the United

States. And that meant Genovese was in real trouble, because "the Hawk" had come up with another witness to the Boccia shooting, a salesman, Peter La Tempa, who had overheard certain conversations and could implicate Genovese.

This fact did not exactly guarantee a long life-span for Peter La Tempa.

THE GUNS

The police guard outside Peter La Tempa's jail cell heard the man inside groan in pain again.

La Tempa was in agony from gallstones. The prison doctors were arranging for surgery, but meanwhile the pain must be terrible. The guard could tell from the constant sounds coming from the room. He looked through the bars and saw La Tempa, white and weak, waving his hand at him. The guard went inside. "You OK?" he said to the man in the bed.

"Jesus, it hurts," La Tempa said. "You better bring me some of that medicine."

The prison doctor had prescribed a pain-killer. The guard disappeared, the cell door clanked open, and the policeman came back with a glass of water with the pain-killer dissolved in it. He handed the glass to La Tempa who gulped half of it down, rested a few seconds, then finished off the glass. "Thanks," he said to the guard—then he started to stiffen. "Oh God," he cried, and fell back trembling. The guard ran out of the door and called for help. In minutes a prison nurse was there. La Tempa was dead from some very strange medicine.

Vito Genovese would be freed in 1946 owing to the death of a corroborating witness, and he would be back in action in New York.

At first he would lie low, moving into a mansion in Atlantic Highlands, New Jersey. In those days, when I saw him with Frank, he was always very friendly to my client—and when Genovese got into trouble in his divorce case Frank asked me to advise him, as a favor, which I did.

But of course Genovese could not help feeling, I'm sure, that fate had dealt him a bad hand, that he, the appointed successor to Luciano, should be under the "smoothie" from uptown, Frank, just because of that stupid Boccia incident.

From what we know now he began almost from the minute he arrived to undermine Frank in every way he could.

But at first he had to move softly.

14

"You can't go down there, Frank. I won't allow it," I said.

"I got to go," Frank replied. "It's the right thing."

The "thing" was to attend the departure of Lucky Luciano for Italy. He was sailing for Italy from Pier 7 at the Bush Terminal in Brooklyn the next day, February 9, 1946. "Every reporter and photographer in New York will be there," I said, "and you'll be the No. 1 target of the press."

"He was my friend. What's so wrong about paying a little visit to the boat when he goes. You're blowing this up, George."

"For three years you've been accused of being the No. 1 man in crime in America. We've done everything we could to change that image, but always they come back with the answer, 'Look at his friends.' And they name Luciano, Adonis, Anastasia, and all the others. Now what's going to happen tomorrow?"

Frank was getting a kick out of this conversation, which only made me angrier. "What's going to happen?" he asked. "Go on. Tell me."

"Every one of those men and more will be at the boat, too. It will look like a convention of the top criminal leaders. And there you'll be right in front of the cameras."

Frank said nothing for a while, then he finally remarked, "There's only one thing you don't know, George."

"What is it?"

"I got to go."

What happened the next day was a nightmare. One reporter described the scene as "one of the most brazen public expressions of Mafia power and contempt for the law in American history."

A huge crowd of photographers and reporters had descended on the office of the Immigration Bureau's security division to ask for passes to board the ship and interview the famous criminal. Harry Ratzke, the assistant superintendent of security, was cooperative. He issued the passes and then personally led the crowd of press people to the pier. To his surprise, there were fifty ferocious-looking dockworkers standing in a line across the pier, all of them holding sharp-edged baling hooks.

Just then Luciano arrived and was let through the line with cheers from the workers. But when Ratzke attempted to follow with the reporters the line closed up. "Nobody goes on that boat," one of the dockworkers said.

"But I'm from the Bureau of Immigration," Ratzke insisted, "and I'm taking these reporters to see Luciano."

The dockworkers crowded menacingly around Ratzke and the reporters, one of whom stumbled and almost fell into the water. At this point Ratzke's behavior changed. He humbly asked if he alone could go aboard. The dockworkers huddled, then one of them said, "OK. But no reporters."

Ratzke went up the pier and boarded the little Liberty ship *Laura Keene,* and the reporters were left to mill in the sun. But they were not entirely disappointed. Many of the guests came with hampers crammed with wines and liquors, lobsters and caviar—and no doubt money. They included Frank Costello, Joe Adonis, Albert Anastasia, Meyer Lansky, and many smaller fry in the hierarchy, plus a few judges and politicians.

The party lasted for hours and reporters could hear the laughter, shouts, and commotion.

The cause of this celebration and expression of loyalty I was not to discover until late that same year. That's when I heard Luciano was coming back to power. He would set up his headquarters in Cuba, where he was protected by the underworld's favorite politician, Fulgencio Batista. Just ninety miles from the U.S., Luciano would issue orders to his underlings in America.

15

On the financial front in those critical years, Frank had to make some adjustments, too. When the crusading new mayor of New Orleans, deLesseps S. Morrison, banned his slot machines from the city, Frank and Phil Kastel had to find other locations throughout the state, and set up all the payoffs and "protection" that were needed.

But it was clear to Frank that the heyday of the slot machines was over. He had, once again, to explore new sources of income. Some underworld chiefs were opening nightclubs in Florida; Frank may have joined them in some of these ventures. If so, he never revealed it to me. But he did have his Beverly Club in Louisiana, and pieces of clubs in Hot Springs, Arkansas, and Saratoga, New York.

Nevertheless, his income would be drastically cut. And so by 1946, he was looking for new investments. Surprisingly, all of them would be legitimate. I personally put him in some real estate deals, and a television company. On his own he invested in some oil well speculations.

But all of this was small-time stuff. The big burst forward into the postwar world was to happen in a desert in Nevada within a few months. Bugsy Siegel would have an idea—and Frank would be the man to bring it to fruition.

Virginia Hill, her chestnut hair falling loosely around her cheeks, leaned over and kissed Bugsy Siegel. "It's going to be great, Ben," she said.

Virginia was Bugsy's girl—of the moment. Before Bugsy, Virginia had been the darling of more than a dozen top mobsters. Voluptuous, sexy, with luminous green eyes, she had begun her life as this country's most storied "moll" as a protégée of Joe Epstein, a Chicago bookie. But Joe was soon left behind as she climbed the status ladder of the Mafia until the day she met handsome, wavy-haired Bugsy Siegel and fell in love.

Bugsy (no one ever called him that to his face) had taken Virginia on a ride that day, direct from downtown Las Vegas to the airport, three miles away. In 1931 Nevada had legalized gambling, the only state in the nation to do so. In Vegas small gambling saloons had sprung up in the tradition of a Western town in the gold rush days. But Bugsy saw more. He envisioned that three-mile strip to the airport lined with great luxury hotels containing posh gambling casinos, all legal. It would be an unbelievable opportunity.

But he needed money, *big* money, even in underworld terms. Millions and millions of dollars.

Some of it he could siphon off from that racetrack wire he had stolen from the Chicago boys. But he needed more, no doubt about it.

The next day Bugsy kissed Virginia Hill good-bye and boarded a flight to New York. He had a date with Frank Costello. It was an appointment that would end with Siegel's murder, and near death for my client.

Once in New York, Bugsy saw not only Frank but other top leaders in the Mafia. All of them saw the great good sense of the proposition, although I have no doubt that—at least from Frank's angle—they would have preferred a solid businessman type to be in charge instead of the excitable, flamboyant Bugsy.

The construction of the Flamingo Hotel, first of the Vegas luxury hotels, began on the desert sand. And almost immediately it became apparent to the money men in New York that there was going to be trouble. The cost was originally estimated at slightly less than two million. But the construction costs started skyrocketing.

One of the reasons for the increased costs was Bugsy's insistence on the "best." The plumbing bill alone came to $1 million. Bugsy thought it was class to equip every bathroom with its own private sewer line. The Del E. Webb Construction Company of Phoenix, Arizona, was the contractor, and Webb's people had their hands full with Bugsy. He was demanding materials impossible to get in the postwar priorities days. Bugsy solved this problem by going into the black market—with the New York backers' cash—and buying steel, copper, tile, whatever was hard to get.

Vegas is hot and sunny; Bugsy had to have concrete walls. All the woods were imported, as was the marble—and the money. The cash flow stopped, except for Frank Costello.

16

In 1946 I was in Chicago to see a client who was accused of illegal stock activities (I'll call him Jim Layner, which is not his name) when suddenly the door burst open and there was Phil Kastel, Frank's slot machine partner in Louisiana.

Phil looked bad. He was obviously fatigued; his eyes were bloodshot. I learned later from Frank that Phil had just gone to Vegas to take a million dollars *in cash* in two suitcases to the voracious Bugsy—and discovered that Bugsy needed more.

After we all said hello, Phil said to Jim, "Can you come up with a million dollars in cash?"

To my surprise, Jim said yes, without blinking an eye. "What do you need it for?"

"The Flamingo. We'll sell you a piece of it."

"I can get it for you in a day," Jim said, "but I want forty percent of the deal."

"Forty percent?" Phil was angry. "That's a shakedown."

I saw things were getting out of hand and I asked Phil to excuse us because I had a legal matter to discuss in private with Jim. The two of us went into Jim's back office while Phil remained outside. "Jim," I said, "that man is in a desperate state, you can see that. Be reasonable. If you don't want the deal on their terms, don't lead them on."

My remarks only made Jim angry. "Mind your own goddam business," he said. "What do you mean by butting in?"

"Phil Kastel and Frank Costello are my clients and I know the situation and I don't want them to get into trouble."

"You butt out of this," Jim snapped.

He went back into his main office where Phil was waiting and repeated his 40 percent offer. Phil said, "That's crazy. I believe we can get the boys to give you ten percent but Frank will have a hard time doing even that."

The meeting ended with Jim and Phil arguing furiously. Phil felt—with good reason—that Jim wanted to take advantage of him and Frank when they were in financial trouble.

Finally, Phil stormed out of the office, and Jim finally calmed down. But back in New York, when I mentioned this scene to Frank, he was still sore. "I hate a jerk like that," he said.

What worried Frank was that many members of the mob had put in money on his say-so . . . and Frank had a reputation as an absolutely straight shooter in business deals. Now that crazy Bugsy in Vegas was swallowing up millions and the damn hotel would never be finished and even if it was, it would be so deep in the red it would go bankrupt.

So it looked to Frank, and then the worst blow of all happened. The hotel opened.

17

It was December 26, 1946, and a cold rain swept the Los Angeles airport. Fog, creeping in from the Pacific, imprisoned the chartered Constellations waiting for their passengers.

The airport was crowded with movie stars and glamorous Hollywood figures all eager to fly—at Bugsy Siegel's expense—to the opening of his exciting new hotel, the Flamingo. But the bad weather held. No planes could take off. Gradually the disgruntled celebrities returned to their chauffeured cars and were driven back to Hollywood.

In Las Vegas, Bugsy heard the news by telephone and was furious. For months he had planned this opening down to the smallest detail. It had to be the biggest in history, and the Hollywood stars he had cultivated all these years would make head-lines across the country.

Grimly, Bugsy dressed in a swallowtail coat and white tie while Virginia Hill fitted herself into the flamingo gown she had especially ordered for the occasion. And precisely on time Bugsy and Virginia threw open the doors of the great hotel.

The hotel wasn't finished, but the theater, casino, lounge, and restaurant were ready for action. Bugsy had imported top enter-tainers: Jimmy Durante and Eddie Jackson, Baby Rosemarie, the Tunetoppers, and Xavier Cugat's music to keep everyone happy.

But where was the excitement? No stars, unless you counted George Raft and Sonny Tufts (Sonny Tufts?). The crowd was disappointed—and, even worse, there were no real gamblers among them. The people had come for the thrill of an opening night when they could see celebrities. Very soon the crowd started to melt, half the tables were empty, and that very first night the casino went deeply into the red.

Back in New York, the boys got the word by phone, "It's a washout."

Two weeks later, with casino losses already more than $500,-000 and climbing, Bugsy closed the hotel and went back to L.A. with Virginia to think things over.

There was even more furious thinking—and recriminations —in New York. Who was to blame for the fiasco? The eyes of the underworld fastened on two men, Frank and Meyer Lansky, Bugsy's longtime friends.

I do not know what role, if any, Lansky actually played in the Flamingo affair. Early in 1947 I got an inkling of Frank's situa-tion. He wanted me to approach some of his former friends for loans. It seems he needed several million dollars to pay back the boys who had gone along with Bugsy on Frank's word.

By that time I had grown so fond of my client I was worried about him. I asked, "What happens if you can't raise it?"

"Part of it's already happened," he said enigmatically. I knew better than to press him with questions, especially when he was under stress, and it wasn't until years later I learned from him what had happened.

Lucky Luciano had reappeared in Havana, taking a luxurious

penthouse in the Hotel Nacional, and some of the boys who had lost their money with Bugsy through Frank had been making pilgrimages to Cuba to air their complaints. Frank and Lucky had been through a lot together, and as a result Lucky held fast. "Give him a chance," he told the angry underworld leaders.

Frank flew to Havana to see Lucky, and was told Luciano's ruling. "You got to get the money up somehow, Frank. Otherwise I can't hold them back."

"I'll get it," Frank said.

"And meanwhile, you retire as head of the commission. Genovese takes over."

"OK."

"But I told the boys—and they agree—as soon as you get the money back, you take over again," Lucky told Frank. "I want you there."

"What happens to Bugsy?" Frank asked.

"Him I can't help," Lucky said.

THE GUNS

18

It was June 20, 1947, and Bugsy Siegel looked great. He and a close friend, Allen Smiley, were dining at Jack's on the beach in Santa Monica and Bugsy was telling Allen the good news. The Flamingo, which he had reopened a few months ago, was now in the black. In May it had made $300,000 profit.

But, personally, what he wanted to do now, he said, was retire. The hotel would earn back all the money everybody thought had been lost, and meanwhile he could go to Europe with Virginia Hill and forget the whole nerve-racking experience of the last few months.

The two men walked out of the lobby of the restaurant and Bugsy picked up a free copy of the Los Angeles *Times*. A card clipped on top of the paper said: "Good night. Sleep peacefully, with compliments of Jack's."

They got into Bugsy's car and drove to a pink Moorish mansion in Beverly Hills, which Bugsy maintained for Virginia Hill. It was quiet when they arrived, that refined silence of Beverly Hills when the air is soft and afar off the hum of cars is muted.

The killer had been told Bugsy would be back an hour ago. Now he sat on the ground inside a rose-covered pergola, a .30 caliber army carbine nearby. Then the roar of a car in the driveway and white headlight beams brought him alert in a hurry. He stood up, quietly, and waited.

Bugsy and his friend got out of the car and in a minute lights were on in the living room. The killer had chosen his spot carefully. The picture window gave him a view of the whole room, and the pergola was a perfect cover. Now he saw Bugsy sit down on the chintz-covered sofa, where he began reading the *Times*. Smiley plunked himself down at the other end.

The killer poked his carbine through the latticework, rested it on a crossbar, and carefully aimed.

Nine times he fired. Glass was flying. Bugsy's head jerked once, twice, as two bullets smashed into his face. One crushed the bridge of his nose and ripped into his left eye. The other passed through his right cheek and sent the other eye fifteen feet through the air to land on the carpet near Bugsy's friend.

Three thousand miles away, in New York, Frank did not despair when he heard the news. Bugsy had broken every rule in the book. It was believed by the underworld that Bugsy had himself profited in kickbacks from the millions that flowed through his hands.

Frank had taken part of the blame, and gone in hock himself to pay back the boys who felt they had been cheated. Now with the hotel starting to pay off, he might recoup some of that money himself.

Costello didn't know who killed Bugsy—it could have been anybody—but it solved a problem for him. His repayment of funds had met with the approval of the underworld, and Lucky had ordered his reinstatement in good grace as head of the commission. Without that crazy Bugsy to cause trouble, things would be peaceful again.

But who did kill Bugsy? And why at a time when the Flamingo was starting to pay off?

So far as Frank was concerned, the reason was, as I have said above, that Bugsy profited on under-the-table deals, a no-no in the underworld. But Frank's friend the Professor recently sent me a letter which reveals, for the first time, a new suspect, Joe Adonis, and a new reason, jealousy. And, according to the Professor, Frank Costello was indirectly the cause of the friction which led up to the shooting.

At center stage was lusty, busty Virginia Hill. Let the Professor tell the story in his inimitable fashion:

> Virginia Hill of Slovak origin left Bessemer (Alabama) and set out for Chicago with indefined but determined intentions of making money to help her poor family's living. She soon became a party girl and her sex appeal was noted by big-shot gambler Joe Epstein. He showed her a gold mine from where she could get any money she wanted to buy fine clothes, furs, and jewels. But it wasn't enough for her. She wanted more and more. She was only fifteen years old then and full of ambitions, a revelation of charm and humor, always desirable as a date. Joe Epstein was her first gold mine and she was for him a messenger and go-between in the underworld. She met all the big-shots of Chicago and among them New Yorker Joe Adonis, and soon she was welcomed as his girl friend. Virginia reciprocated because in Joe Adonis she saw the way to arrive to Costello, considered by her the big-shot of all the big-shots she ever met. *But it wasn't so as she never conferred with Costello.* This story is true as I was a protagonist of an undenied fact. Virginia burst on Broadway as a star and to give a big impression she used to invite people to nightclubs every evening and spend more than $1,000. She suggested Joe Adonis, who liked the idea, to open the Hurricane Restaurant at 49th Street and Broadway. Frank Mario had the checkroom and he offered me a job to help him. As usual I went to Frank to tell him about Frank Mario's offering to me. NO, he said to me. You are not going there. The Hurricane can't last

long. *Virginia Hill is a big Bitch and if she remains here she would call many dogs in New York.* She must go away.

He called Joe Adonis and he gave him an *ultimatum.*

She was there only two nights and then moved to California where the syndicate was extending its way into Hollywood taking over the movie stars. Virginia was Bugsy Siegel's girl friend. Joe Adonis got mad and a war started between the two of them. It was finished with the death of Siegel in Virginia's home. Years later Joe Adonis was deported to Italy and he died in 1972 by heart trouble.

Whether this story is true or not, I don't know. It sounds a bit romantic to me, the tale of a "true love" revenged. I doubt that Adonis and Virginia were that close, if they were close at all. But whatever the motive for the killing, the result was the same. The troublesome Bugsy was gone. Phil Kastel had already come to Costello with a plan to build their own hotel in Vegas. They would not have to contend with someone like Bugsy to run up costs. And with Lucky running "family" business from Havana, Frank would now have time to get back to the business he enjoyed, making money.

But the bullets that ripped into Bugsy Siegel also ripped into this dream. For those same bullets shot down Luciano for good as Boss of all Bosses.

19

Bugsy Siegel's gangland-style killing in California convinced Americans that organized crime was now nationwide in scope. No longer would street killings and assassinations be confined to the streets of Chicago and New York. The killers roamed even in sunny Beverly Hills.

Columnists such as Drew Pearson and Robert Ruark pointed to the coincidence of the former Mafia leader, Lucky Luciano, ensconced in Havana so near by, and the criminal leaders "visiting" him there.

Ruark, particularly, became so abusive—reviving accusations against Dewey for releasing Luciano—that some of his columns were killed by the newspapers that were supposed to run them.

Lucky's presence in nearby Havana was now a clear embarrassment to American officials, and inside the government the Bureau of Narcotics was making charges that Lucky was organizing drug traffic. State Department representatives spoke to Cuban authorities, requesting that they get Luciano to leave Cuba. At first they got nowhere with the Cuban government. But eventually it yielded under what pressure I do not know, although I have heard that the U.S. government threatened to stop all shipments of legal drugs to Cuba if Luciano was not sent away.

In any event the Cuban government could not withstand the American pressure which began with Bugsy Siegel's murder. The Cuban leaders finally had to tell Luciano he was no longer welcome, a scene that must have proved most disturbing for the "lucky" one. For while he would sail back to Italy, survive an attempt to deport him to Sicily, and end up finally in Naples—and though he might get his share of underworld profits for the rest of his life, as has been reported—he would never again be in power in the U.S., never again be the Boss of all Bosses.

Frank Costello stood alone. He was fifty-six years old.

20

How does a man like Frank Costello feel when he reaches the pinnacle of underworld power? Does he ever reflect on the circumstances or events that led him to a position which is denounced almost daily by citizens and newspapers, a position where he is branded the No. 1 criminal in the U.S.A.?

On a balmy June day, after Luciano's final departure from Cuba, Frank Rizzo, the Professor, picked up Costello in a sedan.

They were driving out to Long Island where Frank was going to play golf with the "better" people.

In that sedan, Frank started to talk about his life. In a letter to me the Professor recounts some of Frank's conversation. Frank said:

> The first thing I dreamed in my life, when I was ten years old, was to become a policeman, mayor of the city, some big shot. My world, instead, went in a different direction. There are moments in life where no one is able to stop, to deviate to other aims. All of my life, of which everyone is talking today, was born that way, without thinking of what it meant.
>
> Would you like to have an image that will give you an idea of my life? There is a person at the wheel of the car on a road unknown to him. He is unable to stop the car. The things passing through are unexpected, new, different from the trip that he wanted to make. It is terrible for the man who is at the wheel of his own life to realize that the brake doesn't work.
>
> So many times I confided to my wife the secret projects, the dreams of my life. Not one has been realized. I wanted them. I spit on my life, and yet the life gave me everything. I spit on my life, denying it when it was wonderful for me to live it. It isn't nice being called the prime minister of the underworld. Yet what can I do? I would like to know from others what should have been done in my place when everything I have touched turned into money, and in a blinding rhythm of life.
>
> It is seen that I wasn't born to be a saint, even if in my youth I had the image of St. Francis on my neck, given to me from my mother. Perhaps St. Francis is watching me. Don't you think so, Professor?

Frank Costello in power as the Boss of all Bosses.

I saw Frank almost every day during those years when he was the absolute ruler of the underworld; I came to his famous "breakfasts" in his apartment along with the high and mighty from both political and Mafia circles; I sat with him at lunch in East Side restaurants and watched the parade of sinister men come to his table and whisper in his ear, a fascinating ritual to watch, one man after another, waiting his turn. Frank would nod without saying anything, or turn and sharply rebuke the man. The man would go away to be replaced by another who quietly waited his turn. Lunch was an important time for Frank, always with some associate on business matters. And the telephone hours when he spoke across the nation to family leaders or business associates were also rigid. For at least an hour before his breakfast every day he was on the phone. Everyone who dined with Frank in the evening knew that at precisely eleven he would leave to go home to make his evening round of calls. (The people who eventually tried to kill him knew this schedule, too.)

Frank never had a real business office after his bootlegging days. All mail to him was forwarded to my office, where I would screen the letters and prepare answers for Frank. But this is hardly surprising; no Mafia leader I ever heard of operated out of a business office.

But Frank's method of running the underworld was certainly unique in another perspective. It was so public. There he was every day right in front of the world, consulting with known criminals. And his phone from his apartment could be tapped, although Frank paid technicians to "sweep" the phone and let him know when it was clear. The restrictions at the time on wire-tapping were so confining that the authorities rarely bothered, and when they did they had to have hard evidence of some particular crime in the offing.

But even wiretapping didn't concern Frank because he—alone of all major underworld figures—was "protected" from bottom to top in New York City political and judicial circles. The roll call of guests at the Salvation Army dinner he sponsored tells it all—judges, congressmen, political leaders. All underworld leaders, before and since, have had various public officials on their payroll, taking graft, but no one carried the art of corruption as high and as successfully as Frank. He was famous for it.

And so New York was treated to the spectacle of its underworld leader running his life and business right out in the open. No secluded, guarded mansion in New Jersey or Long Island, no fortress, no hideaway. Frank Costello, New York citizen, awoke every morning in his apartment at 115 Central Park West, and quietly began the daily routine of running his business, which happened to be the Mafia.

Rising from his bed, Frank would slip into a silk dressing gown and have a cup of coffee. Then the telephone would come to life: Bugsy Siegel in Los Angeles with a problem concerning Willie Bioff; Albert Anastasia in New Jersey asking advice about a dockworkers' contract; Jake Lansky in Miami explaining the financial setup of a nightclub in Florida; Phil Kastel in New Orleans asking him to make a move on a Scotch distributorship.

And all interspersed with local calls from men like bookie Frank Erickson, Brooklyn leader Joe Adonis, Bronx chieftain Joey Rao on various underworld matters.

In about an hour the guests would begin to arrive for breakfast. You might find a Tammany Hall leader, a mobster like Tony Bender, a businessman, all rubbing shoulders and enjoying bacon and eggs, while Frank sat at the head of the table in his dressing gown. If there was underworld "business" to discuss in which everyone was involved, it would be straightened out at this breakfast. When there was no business pending, the breakfasts were held anyway, often just to introduce people to each other, a gangster to a politician who might later help him.

Breakfast over, the Boss of all Bosses slipped into one of his conservative blue double-breasted, hand-tailored suits, with a dazzling white handkerchief peeping from the breast pocket. At this point someone like the Professor or Jim O'Connell or another trusted friend would appear to drive Frank over to the Waldorf Astoria for his daily morning shave. If no one was available for the drive, Costello would be on the street crying "Taxi!" just like other New Yorkers.

He would arrive at the Lexington Avenue side of the Waldorf and unobtrusively slip into the barbershop. There he would sit in a chair reserved for him, and soon towels and lather would be applied, while a manicurist worked on his fingers and a bootblack polished his shoes.

After his daily shave, Frank would appear either in the Waldorf Grill or another restaurant where more business would be conducted. Frank Erickson would be there at least twice a week to discuss their bookie operation; other frequent guests were Vincent (Jimmy Blue Eyes) Alo, who was Frank's man in Harlem, Joe Adonis, Frank's key man in Brooklyn, or any of the leaders of various families who had problems to discuss.

After lunch he might go to the Biltmore Hotel for a steam bath and a massage; or to the racetrack, in season; or to Sands Point for a golf game. Frank Costello loved golf, although he never mastered the game as well as he did underworld politics.

Playtime over, it was back to business at various cocktail lounges throughout the East Side, most notably the old Madison Hotel and the St. Regis King Cole Room, and once again the parade of underworld people with things to discuss. Then Frank would call his wife, Bobbie, who would meet him, and off they would go to dinner until, promptly at eleven, Frank would excuse himself and head back to his apartment for the telephone calls he knew would be coming in.

His life as head of the underworld was a commingling of three interests: his personal businesses which brought him his income; underworld problems and frictions which he helped resolve; and New York political corruption which he constantly worked on, for it was the basis of his influence. It is interesting, from my knowledge of Frank, that the press dubbed him the "prime minister" of crime, instead of just "the boss," for my personal knowledge showed him to be just that. The underworld is a series of families linked by two common concerns: profit and survival. Of those family leaders Frank was "first among firsts." That meant he was the man to see for a decision involving major family disagreements. However, before making such a decision he would first consult the council of Mafia leaders around the country. As to the multitude of smaller problems which came to him he could only give his advice, mediate, assist in any way—but if a family leader had trouble with one of his underlings and was determined that nothing, no commission meeting, no word from Frank could stop him, that underling would be murdered.

Interestingly, during Frank's reign this rarely happened, and that is indicative of the kind of advice Frank was giving. Even Albert Anastasia, the erstwhile head of Murder Incorporated, quieted down under Frank's influence. In Valachi's words, everything "was peaceful" under Frank.

It is an evening in the late Forties at the Copacabana. Frank and his wife Bobbie, who is clad in an elegant mink coat, come through the door with some friends, my wife Mina and I among them. A murmur in the room as everyone watches Frank, and we are taken to the best table, seated with a flourish, a gaggle of waiters in attendance. Frank is smiling, then laughing at a joke one of his friends has just whispered in his ear.

The Copa is his favorite nightclub and perhaps that is why, seated in the dark around the room, there are some underworld associates, perhaps looking in envy at the Boss of all Bosses, and wondering how *they* might some day rise to the top.

Joe E. Lewis, the performer, comes on stage, a glass of Scotch in his hand. Soon his patter is breaking up the audience: "Behind every successful man is a surprised mother-in-law," and, as he watches a shapely girl walk by, a follow-up joke: "Behind every great woman is a great behind."

Frank laughs; someone whispers in his ear; he laughs again. The Boss of all Bosses is enjoying himself—until eleven o'clock and those phone calls.

21

A clear demonstration of Frank's political influence in those years was the famous Salvation Army dinner, which provoked a scandal. What made it especially embarrassing to me was that my wife and I were the acting hosts of the dinner, on behalf of Frank.

It all began innocently enough when a letter addressed to Frank arrived from Walter Hoving of the Hoving Corporation.

> At the request of Ray Vir Den who, as you may know, has accepted the Chairmanship of the Salvation Army

1949 campaign I have agreed to head up the Men's Committee.

I am asking key people in New York to be Vice-Chairmen of my committee. I am most anxious to have you join me as Vice-Chairman. I'll guarantee minimum demands on your time.

The letter was addressed to Frank at the 79 Wall Street Corporation, and I was delighted. My plan expressed to Frank a few years before to use the funds from rentals at 79 Wall Street for charity had been more than amply fulfilled in the past. All rents were collected by an agent who, after deducting taxes, maintenance, and her own commission, would send me a check for the balance, which was deposited in the corporation account. Virtually all charity donations were drawn from this account. What's more, Frank would advance in cash sums for charities when the fund did not hold enough.

And I think it is not inappropriate here to point up just how much Frank did contribute to various charities, ranging from religious and youth activities to his home town in Italy, to contributions to every sort of charity in America. This activity on the part of a man like Costello may be derided by some as "frosting"—but I think the skeptics are wrong in Frank's case. There is no question, and I have the records, that he contributed many thousands of dollars over the years to various charities, much more than mere "frosting"—and he enjoyed doing so.

Now, with Hoving's letter, I saw an opportunity to bring this side of Frank's character to the public. I advised Frank to let Mr. Hoving know that he would be honored to serve as vice-chairman in the drive. I further suggested that Frank run a fund-raising affair at the Waldorf, to be conducted without a fanfare of publicity, that he invite 100 people, each to contribute $100—and that he pay all expenses, thus being able to raise $10,000 net which he could turn over to Mr. Hoving. He was enthusiastic about the idea.

So far so good. But then the event started to plunge to a disastrous course.

Loyalty was a way of life for Frank, and it showed when he visited me next with his proposed guest list. What a list! It began with the mayor, included practically every political leader and judge in the city, then went on to include dozens of top gangsters. All at one cozy party.

I remonstrated with Frank. I pleaded. Nothing I said could change his mind. Those so-called "gangsters" were his friends. Furthermore, forget the Waldorf. The dinner would be held at the Copacabana.

I hoped only that somehow, by some miracle, the newspapermen wouldn't hear about the affair. I also made a call to Mr. Hoving, just in case that aristocratic fellow didn't know what he was getting into. I told him I wanted him to be sure, before we went any further, that he knew who FRANK COSTELLO was. I went into his antisocial activities. Mr. Hoving assured me that he knew all about Costello and that, after all, "this is a charity drive and no one can be criticized for doing good."

That's what *he* thought.

The dinner was held, and I must say it was a beautiful party. The mayor and the politicians mingled with gangsters in their finest outfits; nary a gun in sight.

But outside the door a horde of photographers waited. When the distinguished guests exited, one by one, the flashbulbs exploded. Guests such as Mayor Impellitteri, Congressman Arthur Klein, five judges of the New York State Supreme Court, at least three other judges, and a whole slate of Tammany Hall luminaries headed by Hugo E. Rogers, president of the borough of Manhattan.

The publicity reached Washington and beyond. A U.S. Senator who sported a coonskin cap in his political campaigns thought Frank Costello just might be worth investigating. The Senator was Estes Kefauver from Tennessee.

BOOK IV

The Kefauver Hearings: America Meets Frank Costello

1

Kefauver's famous hearings on organized crime were preceded by another hearing in front of another Senate committee, which Frank once referred to as "a warm-up session."

By now the constant coverage by the daily press had made Frank a legend. He was, according to all reports, the No. 1 man in organized crime.

This rankled Frank, even though in an underworld sense it was true. What made him most angry was that the crimes committed by other underworld leaders, such as narcotics pushing, were imputed to him merely because of his notoriety. Time and again some politician or government official would hold a press conference declaring that Costello was behind the drug pushing, or the latest murder in the community. Time and again he would be on the phone, angrily telling me to issue a statement denouncing the charge as a lie.

Despite all the denials, by late 1949 Costello reached such fame that the Greater Los Angeles Press Club asked him to be the honored guest at their annual Eight-Ball dinner. Previous guests had included President Harry Truman, Vice President Alben Barkley, and General Mark Clark.

Frank could see all the "paper" (headlines) that would come out of *that* dinner, so he asked me to decline. And I wrote a rejection, in his name, which caused some amusement.

While I deeply appreciate the great honor conferred on

me, I cannot accept. I never made a speech in my life and
the very thought of it almost scares me to death. Even the
idea of facing members of the press gives me the shivers.

Evidently you folks are not satisfied with the countless
crimes that have been laid at my door; but you are now
egging me on to commit the most serious of all crimes—
murder—of the English language. That is one charge to
which I would have no defense—so my barrister advises me.

Early in 1950 a request—not a subpoena—came to the office
from a subcommittee of the U.S. Senate's Commerce Committee.
The subcommittee was investigating gambling in America and
wanted any information Frank could give them.

I advised Frank that this would be a good way to show that he
would voluntarily cooperate with the authorities and had nothing
to hide. He agreed and I contacted the subcommittee, telling the
Senators Frank would be happy to testify.

I understand some of the Senators, especially Charles W.
Tobey, from New Hampshire, were stunned by this quick ac-
ceptance. And so, apparently, was the whole city of Washington.
The excitement was intense. Costello, in the flesh, was coming
to Capitol Hill!

Frank and I took the train to Washington and stayed at the
Mayflower Hotel. The morning of his Senate appearance he was
just a trifle nervous. He appeared in the dining room in a blue
pin-striped suit, a conservative patterned tie, and shoes with a
mirror polish. But throughout breakfast he kept glancing at his
watch. "I want to be right on time," he said. "It's only proper."

I noticed that he hardly touched his breakfast. When he was
finished, he wrapped a napkin around his forefinger, massaged
his teeth and gums, and announced he was ready.

Crowds jammed the caucus room where the hearing was to
be held. The committee chairman announced that the purpose
of these hearings was a bill that the Senate was considering which
would outlaw racing wire services for gambling information.
Frank lighted up one of his English Ovals, and in his raspy voice
told the committee that, as to racetrack wires, "I have very little
knowledge . . . I don't feel I qualify."

"Didn't you have anything to do with bookmaking?"

"Nothing," he said.

The Senators wanted to know what he did do.

"I am in the real estate business. I am interested in a nightclub in Louisiana, and I have some oil leases in Texas."

Wasn't the nightclub in Louisiana actually a gambling casino?

"There's a little gambling in the club," Frank said. Noticing the disbelieving look the Senators gave him, Frank went on to explain, "Just to make it clear, they play the roulette wheel and dice."

Senator Tobey, who had called down the wrath of the heavens on Erickson a few days earlier, now let Frank have it. "Have you ever greased the palm or paid protection in any state in the union?"

"No, sir."

"Then why do all the witnesses who have come before this committee keep referring to you as the 'big shot?' "

Frank replied, "The fantastic write-ups I'm getting. The newspapers have a great investment in me just like Coca-Cola. The newspapers want to get off the nut. With them I'm No. 1."

Another Senator asked Frank if he thought the proposed bill would end bookmaking, and Frank responded, "Ninety-nine percent of human beings is gamble-minded. Passing a law is not enough. There is always an angle on how to skin a cat. There is no way to wash the spots off a leopard. If a man wants to gamble, he'll find some trick to do it."

That answer skewered the committee's whole reason for existence. But Frank was something of a hit with most of the Senators. Tobey, of course, excepted. The Senators thanked him profusely for his expert testimony, and Frank was rather set up when we came out into the hall. He even made me stop so he could admire the paintings on the Capitol's ceiling on the way out.

But his success was to bear bitter fruit. For other Senators noticed the great publicity which the subcommittee had garnered in their exploration of crime. I do not mean to say that Senator Kefauver launched his hearings for this purpose alone, but one would have to be a naive person to deny that publicity had something to do with the establishment and subsequent conduct of the Kefauver hearings.

The fact that the Kefauver hearings were scheduled almost

exactly like a Broadway show, with out-of-town tryouts building to the climactic appearance in New York, has to confirm that opinion. But that does not gainsay some very substantial benefits that the congressional probe inspired. Gambling clubs throughout America (except for Nevada where gambling was legal) would go out of business, thanks to the public clamor the televised hearings inspired. The national coalition—or syndicate—of crime would be pinpointed by the hearings held in different cities, and the evidence showed that all the major crime figures seemed to know each other rather well, even though they were thousands of miles apart.

And very early on one fact became unmistakably clear: the chief target of the whole hearings was one man—Frank Costello.

2

The Kefauver hearings were to be the climax of Frank's life. Everything after, the trials, the prison sentences, even the attempt on his life, was to be anticlimax. For the promised television appearance of Frank Costello—right on camera, the most feared criminal in America—created a sensation.

Frank did not disappoint the audience. The highlight of his appearance, as far as the public was concerned, was, first, the request by an angry lawyer, me, that Frank not be televised at all. The resulting compromise was an unforgettable close-up of Frank's hands drumming on the witness table throughout his days on the stand. This dramatic picture was invariably accompanied by his rasping voice.

The second highlight was Frank, after days of testifying, suddenly announcing that he was taking a walk and leaving the committee room while enraged Senators shouted at him.

The third highlight was Frank returning to testify for reasons not explained at the time and then—after voluntarily testifying to everything asked of him—making a final refusal to divulge his net worth, and being cited for contempt.

These spectacular acts by Frank would make him the star of

hearings that were not without other stars: the lovely Virginia Hill bringing gasps and then laughter as she detailed her flamboyant life as a gun moll with a "what's new?" attitude; Willie Moretti, Frank's cousin, making unwitting but funny remarks in the style of a later witness at another hearing, Tony Ulasewicz; and, finally, an unexpected drama in the sudden revelations about Bill O'Dwyer, then the Ambassador to Mexico, who came on as a confident, relaxed senior statesman, and saw the darkest secrets explode in his face.

But Frank Costello's appearances were always tops in audience appeal. The TV close-up of his hands somehow made him seem even more mysterious, more frightening, than the public anticipated.

And I will tell now, in these pages, for the first time the inside story of Frank's mysterious actions at the Kefauver hearings, from beginning to end—quite a different affair from the version made public by Senator Kefauver after the hearings were over.

This is what the Senator told the American public in his book *Crime in America:* *

> In eight days of public hearings in New York City . . . the Senate Crime Investigating Committee . . . became a national phenomenon. The hour-by-hour television coverage of the proceedings . . . reached an estimated audience of between 20,000,000 and 30,000,000, and the effect was unbelievable. In New York City itself, some merchants wrote us, their businesses were paralyzed; many movie houses became "ghost" halls . . . and housewives did their ironing and mending in front of their TV sets. . . .
>
> For sheer drama, for wholesale peeling back of layers of deceptive camouflage and perjury about the activities of criminals and certain politicians, the New York City open hearings were the climax. . . . Frank Costello, described in testimony before us as "the most influential underworld leader in America," [did] a remarkable job of demolishing, through his own testimony, his pose of present respectability and veracity . . .

---

* Estes Kefauver, *Crime in America,* edited and with an Introduction by Sidney Shalett (Garden City, N.Y.: Doubleday & Company, Inc., 1951).

Of all the witnesses from the crime world summoned before us in New York, Frank Costello was the focal point of interest. The remarkable thing about his appearance before us is that Costello, the vaunted "prime minister" of the underworld, made himself out—and needlessly so—to be unintelligent. This in itself is a paradox, for it is hard for anyone who has studied Costello's persistent criminal activities, his influence in criminal and political circles, and the skill with which he has covered up the tracks of some of his operations, to believe the man really is a fool. In this case, it is obvious that he was the victim of outraged personal vanity; the "elder statesman" of crime probably has come to believe the picture he has painted of himself as an important character. Possibly, too, he and his legal counsel had some misguided ideas on what they thought Costello might be able to get away with before a committee of the United States Senate.

But Costello's strategy didn't work. We trapped him in what the record shows are a certain number of outright lies, and in other "evasions" almost too numerous to count . . . he also exposed himself as a whiner and something of a crybaby; he did not even particularly display courage, for, after threatening twice to walk out on the committee, he lost his nerve, came back and abjectly answered most of our questions in a manner that indicated his defiance was gone. . . .

. . . At the outset, he looked younger than his sixty years; his hard, sallow face was set in impassive lines and he obviously sought to control both his facial expressions and his language. Under the relentless questioning of the committee's chief counsel, Rudolph Halley, Costello broke and became an old, beaten man.

Well, not quite, Senator. The real story was a drama played behind the scenes in which the eventual focus was a man the committee never connected with Frank's walkout, Bill O'Dwyer. But let's go to those January days in 1951 when the hearings loomed ahead, and Frank was, indeed, a very nervous man. As Mr. Kefauver said, he was intelligent. More than the Senator

1. The house where Frank Costello Francesco Castiglia) was born in Lauro-oli, Italy, is still standing today.

2. Newly arrived in America, Frank's parents, Luigi and Maria Saveria Aloise Castiglia, opened a little store in Harlem.

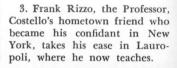

3. Frank Rizzo, the Professor, Costello's hometown friend who became his confidant in New York, takes his ease in Lauropoli, where he now teaches.

4. A rare photograph of Frank Costello as a young man, standing in the doorway of his mother's home.

5. A typical rum-running schooner of the Frank Costello era which sailed the high seas and engaged in fantastic sea battles with Coast Guard destroyers and underworld pirates.

6. The small boat alongside the schooner is part of the bootleggers' famed "Sunset Fleet," fast little craft which set sail from hidden coves at sunset to reach the outlying rumrunners, unload them, and speed back to the beach.

7. Sometimes the Coast Guard won the battles, and the liquor was confiscated. Another victory for the "Drys."

8. Al Capone's murder rampage in Chicago was punctuated by idyllic trips to Florida as his fame and wealth grew.

9. But the most famous underworld "hit" in history, the St. Valentine's Day massacre, caused Frank Costello to call a halt. With Capone's old boss, Johnny Torrio, Costello convened a Mafia peace conference in Atlantic City in 1929, and Capone wound up allowing himself to be arrested and sent to prison while things cooled down.

10. Mayor Fiorello La Guardia drove Costello's slot machine business out of New York with a sledgehammer approach. Standing beside La Guardia, the man who has been called "the best mayor New York ever had," is Police Commissioner Lewis Valentine, considered by many to be the best New York ever had in his job. Things looked bleak for Costello.

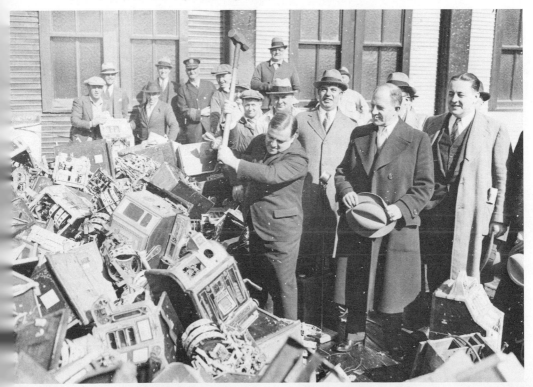

11. Costello, adept as ever, found another colorful politician, Governor Huey P. Long of Louisiana. Long, seen above leading cheers at an LSU football game, led Costello into New Orleans with an opportunity to place his slot machines all over the state, cheering news for Costello.

12. Thomas E. Dewey, the vigorous and ambitious special prosecutor of crime and corruption in New York, became the nemesis of top criminal leaders, among them Dutch Schultz. Despite Costello's warnings, Schultz was determined to kill Dewey.

13. On October 23, 1935, in the Palace Chophouse in Newark, New Jersey, two Mafia hitmen, acting on the orders of Lucky Luciano, gun down Dutch Schultz to save Dewey from assassination.

14. George Wolf represented Lucky Luciano in the controversial case which won him freedom from prison. Luciano's deportation to Italy brought Frank Costello to power as Boss of all Bosses.

15. After World War II Costello joined forces with Frank Erickson, the legendary bookmaker. Erickson had the legend; Costello was the man behind the scenes.

16. The Flamingo Hotel and the famed Strip in Vegas were the creation of handsome, jaunty, vicious Bugsy Siegel, shown here with actor George Raft. Costello helped bankroll Siegel, but soon the hotel ran into trouble.

17. And so did Bugsy.

18. Frank Costello lost his position as Boss of all Bosses during the Siegel fiasco. In a story never revealed before, George Wolf tells how Costello won his position back, and who saved his life. This is Frank as he appeared at the height of his power as the Boss of all Bosses.

19. Frank was so powerful that J. Edgar Hoover negotiated with him, through intermediaries, to force Louis "Lepke" Buchalter (center), a New York racket leader, to surrender. A columnist, Walter Winchell, claimed credit for the surrender, but Lepke knew better. The only underworld leader ever to be executed, he told newspaper reporters that Costello had "betrayed" him.

Chairman,
County Committee,
Democratic General County Committee,
New York, N.Y.

Dear Sir:

I hereby tender my resignation as Chairman
of the Committee on Organization and Elections of the
Democratic County Committee of the County of New York,
same to take effect at once.

Very truly yours,

Francis X Mancuso

20. Costello's power in politics was as strong—and efficient—as his power in the Mafia. Tammany leaders and other city officials had to deposit signed resignations with Costello before they took office, such as this one signed by Francis X. Mancuso, who later rebelled against Costello.

21. In Costello's reign, everything was peaceful and businesslike in the Mafia. But then came a Senator with a coonskin hat, Senator Estes Kefauver. The famous Senate crime investigation was launched.

22. Frank Costello's appearance before the Kefauver Crime Committee created a sensation—even more so when George Wolf demanded that his client not be televised, and the TV cameras, unknown to Wolf and Costello, carried instead an unforgettable close-up of his hands during hours of testimony.

23. One of Costello's many "off-mike" conferences with Wolf. After one of these sessions Costello showed Wolf a bruised shin, the result of vigorous kicks from his lawyer trying to caution his client.

24. Lovely, lusty Virginia Hill created a sensation of her own when she detailed her days and nights as the premiere "gun moll" in the underworld. Some of the details she left out are told in this book.

25. The famous "walk." Reporters cluster around Costello and Wolf after the underworld leader stunned the committee by walking out in the middle of a session. Wolf claimed that his client had laryngitis, but even Wolf did not know at the time the real reason for the walkout.

26. Costello tried to protect his cousin, Willie Moretti, who talked too much. But the underworld feared Moretti's tongue more than Costello's power—and this funeral was the result, one of the most elaborate in underworld history.

27. The Kefauver hearings, and resulting legal complications, weakened Costello's position, and this man, Vito Genovese, was anxious to dethrone Costello.

28. In the lobby of Costello's apartment house on Central Park West, a hulking figure waited on the evening of May 2, 1957. He fired. Minutes later a blood-spattered Costello was on his way to a hospital.

29. The man behind the gun was reputed to be Vincent "the Chin" Gigante. The man behind him, according to Costello, was Genovese. George Wolf was surprised some months later to attend a dinner at Costello's home and find Gigante one of the honored guests.

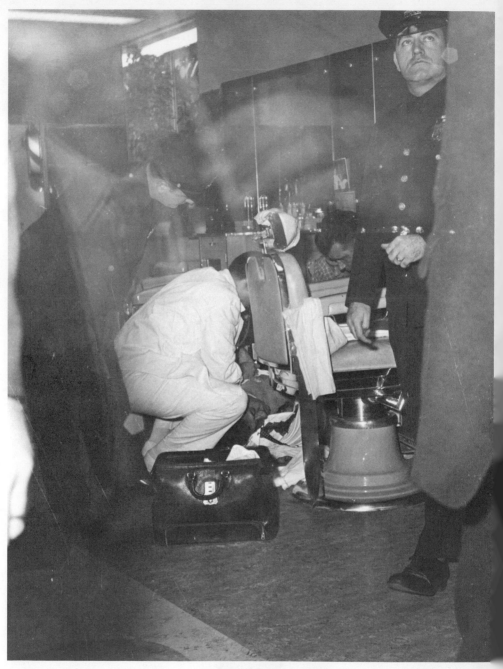

30. Genovese struck next at Costello's friend and enforcer, Albert Anastasia, in—of all places—the barbershop of a midtown Manhattan hotel. Anastasia's death led to Costello's remark to Wolf: "It looks like I'm next."

31. But he wasn't. Costello survived the turmoil and the bullets and lived many years. He died peacefully in bed in February, 1973. His widow, Loretta, shown with her brother Dudley Geigerman, listens as a priest bestows last blessings.

32. But the legend of Frank Costello grew even after his death. One year later in a mysterious incident his mausoleum was bombed, and police authorities speculated that it was a symbolic gesture of an ambitious underworld leader who wanted to dethrone the current Boss of all Bosses.

realized, he knew what those hearings could mean to his career. And the man he feared was not Kefauver or Tobey or Rudolph Halley—but Bill O'Dwyer.

3

It was a snowy afternoon in January and Frank was in my office, smoking. I finished dictating a letter to my secretary who then left the office, glancing curiously at Frank before she closed the door behind her.

Frank was obviously irritated. One of the morning papers had linked him with a drug ring. "It's the same old crap," he said angrily. "And every time I tell one of the news boys I'm not in drug traffic, he just laughs and prints what he wants. Dammit—"

I held up my hand. "Forget the article, Frank. We've got more important business. The Kefauver committee wants you to testify at an executive session on February 13th."

"So that's why I'm *here*, ain't it?"

"Right," I said. "But, Frank, you have to make up your mind as to whether to claim immunity against self-incrimination."

"I've got nothing to hide," Frank said. "I'm in gambling and slot machines, everybody knows that. But I'm not in dope and I'm not okaying murders, so why should I hide behind the Fifth?"

"Frank," I said, "you've been charged with crimes such as engaging in narcotics traffic and assassinations. I don't like to take the responsibility for advising you. If I were in your place I'd gladly waive immunity. But you're in a different situation. Rather than take my advice, I must ask you to consult some of the judges, some of the business people like your friend Gene Pope [the newspaper publisher], to see what you should do."

"I'll be back to you, George," he said and left.

A few days later he came to me with the news that he had seen the people he respected and they all advised him not to claim immunity, to tell the truth. They thought by so doing he might end those rumors which dogged him about narcotics.

It is interesting to note here that had it not been for Frank's determination to be disassociated from drug traffic, he might well have claimed the Fifth Amendment at the hearings, and escaped the trials and prison sentences which awaited him.

On February 13, 1951, we had our executive session. For a while, everything seemed to be turning out just as Frank and his friends had hoped. Kefauver asked a few questions about Costello's gambling, slot machine, and bootlegging activities and he answered them.

In the same forthright fashion when asked about narcotics he answered with a loud "NO."

The atmosphere warmed up even more when I, on behalf of Frank, promised to turn over all of Frank's financial records, including a statement of his net worth, at the open hearings.

But then Frank made what may have been the biggest mistake of his life. It happened when Rudolph Halley, the committee counsel, asked me to step into the corridor. He complained that Senator Kefauver was not getting enough publicity and he wanted to know if we would permit a photographer to take pictures of Senator Kefauver in the act of interrogating the famous criminal, Frank Costello.

After consulting with Frank, I told him there would be no objection. I told Halley that a prominent *Life* magazine photographer was a friend of mine and I would have him take the pictures.

Senator Kefauver happily plunked himself down at the end of the table and, suddenly, as the camera was about to shoot, waved his forefinger angrily at Frank as if the Senator was telling Frank where to go. But Frank just as swiftly waved his finger in front of Kefauver's nose, grinning.

In later years I came to think that Kefauver was a great Senator, but I doubt if anyone ever commended him on his sense of humor. Instead of taking Frank's gesture as a small joke, he became angry, the blood rising in his cheeks. He jumped to his feet and shouted to the photographer, *"Forget the picture."* Then he turned to Frank and said, "You've had your laugh, Mr. Costello, but you'll live to regret this."

And he stormed out of the room, followed by Halley. I said to my client, "Frank, a picture isn't worth a jail sentence."

But Frank was unruffled. "If he does that finger bit with me on television, I'll give him the Italian salute."

4

But things were to get worse, and I don't know how much that antagonism in the closed sessions contributed to later events. But what galled Frank—and me—more than anything associated with the hearings was the issuance of an official interim report by Kefauver's committee (before Frank had any opportunity to testify in open hearings) in which the committee announced its preconceived conclusion that Frank Costello was the No. 1 man in the crime syndicate, and that he was involved in every kind of criminal activity including drug traffic.

This infuriated Frank, and we had another sitdown before the televised hearings began. This time we were in complete accord. "They're out to get you, Frank," I said. "They've announced it in public. You're their No. 1 target."

"So should I take the Fifth?"

I had given this a great amount of thought. On the one hand I considered the favorable impression Frank made when he testified openly. Plus the fact that I believed him when he said he was not involved in drugs—and the gambling evidence they would bring out was all old hat. But the net worth question—which in the early ambience of the closed hearings I had promised to produce—was quite another matter. I had now changed my mind.

Net worth, as many citizens know who have brushed with the Bureau of Internal Revenue, is a very tricky legal trap. For the government agents have other ways to estimate your net worth than your mere statement. And if their estimate disagrees with yours, you are guilty of perjury, and tax evasion.

For example—as later happened to Frank—they can accumulate evidence of your expenditures, the cost of your home, your standard of living over a period of years, and tie this together with your known or suspected sources of income to make up their own net worth estimate.

Worse yet, with a man like Frank Costello, a net worth statement would enable them to ask specific questions about the amount stated. That is why the net worth statement was so dangerous for Frank, especially. If he estimated a low figure, they could dig up evidence of expenditures to prove he had underestimated his net worth and was guilty of tax evasion. If he gave a high estimate, they would want to know just where all the money came from.

"Frank," I said, "I'm going to ask you to gamble."

Frank smiled. "A funny thing for you to say to *me*."

I smiled, too. Then I said, "It's the question of your net worth. If the committee is out for your blood, as it appears to be, that net worth statement will send them off on a hundred trails, open up all kinds of leads. I advise you to take the Fifth on your question of net worth. Everything else you testify to."

"I got news for you, George," Frank said. "I wouldn't have told them my net worth anyway."

"Why not?"

"I don't know what it is."

I laughed, but I remembered what the Professor once told me about Frank's bootlegging days. He had come upon Frank making little circles, slanted lines, and dashes with a pencil on a crumpled piece of paper. Each mark stood for a different mathematical factor. And the Professor said Frank always knew to the penny what he was worth.

Frank asked, "Suppose they come at me for contempt of Congress?"

"That's the gamble. You'll have your day in court, and the courts have traditionally protected the Fifth Amendment. And even at the worst it's a light sentence, usually less than a year. If they dig up something from your net worth statement you'll be in for far more trouble."

"OK, George. When do we go to war?"

"March 13th."

"If you see Kefauver," Frank said, "tell him to keep his hand on the table."

5

The televised hearings had begun in December, 1950, and they were building in suspense toward Frank's appearance. One witness who appeared was to play an important role in Frank's own testimony, and his later life-and-death struggle for survival. He was Willie Moretti, the New Jersey mob leader who was a cousin of Frank's, and who caused Frank nothing but trouble for years. I never knew whether Willie suffered from syphilis, as has been reported, but I did know he had a loose tongue, which was a dangerous flaw in the underworld. Frank kept protecting him, sending him out of harm's way. But the dragnet of the Kefauver hearings had brought him in, and here are just a few of the highlights of his testimony which had people laughing throughout America. They also provide examples of his need to talk, which eventually led to his death. In Damon Runyon language, he defined the Mafia, in his own terms:

Halley: "These people come from a great many different cities around the country . . . How do you get to meet all of these people from all over the country?"

Moretti: "Well, you go to the racetracks and you go to Florida and you meet them; and a man that is well known meets everybody; you know that."

Halley: "Are these the people you are thinking of when you are talking about the mob?"

Moretti: "Well, the newspapers calls them the mob. I don't know whether they are right or wrong. If they would be right, *everybody* would be in jail; is that right?"

Halley: "Is that what you mean when you say the mob?"

Moretti: "People are mobs that make six percent more on the dollar than anybody else."
(LAUGHTER)

Halley: "I am sorry; I just did not hear that."

Moretti: "They call anybody a mob who makes six percent
            more on money."

Where Moretti got that magic figure of 6 percent I don't
know, but I do know he was an underworld leader in New
Jersey and maybe the figure came close to representing the
Mafia leader's actual take, after those "protection" expenses.

Halley followed this line with questions about underworld
leaders but was stopped once again when he asked, "Did you
know Al Capone?"

Moretti: "I knew him very well."
Halley: "Who introduced you?"
Moretti: "Listen, well-charactered people, you don't need in-
            troductions; you just meet automatically."
Halley (after a pause): "Let us get this again. *Well-charactered*
            people you say?"
Moretti: "Don't need introductions; they meet automatically."

The committee had a new definition of character. Now it got
an inkling, once again in Moretti style, of how the underworld
moved in on legitimate business. Moretti and some of his boys
had bought a company called the U.S. Linen Supply. Amazingly
enough, as Moretti testified, "from a $200-a-day business I
brought it up to $13,500-a-week business."

Halley: "And what percentage of the company do you own?"
Moretti: "I used to have twenty percent. Now the business
            that gave me a lot of trouble, the Noxall that I took
            some business away from because I was—"
Kefauver: "I did not understand that, Mr. Moretti."
Moretti: "The Noxall Linen Supply Co. of Hackensack, a
            corporation, a big firm of consolidated laundries.
            Their president gave me a lot of trouble. They had
            a big meeting once, and they accused me of taking
            their business away from them, and they're the ones
            made the complaint, and I was hit with it in 1939
            before the grand jury . . ."
Halley: "Did you ever have an interest in the Noxall Co.?"
Moretti: "No, sir . . . this fellow that made all the com-
            plaints, he was the president of the association . . .

Fortunately God helped me and this fellow went
horseback riding, got kicked in the head by a horse
and died, so his company became my partners after
he died."
(LAUGHTER)

Halley: "They joined your company?"
Moretti: "Yes, sir; and they made me vice-president."
(LAUGHTER)

Moretti's comedy rating soared ever higher with his garrulous
Damon Runyon testimony. But Frank Costello, waiting his turn
to take the stand, grew increasingly nervous. It appeared Willie
would soon be a dead man. How could he save him?

6

The Kefauver hearings, carefully orchestrated, built in suspense
until the climactic drama of ten days in March, 1951, when
Frank Costello would move onto center stage.

I do not deny that, as Frank's attorney, I was angry at this
carefully structured drama, which might well prove tragic for
my client. During months of hearings the Senators had missed
no chance to link witness after witness to Costello, and had
charged him with being guilty of almost every kind of crime.
The reason was obvious: Frank Costello got "space" . . . no
one else in the underworld approached him in charisma, no one
else commanded the front covers of magazines and the front
pages of great newspapers as he did.

The crowds in Foley Square in lower Manhattan when Frank
and I arrived were enormous; the room was jammed to capacity
with reporters, television crews, and those who could get seats.
This is all now familiar stuff to Americans who have witnessed
the Army-McCarthy hearings and the recent Watergate sessions.
But remember, in those days television was in its infancy. I fore-
saw my client being stormed at, and accused of crimes of all

kinds, before millions of people. How would Frank react if he knew the cameras were sending his every word, and picturing his every facial expression, before a voracious public?

And in this respect I can say for the record that few attorneys ever had a more difficult client to represent at a hearing. Frank was almost impossible to coach. I never knew what he might blurt out in answer to questions directed at him. (The famous "Joe Kennedy" response at another hearing was a good example.) My "coaching" consisted of two dictums: Don't perjure yourself, and tell the truth.

As we took the witness stand together, I noticed the actor Robert Montgomery sitting behind us. He had wangled a job as a radio reporter doing commentary on the hearings, and it is amusing to me that his reports said that I constantly whispered all the answers to Costello before he made them. Actually time and again I would hear my client blurt out an amazing untruth —just to show the Senators who's boss, or thinking he would evade the issue. I would kick him sharply in the shins every time he made false and perjurious responses. In many instances the truth would have proved harmless. After one session we were in a taxi and I remember Frank pulling up his trouser leg and showing me black and blue marks, saying, "Dammit, you're killing me in there, George! Take it easy."

And so, with these considerations in mind—my uncertain feeling as to how Frank would react to TV cameras, and my knowledge from past hearings that he might lie and get caught—I stood up at the beginning of the hearing and made a request, which I considered routine but which apparently made television history.

Wolf: "I am appearing as attorney for Mr. Costello and I would like to know whether you intend to televise this proceeding."

Senator O'Conor: "The proceedings have been televised. May I ask whether you have any objection?"

Wolf: "Strenuously object."

O'Conor: "Upon what basis do you register objection?"

Wolf: "On the ground that Mr. Costello doesn't care to submit himself as a spectacle. And on the further ground that it will prevent proper conference with his attorney in receiving proper advice during the course of his testimony."

O'Conor: "Would it in any way have effect upon his giving a complete and full statement to the committee, and of answering questions freely?"

Wolf: "I think it would interfere with Mr. Costello testifying properly."

O'Conor: "I see. Well, under the circumstances, then, it is the view of the committee, counsel, that the defendant not be televised . . . at this time."

When that colloquy was finished I was satisfied that Frank would not be televised. It was only at lunchtime when I called my wife that I realized the television directors had come up with an idea that was to fascinate the public: to focus on Frank's hands. And so our objections went for naught; those writhing, twisting hands were hypnotic to viewers, and possibly betrayed just as much emotion as his face. Nevertheless, the die—and the hands—was cast and I did not feel it worth while to make further objection. Perhaps the TV geniuses would then have focused on his right ear.

The questions had no sooner started than we were in trouble. Frank just did not understand the difference between being cautious and telling a needless untruth. His very name started him into legal difficulties: Halley asked him if he had ever used the name Severio.

Costello: "I might have used it; yes."

Halley: "I will not accept that answer. Did you or did you not use it?"

Costello: "Well, I don't know. I won't say I didn't."

Halley: "You are not willing to admit that you *know very well* that you did use it?"

Costello: "Why should I?"

Halley: "You were convicted of a crime under that name, were you not?"

Costello: "I beg your pardon?"

Halley: "You were convicted of a crime under that name, were you not?"

Costello: "Thirty-five, thirty-six years ago; yes."

This was one of my shin-kicking sessions with Frank. But we were heading into deeper waters. Halley now had Frank's naturalization papers in front of him. He asked Frank if he remembered having been asked, in the course of his naturalization proceeding, whether he ever used any alias or any other name. Frank said he couldn't remember. But Halley showed that, although Frank had been convicted in 1915 in the name Frank Severio, years later he lied on the application form for naturalization by saying his name was Costello and swearing he had never used an alias.

But that was just the beginning of Frank's troubles on the naturalization form he had filled out. I whispered to him to tell the truth about the other items and claim it was faulty memory at the time he filled it out. But Frank wouldn't listen. I can only explain his responses at this time by saying that he was less afraid of a perjury charge than deportation. A sample of the questions and answers reveals what was being developed:

Halley: "Then the next question was: "My present occupation is" and the answer appears here to be "Real Estate" . . . You were in the liquor business at that time, were you not?"

Costello: "I don't believe so."

The naturalization papers were filed in 1925 when Frank was thirty-four years old. Frank was now testifying that he had not been in the liquor business at that time. Beautiful, I thought. And Rudolph Halley bored in quickly with the revelation that not only was Frank in the liquor business but he had been brought to trial for bootlegging in 1926. Frank's answer, I must admit, was disarming. "I wasn't convicted, was I?"

"No."

"Then I wasn't in the bootlegging business."

That set the committee back for a few moments, but then they were asking about the two witnesses on Frank's naturalization papers: Frank Goss and Harry Sausser. On the naturalization forms, Frank had stated that Goss was in real estate and Sausser was "a railroad man." Halley brought out that they had both been charged with bootlegging, and he had obviously lied again on the naturalization papers.

But Frank led them a merry chase on that Harry Sausser name, which apparently fascinated the committee. Especially when Frank claimed there were *three* Harry Saussers.

Halley: *"Three* Harry Saussers!"
Costello: "Yes . . ."
Halley: "In any event, we have one Harry Sausser in Plandome who was in the railroad business?"
Costello: "Yes."
Halley: "Where were the other two Harry Saussers?"
Costello: "Well, I wouldn't say two exactly, but one more I would say stopped at the McAlpin Hotel."
Halley: "Now, you mentioned that there might have been a third Harry Sausser?"

This was where Senator Tobey broke in: "Perhaps the third one could have been a flying Sausser."

All amusing at the time, but the committee was building the case which would eventually result in a deportation trial for Costello, based on misinformation he filed on the forms. But the committee now touched even more dangerous ground—Frank's net worth. This was the question on which we had decided he would claim the protection of the Fifth Amendment. When Frank did so, the Senators were furious and turned their wrath on me. I had promised them the net worth statement at the closed hearing weeks before. Now I was in their word "reneging."

Halley: "Mr. Chairman, I believe the witness has fully waived his rights by testifying in great detail about his financial status and by telling the committee he would provide such a financial statement at the last hearing. He was represented by able counsel who, as I believe the committee can see, has taken advantage of every proper technical point in his favor; and under the circumstances I ask the committee to require the witness to answer the question."
O'Conor: "Counsel, we will be very glad to hear you."
Wolf: "Why it's very obvious that the witness has a right to

stand on his constitutional right, if he fears that the question might tend to incriminate him, to take advantage of that right.

"Now on the question of waiver: there has been no waiver about that. Mr. Costello was asked if he would furnish a financial statement. He intended to forgo any claim of constitutional privilege. He has changed his mind about that. I think he is justified in changing his mind about that, but that's something that is for him to determine."

Tobey: ". . . Then how far can the committee proceed on the assurance of counsel! . . . that they are going to do a thing, and then have them . . . later renege upon it?"

Wolf: "Well, Senator, it's very obvious if you had known the facts from Mr. Halley. . . . When the interim report came down—I . . . told Mr. Halley that this witness would not supply a financial statement . . . I presumed that when this man was testifying . . . fully, completely, that no report of this committee would be made until he had completed his testimony, when this interim report came down."

O'Conor: "Mr. Wolf, of course there is a marked difference between what a witness's rights are and what he may elect to do out of displeasure, or otherwise."

Wolf: "I agree with you wholeheartedly. It isn't based upon displeasure . . . [but] the very report, Senator, indicated that most of the individuals named in the report were guilty of income tax evasion. As a matter of fact it criticized the various income tax bureaus for not more rigidly investigating or . . . prosecuting these individuals . . . The sole question that this witness is concerned with is whether or not the answer to the question is going to violate his constitutional rights.

"He believes so . . . And I believe that as a matter of law you should recognize that claim."

Back and forth we went, culminating with this exchange:

Tobey: "We now find you are covering up behind the bush
. . . You are now saying since we issued the report,
you are not going to give us the statement."

Wolf: "That was more than a bush, Senator. It is maybe a
tree. . . Now when the question was first asked him,
he was cognizant of the fact that the answer might tend
to incriminate him. He was willing to take his chances
then. He will not take his chances now, Senator."

In the end the committee formally directed that he answer
the question of his net worth, and Frank formally refused. The
groundwork was laid for a contempt of Congress charge, but the
infinitely more hazardous charges that might have arisen out of
the analysis of a net worth statement were avoided, at least for
the time being.

And now, denied the statement, they went at Costello hammer
and tongs to discover as much as possible about his sources of
income. The slot machine company in Louisiana was probed,
but all they got out of that was a startled look on Senator
Tobey's face when he learned that Huey Long, the Governor
of Louisiana, had been involved with a gambling man. This
prompted Costello, to my astonishment, to come to the defense
of the dead governor. "I think you misrepresent it, sir," he said
to Tobey, "with all due respect to you; that you say that a governor of Louisiana tried to violate a commercial purpose—which
is not [so]. He did it, just like you have a racetrack up in New
Hampshire, and if you went there and passed legislation, you
are doing it practically for the state. You are not doing it for a
selfish purpose."

What about the Beverly Club in New Orleans? Frank admitted he earned $1,500 a month from that. What did he do for
that salary?

"Well, I helped to get different acts, and I solicited some business. In other words, if someone was going to Louisiana I
would recommend a place. I was just a good will man for them.
And I would recommend different acts for the club."

Halley: "In other words your recommendations to your
friends were worth $18,000 a year to the Beverly
Club?"

Costello: "Well, it wasn't just a recommendation. I had to go around and look for acts, also."

The committee obviously had a hard time believing Frank's efforts for the club were worth $18,000 a year—but more revelations like that were to follow. Frank, it turned out, may well have been the best-paid "good will man" in history.

After it was brought out that Frank on various occasions borrowed money from Frank Erickson, counsel asked, "You had an income in 1949 from George M. Levy, $15,000. Would you mind telling the committee again what that was for?"

Costello said that he had met Levy at the Yonkers Raceway. Levy was president of the racetrack. "He thought that he might lose his franchise; bookmakers were there and the racing commission told them if he didn't clean it up, he might jeopardize his license . . . I says, 'Well, what I can do, George, I can spread the propaganda around that they're hurting you there and you're a nice fellow, and I can tell them that if there's an arrest made, it's going to be very severe. I don't know how much good it's going to do you, but I'll talk about it.'"

Halley: "Where did you talk about it?"
Costello: "Oh, in Moore's Restaurant, Gallagher's Restaurant, a hotel, a saloon, as you would call it, any place, or a nightclub, whenever I had a chance, just in general."
Halley: "Did you think that your services were worth a total of $60,000 over four years?"
Costello: ". . . No, I didn't think so."
Halley: "What did you do in 1946 to earn $15,000?"
Costello: "Practically nothing . . . outside of just talking about it, that bookmakers are going to hurt this man's license . . ."

A glimpse of Costello's fascinating life-style came to light in this testimony, creating a surprised reaction among some of the Senators:

Halley: "What other places, Mr. Costello, did you spread the gospel, in what other restaurants?"
Costello: "Maybe half a dozen restaurants . . . the Waldorf or—"

Halley (stunned): "When you go to the *Waldorf,* there are book-
        makers there?"
Costello: "The Colony, anywhere where I had dinner, or lunch,
        or something."
Halley: "How many bookmakers have you had to dinner, or
        lunch, at the Colony?"

Costello loftily reminded Halley that he had not dined with
bookmakers there, he just talked to "people" and those people
somehow passed the word.

And it was at this time that the committee sprang a series of
wiretaps it had obtained, part of the catch when Hogan's people
had overheard the famous Aurelio conversation. The first one
was a beauty. The state had insisted on George Levy hiring the
Pinkerton agency for his racetrack. Levy was incensed. Excerpts
from the wiretapped phone call to Costello, as read in the hearings:

Levy: "Pinkerton sent us a contract and it is the blankety-
        blank thing you ever saw. They can refuse to let in
        anyone that they choose . . . We can't jeopardize the
        bookmakers . . ."
Costello: "If they make any errors, you are subject to a suit."
Levy: "As boss, you should be able to tell them—the way it
        stands now, you better tell George."

I don't mind saying I sat straight up when this wiretap was
read. That sentence, "As boss, you should be able to tell them,"
seemed damning on its face. But meanwhile Halley was having
fun with me. He asked Costello, "By the way, can you identify
George from this wiretap?"

Costello: "No."
Halley: "It, of course, wasn't George Wolf your attorney
        here?"
Costello (after smiling at me): "No."

The committee was sure they had caught Frank in another
lie. He had testified he received $15,000 a year from Levy to
keep bookmakers away from the track—and here was a wiretapped call which revealed Levy was saying "We can't jeopardize

the bookmakers" and apparently was worried that the Pinkerton agency might bar them from the track.

But Costello insisted it was no lie. He had tried to keep book-makers off the track, no matter what the wiretapped call implied. And he gave the Senators some racetrack information. "If I am a $1,000 bettor and I go to a small track where they don't have a million, and if I am in the mood of betting $5,000, my 8 to 5 goes down to 3 to 5, and if I give it to the bookmaker he takes care. He is going to hold it and keep my price up.

"So the machine at the track gets nothing," Frank said, "so I imagine all these racetrack owners, they just don't like it."

But Senator Tobey was still not satisfied. "Mr. Halley, may I point out that . . . in the fourth paragraph, he says 'We can't jeopardize the bookmakers,' and yet, as I understand the testi-mony of the witness today he received $60,000 to put the bookies out of business. Is that consistent? In one case they can't jeop-ardize them, and yet he paid this man $60,000 to put them out of business. What do you say, Mr. Witness, to that?"

Costello: "I really don't know how to answer that question."

Halley wanted to know what the reference to "as boss" meant.

Costello: "Well, there is an error there somewhere. I was never a boss; never had any interest."

Surprisingly, Halley didn't press that issue. Perhaps he felt Costello's testimony that he earned $15,000 a year just to "pass the word" to bookmakers established the fact that he was a boss more emphatically than the words of the intercepted call.

A word about George Levy is in order here, I believe. George is a fine man and a good friend of mine. He was a distinguished lawyer before becoming involved in a grand passion, harness racing, which he established in New York and has pioneered ever since. George sent telegrams to the committee upon hearing the testimony about the intercepted call, and demanded time to give his version of what the words meant.

The television cameras, the skeptical Senators, and the crowd pressure all conspired to make George's explanation less than convincing. Recently I visited with him, and heard the story again. George's version, as recounted to me, has a ring of authenticity about it. He says he paid the $60,000 purely from fear that Costello would ask for *more!*

What happened, he said, was that the state racing commission was convinced there were bookmakers at his little track. The commission told George Levy it would close down the track if the bookmakers weren't removed. George was in a panic. Bookmakers don't wear uniforms or badges. Of course he knew several, as any racetrack owner would, but he certainly didn't know *every* bookmaker in New York, so how could he guarantee no bookmakers were in attendance. Then he thought of Frank Costello who golfed at his country club in Sands Point. He said to the commissioner, "What if Frank Costello guaranteed there will be no bookmakers?"

The commissioner was impressed. "That would do it," he said.

Levy asked Frank to help him and Frank said he would. Some time later, a terrible thought struck George. He hadn't made a money deal with Frank. Suppose Frank thought his services were worth hundreds of thousands of dollars. Costello would be a hard man to refuse.

So, eventually, he came to me, as Frank's lawyer. After consulting Frank, I told George he wanted $15,000 a year, which would be paid retroactively for the two years. George was relieved.

As to the "boss" mention, Levy patiently explains it as he explained it to the committee. He was referring to himself as the boss, saying, "As boss, you should be able to tell them" (meaning the Pinkertons).

As I say, I believe this story to be true, especially since I was present when the actual money negotiations were made. In fact, Levy later got a letter from the committee exonerating him of all such charges.

But meanwhile the committee counsel, Halley, was brandishing more wiretapped calls in front of Frank. Calls to Phil Kastel about the slot machine operation which showed that Frank had "lied" when he said he didn't run the company, but just shared an interest.

More significantly, he came to the phone calls between Frank and Willie Moretti.

Willie Moretti's case was to become an increasing problem for

Frank. Willie was Frank's cousin. They had grown up together, and Frank, who was always strong on loyalty, felt an even stronger loyalty toward Willie.

Willie had become, with Frank's help, one of the leading underworld leaders now ensconced in north New Jersey. But his loose tongue worried his fellow mobsters; time and again their threats came to Frank's attention—and every time Frank would whisk Willie to the Far West for safekeeping until the storm blew over.

When Moretti would "disappear," Frank remained in constant touch with him. The phone tap in 1943, for example, revealed more than 130 calls in a two-month period. Some of the calls were now brought out by Halley.

Halley: "Now, Mr. Costello, is it a fact that Willie suffered some kind of injury or accident and began to talk too much?"

Costello: "I don't know what you mean by talking too much. I know he was a very ill man."

Halley: "You gave certain instructions for Willie Moretti to keep from talking; isn't that right?"

And he read an intercepted call:

"Willie in California called Costello, and Willie said, 'Hello, Chief.' . . . You asked him 'How do you feel?' Moretti said 'Great.' . . . and you said, 'Now, Willie, just rest and don't call me so much.' . . . Then he said, 'I worry about you. How about you calling me?' . . . Then you said, 'OK, I will do that. Put your wife on.' And the lady got on the phone . . . And she said, 'Hello, Frank.' And you said, 'Hello, how do you like it?' And she said, 'Fine. Willie is feeling much better now. He was terrible when we first came here.' And you said, 'Tell him to stay away from the telephone. When he talks so much, he gets upset.' . . . *You didn't want him talking?*"

Costello: ". . . For a man, if he is a sick man, and he probably started to talk for hours . . . Just a little advice I was giving him."

Halley: "Well, did you ever say, 'I'll let you talk to somebody, but don't talk too much. You know.' "

Halley had a transcript of that call, too, and one to a doctor whom Frank asked to "call him and see what you think of his conversation and let me know."

Halley's purpose was to show that Frank, as the almighty boss, could shift people hither and yon across the country. What he didn't know—and I didn't know at the time—was that Frank and Willie were related, and Frank was worried much more about the illness which comes with a bullet through the stomach.

But after a few more questions this first long day of Frank's testimony came to an end. It had been quite a day for the committee. They had laid the groundwork for a contempt of Congress citation (on failure to reveal net worth), perjury (on various and assorted "lies"), and denaturalization (on factual misstatements on his naturalization papers).

Outside the crowds waited for the man who now had the most famous hands in history. But Frank, for once, was in no mood to josh with the press. That Willie Moretti business had angered him. In the cab going uptown he said, "I take care of a sick guy, even ask a doctor to check on him, and they make a federal case of it."

But the next day was to provide even more bombshells.

7

The day's testimony was just getting under way when Halley, almost unnoticed, slipped in a few questions which later were to loom large in the committee's version of Costello's walkout. In this little exchange, the committee thought they caught Costello lying.

Halley: "Did not Mr. Irving Sherman [a bookmaker] introduce you to a man named James McLaughlin who worked for the telephone company?"

Costello: "Not to my recollection."

Halley: "And didn't James McLaughlin check your telephone wires at your request?"

Costello: "Not to my recollection. I never give anybody a con-
             tract to check my wires."
Halley: "That is your sworn testimony?"
Costello: "Yes."

Halley dropped it there and went on to the matter of the
imported Scotch distribution deal, which seemed to fascinate
Senator Kefauver in particular. The Senator took up the questioning. The facts brought out were that Frank and his partner
Phil Kastel had endorsed a note for a man named Abe Hellis, a
New Orleans businessman, with which Hellis bought the distribution rights in this country for King's Ransom and House
of Lords Scotch from Alliance Distribution.

The chairman: "Now, what did you get out of this deal?"
Costello: "Nothing."
The chairman: "You mean you would sign a $325,000 note
                 and lend your credit to the note for nothing,
                 Mr. Costello?"
Costello: "Absolutely nothing; pure friendship."

But Halley brought out documents which showed that Frank
in 1938 was negotiating a contract whereby he would get five
shillings on every case of whiskey exported to the U.S. by Alliance Distribution. Once again, Frank was being paid as a "good
will" man. Halley read from the contract:

"And Mr. Costello shall use his best efforts to promote the
interests of the company in the United States by personal contact
with the wholesale and retail merchants, and the consuming
public, by frequenting first class hotels and restaurants and asking to be supplied with the company's brands marketed in the
United States."

Halley said, "Now were you so prominent and popular a man
in this country that you could simply, by going into bars and
asking for these brands of whiskey, stimulate the sales to make
it worth . . . five shillings on every case?"

Frank's answer brought a laugh from the crowd. "Well, Mr.
Halley . . . *they* thought so."

The line of questioning laid no groundwork for charges
against Frank, but it once again emphasized the committee's

overriding purpose: to show the extent of Costello's power. Here was a legitimate company giving him a fancy override just to "pass the word" that bars and restaurants should buy a certain brand of Scotch.

In fact, the deal fell through when one of the attorneys realized that Frank's connection with the enterprise might reflect ill on the company. Or so the records showed. But then another of those intercepted phone call transcripts was being waved by Halley, and it suggested that though the deal supposedly fell through in 1938, Frank in 1943 was still getting money from Irving Haim, one of the partners in the company.

"I think I would like to read you a telephone conversation of June 24, 1943, an incoming call to your house, and it was you calling Mrs. Costello. You said, 'What time will you definitely be home this afternoon, as I expect a package. Irving Haines'— it says here—'will bring it.' . . . It must be Irving Haim, I should think."

Costello: "I don't remember."

Halley: "Was there anything valuable that you would have gotten from Irving Haim after 1938, when this deal fell through?"

Costello: "No."

Halley: "Well, Mrs. Costello said that she was going to the hospital to see somebody—but 'I will be home by five o'clock.' And you said, 'Well, Irving will bring it and it will be in an envelope. You know where to put it.'"

Halley was fishing for more perjury material here, but unfortunately he couldn't prove what was in that envelope. I was beginning to worry about my client on another score. By now Frank had been on the stand continuously for two days and his voice, never strong because of the tumor operation some years previously, was obviously tired. Time and again I referred to my client's fatigue, speaking to the chairman, but each time my objection was dismissed as merely an opportunity to get Frank off the hook.

But events I did not even know about at the time were to cause Frank to walk out on the committee, and cause a sensation. Open defiance—on television!—of the Senate.

The drama began the next day when Halley sprang a surprise witness on us, James McLaughlin, a "wire-man," as they say nowadays. In those days he was called a telephone technician. What he did was tap phones, or—on the other side—check phones to make sure they were not tapped. The day before Frank had testified under oath that he had never paid anybody to check his phones. Now McLaughlin was quizzed:

Halley: "Did Costello ask you to do anything for him?"
McLaughlin: "Costello asked me to look over his telephone—"
Halley: "And did you do it?"
McLaughlin: "Yes, I did."
Halley: "Who paid you?"
McLaughlin: "Frank Costello."
Halley: "How often would you say you checked Frank Costello's telephones to see if they were tapped?"
McLaughlin: "For a period of about three months I checked that, sometimes two and three times a week."

Senator Kefauver would later write that "It was after the McLaughlin testimony, with the threat of a perjury indictment looming, that Costello attempted to stage his first walkout on the grounds that he was sick and 'confused.'"

The one who was confused was the Senator. Frank knew just what he was doing. But he wasn't telling anyone, not even his lawyer. I thought Frank was legitimately sick; his voice could hardly be heard after two days of testimony. Even the Senators remarked on the fact.

So the night after the McLaughlin testimony I was not surprised when Frank asked me to summon a doctor. The doctor said that Frank's voice was so weakened that he should have a rest. In other words, we could ask for a delay.

What I didn't know was that Frank wanted that delay for other reasons. He had heard that Bill O'Dwyer was flying to New York to testify, and for O'Dwyer's sake he wanted the ex-mayor to testify first, before he took the stand again. Otherwise Frank might be asked some questions, and give some answers, which might be used to entrap O'Dwyer into perjury.

And so the stage was set. I was to be the villain who would draw the Senators' anger.

8

Frank was next scheduled right after a crowd pleaser, Virginia Hill, who had the Senators goggle-eyed with admiration, or perhaps just awe. What a life she led. On a vacation in Colorado Springs she spent thousands of dollars in two weeks. Where did she get the money? Friends gave it to her, just good friends.

Now, after the comedy relief, I came in with Frank and raised a long, serious objection. I said that Frank had testified from 10 A.M. to 5:30 P.M. on the 13th, and from 10 A.M. to 1 P.M. on the 15th, and "as this committee has been informed, and is quite evident from the voice and the appearance of the witness, he was suffering from a severe case of throat inflammation and laryngitis . . . No formal request for an adjournment was made on that ground because, as counsel pointed out, such a request coming from this witness would have been misconstrued as an attempt to avoid questioning . . . Because of his illness, the witness was at a decided disadvantage, suffered pain in his throat when he talked, and had difficulty in speaking . . .

"There is no doubt in the mind of the witness that he is here not as a witness, but as a defendant.

"Now he has reached the end and the limits of physical and mental endurance. He cannot go on. He desires to defend himself, and wants the opportunity to do so.

"He asks that this examination be postponed to such time when he is physically and mentally able to continue, and in surroundings and under circumstances where he can testify properly and defend himself."

For a moment no one spoke, then the outbursts began. Halley was furious. He cast aspersions on me, to which I hotly retorted, and the chairman tried to smooth things over. He added, "If the committee should have to delay its hearings of Mr. Costello for two or three weeks, until he feels better . . . we would be expired by that time."

"Mr. Costello may expire, if you don't grant it," I answered.
From then on confusion reigned with everyone jumping in:

Senator Tobey: "If it is in order, I want to apply the words
of Farragut at Mobile Bay, 'Damn the tor-
pedoes. Go ahead.' "

Wolf: "I think in view of the torpedoing about to be
released, I think we should have the protection
against the assault, and the only protection we
can have is by having these proceedings conducted under proper circumstances."

Kefauver: "All right. If the lights bother Mr. Costello,
I hope you will say so, and we will turn them
off him. And if he does not want to have his
hands televised—well, I would leave that to
you, sir."

Frank finally spoke. "Senator, they do bother me. I am in no
condition to testify.

"You heard my statement through Mr. Wolf, and I stand by
it and under no condition will I testify from here in, until I am
well enough."

Kefauver: "You refuse to testify further?"
Costello: "Absolutely."
Kefauver: "You ask questions, Mr. Halley, and we will see.
Now just a moment, just a moment . . ."

The television people were crowding around Costello, creating
an uproar.

Kefauver: "Let us not have the television now on any part of
Mr. Costello . . . Let it be on anything else but
Mr. Costello . . . Is it possible for the lights on Mr.
Costello, is it possible to have that changed; or how
long would it take? That's better now."
Costello: "Mr. Halley, am I a defendant in this courtroom?"
Halley: "No."
Costello: "Am I under arrest?"
Halley: "No."
Costello: "Then I am walking out."

The audience seemed stunned. Halley was angrily reminding Frank that he was under subpoena, and that if he refused to answer questions he would be guilty of contempt. "Now, if you are ill, produce a doctor's certificate, produce an affidavit of a doctor. If you are not ill, testify."

Whereupon I produced such a certificate. "Mr. Halley, this is a certificate of Dr. Vincent J. Panettiere, M.D., dated March 15, 1951. It says:

> "Mr. Frank Costello of 115 Central Park West is confined at home in bed. He is suffering from acute laryng-tracheitis. He should remain in bed and have complete voice rest for several days."

Halley pointed out the certificate said several days, not weeks, and I said, "I would take a week"—but then Kefauver said the certificate was "not enough" to obtain a delay.

Wolf: "Regardless of the certificate, I have stated grounds on which my application is made. It is not only confined to that; that is only a part of it."

The chairman: "Very well. If Mr. Costello wants to risk his chances with this committee and with the Senate, he can do so."

Wolf: "All right."

Frank and I started to leave.

The chairman: "Just a minute, Mr. Wolf; just a minute, Mr. Costello. Just a minute. Sit down a minute."

Halley: "Please, may we have some order . . ."

But in the end, with the Senators bitterly calling after us and the crowd buzzing with excitement, the Prime Minister of the Underworld and his counsel walked out of the hearings. As one newsman said, "Senator Tobey had damned the wrong torpedo."

Next day the angry committee put Dr. Panettiere on the stand. The doctor said he had examined Costello "with the indirect laryngoscopy method—in which we use a mirror, to examine his throat, and found his vocal cords inflamed, and the upper portion of the trachea inflamed."

But under relentless questioning, the doctor said that yes, Costello could talk for a reasonable period without undue risk.

The chairman thereupon ordered Costello to appear at two o'clock, and we did so appear. This time I brought *another* doctor's certificate, from Costello's long-time personal physician, Dr. Douglas Quick, who had previously been unavailable. This certificate stated that "Mr. Frank Costello has had a heavy cold and a laryngitis for nearly two weeks. During this week the laryngitis has gotten steadily worse until he is now unable to talk in sustained conversation, and any effort in this direction will cause further and continuing danger to his larynx."

On Frank's behalf, I asked an adjournment to Wednesday of the next week. The committee, instead, said they would appoint their own doctor to examine Frank and then would rule on when he would return.

And so we left again, this time with permission. And the first hint I got that more than laryngitis might be involved was when a very famous lawyer sitting in the audience approached us on our way out. He was an old friend of Frank's. And he said to us in a low voice, "Why'd you walk out, Frank? They'll hit you for contempt for sure."

"I got to help O'Dwyer," Frank said.

9

The Honorable William O'Dwyer, Ambassador to Mexico, former Mayor of New York, took the stand.* Once described as a man whose smile could melt a skyscraper, O'Dwyer came on

---

* I am sure that Paul O'Dwyer and other members of his family, who are among my oldest and dearest friends and whom I hold in highest regard, will understand why my collaborator and I find it necessary to refer to the actions of his brother Bill in terms that may seem harsh. All of the matters referred to concerning his brother have been the subject of reports of the senatorial and congressional committees and of his own testimony therein, and are therefore in the public domain. To ignore them would be unfair to the reading public of this book and would defeat its main purpose—to tell the full story honestly.

full of charm and confidence. While the committee members fidgeted with impatience, O'Dwyer discoursed at length on prohibition and the causes of crime and on his accomplishments as mayor. But no sooner had he come to his close, than the Senators were after him. As Frank no doubt expected, they were very much interested in that strange visit O'Dwyer had made to Frank's apartment in 1942, while O'Dwyer was still an army major.

The Ambassador said that he had gone there on army business —to investigate clothing contracts for the air force and rumors linking Costello to them.

The Senators did not attempt to hide their skepticism. Quickly, they brought out in questioning that Jim Moran, O'Dwyer's closest political aide and a friend of Costello (Moran was serving in a lifetime job as Commissioner of Water Supply, the job appointment being O'Dwyer's last official act in office), had accompanied O'Dwyer to the meeting with Frank.

That a man named Irving Sherman was there, that Sherman was a friend of both Costello and Costello's partner, Joe Adonis, and that Sherman had later been of help to O'Dwyer in his second campaign for mayor.

That the late Michael J. Kennedy, then leader of Tammany Hall, and Bert Stand, then secretary, also were present.

And O'Dwyer, under stiff questioning, provided the committee with still other links in the chain of evidence tying his administration with Costello. He admitted that, as mayor, he appointed Philip Zichello a deputy commissioner of hospitals, Lawrence Austin a city marshal, and Joseph V. Loscalzo a special sessions justice.

Zichello, it was revealed, was a brother-in-law of Willie Moretti, Austin a cousin of Irving Sherman, and Loscalzo came to his job, a wiretap revealed, after Supreme Court Justice Aurelio had told Costello on the telephone that he "must do something for Joe."

O'Dwyer admitted knowing that "Joe" was Loscalzo. He also admitted he had appointed Abe Rosenthal, another friend of Costello, assistant corporation counsel and Frank J. Quayle, a close friend of Joe Adonis, fire commissioner.

Why had he appointed men who were alleged to be friends of Costello and Adonis? "There are things you have to do politically if you want cooperation," he said.

Costello came off better when the committee turned to the Abe Reles matter. O'Dwyer insisted that Frank's name never came up in the investigation of Murder Incorporated. Frank's was about the only name that did *not* come up.

Former Deputy Police Commissioner Frank Bals had appeared on the stand before O'Dwyer and told a strange story about the death of Reles, the "canary who could sing but not fly." Reles was under guard by no less than six policemen when he went out the window. How come?

Bals said that all six policemen fell asleep at the same time and Reles decided to play a joke on them: he knotted a bed sheet and a strip of wire and climbed out of his room, planning to reenter the hotel by a fifth-floor window, run up the stairs, and awaken the policemen. The bed sheet and wire parted, and he fell to his death.

This was quite a story, told by Bals with a straight face to an incredulous Senate committee. Now they pounced on O'Dwyer. What was his version of the Reles mystery? O'Dwyer said that Bals's story was nonsense, but his own story was hardly more convincing. He claimed that Reles had died while trying to escape. Escape from whom? The guards who were *protecting* him against the Murder Incorporated killers? It didn't make sense. Anyway, the Senators wanted to know, why hadn't the cops prevented the attempt?

"A simple case of negligence," O'Dwyer said.

Halley: "Mr. O'Dwyer, weren't you reported in the newspapers as having appeared at the police trial to defend those same policemen?"

O'Dwyer: "Well, not to defend the particular act of carelessness . . ."

Halley: "Did you feel justified in publicly stating that you were going to the defense of these policemen?"

O'Dwyer: ". . . Why not?"

Then came the knockout punch. The committee revealed that Bals himself had been the man in charge of the Reles guard—

and that O'Dwyer instead of punishing him actually had promoted him.

O'Dwyer was rocking, but worse was to come. Senator Tobey turned once again to the matter of O'Dwyer's meeting during the war with Costello in Frank's apartment.

Tobey asked O'Dwyer if he wouldn't agree with him that the presence of leading and professional politicians in Frank's apartment at that meeting "is a very striking instance . . . about the influence of this man Costello on political affairs in New York . . ."

Then came one of the most famous exchanges of the hearing. It concerned Costello:

Tobey: "A funny thing what magnetism that man had. How can you analyze it? You look him over, you wouldn't mark him except pretty near minus zero. But what is there? What has he got? What kind of appeal does he have? What is it?"

O'Dwyer (after a pause): "It doesn't matter whether it is a banker, a businessman, or a gangster, his pocketbook is always attractive."

It was a statement which explained everything—and would always explain everything in the future—about political corruption in America, ranging from Frank Costello to the Vesco and ITT allegations of today. There was never any question that Frank freely gave money along with his influence to political candidates who would be friendly to him once they were in office. His pocketbook was always "attractive."

And this theme of corruption soared in the Kefauver hearings to a climax as dramatic as ever heard anywhere, unexpected, actually thrilling at the time.

O'Dwyer provided the twist. One of the most popular mayors and one of the most successful ambassadors this country has ever had, he exuded confidence and expertise on his first appearance, as we have seen. Then a longer interrogation began to crack the veneer. But not quite. He remained firm, if shaken.

When O'Dwyer left the stand I know Frank must have breathed a sigh of relief. O'Dwyer had not been positively shown to be guilty of any actions, despite the insinuations. And Frank's claim that he was ill had allowed him to withdraw from the hearing while O'Dwyer testified, so as not to further involve the ambassador, whom Frank liked.

But then the committee turned to another matter: payment by unions in cash under the table to Jim Moran, O'Dwyer's closest political aide. Moran angrily denied the accusations. One of the persons who were alleged to have delivered the payoff, John P. Crane, president of Local 94, Uniformed Firemen's Association, claimed the Fifth Amendment on the question. Moran contended he had received no money from Crane, including any campaign contributions.

The committee was at a dead end. Louis Weber, a longshoreman who was alleged to have made payoffs for the dockworkers' union to Moran, claimed he didn't even *know* Moran.

But then the committee sprang a surprise witness: Gerard M. Martin, fireman, New York City Fire Department. Martin had been employed in a key job, it seemed. He was Jim Moran's receptionist. He testified that Weber in fact came to Moran's office at least eleven times each month.

Moran and Weber had been caught in a bold-faced lie. But still the committee had no proof of just what the mysterious visits of a stevedore to O'Dwyer's aide, the deputy fire commissioner, were for. Obviously, Weber was a messenger; what other business would a stevedore have with the fire commissioner? But then came March 21st, the very last day of the hearings—and John P. Crane, the alleged payoff man, took the stand again.

It happened so suddenly that the committee was literally caught breathless, and the audience was silent in shock:

Halley: "I believe you testified that . . . Mr. Moran
                 told you he was a poor man."
Crane: "I did testify Mr. Moran said he was a poor
                 man."
Halley: "And after he told you he was a poor man, did
                 you take certain action with respect to him?"
Crane: "Subsequently I made him a gift of $5,000."
The chairman: "Now, just a minute. When was this? Let's get
                 the—"

Halley: "Do you recall whether you paid that $5,000
                to Mr. Moran in currency?"
Crane: "It was paid in either $50 or $100 bills, or
                both."
Halley: "Where did you deliver that to him? . . . in
                his own office?"
Crane: "Yes, sir."

Crane said that in 1948 he came through with another $30,000
to Moran "to promote the good will of Mr. Moran on behalf of
the firemen."

Tobey: "To put it very boldly—here I see a total of $35,000
          . . . Let's get down to brass tacks . . . Why did you
          give him the money?"
Crane: "So that the firemen could benefit by it . . . We were
          getting a square deal from Mr. Moran . . . and we
          wanted to make sure it stayed that way."

Jim Moran was one thing. But O'Dwyer was Mayor of New
York. Surely if Moran had been on the take O'Dwyer was igno-
rant of the fact. But then, to a spellbound committee, Crane
told his story.

He said that in 1949 O'Dwyer had been initially cool to the
firemen's request for a raise in salary and pension benefits. The
firemen had hoped that by 1951 O'Dwyer would retire and they
would get a chance to press their salary demands with a new
mayor. But then O'Dwyer announced he was going to run again,
and it was obvious his popularity would make him a sure winner.
So Crane went to Jim Moran and "asked him to take me over
and let's patch up my differences with Mayor O'Dwyer."

"He took me over. We straightened out our differences. He
committed himself to go along on our pension legislation then
pending, and we got on the bandwagon."

Halley: "Did you subsequently meet Mr. O'Dwyer on the
           stairs of City Hall?"
Crane: "Yes . . . I told him I wanted to see him. And he said,
           'Drop up to the mansion.' I can't tell you the date but
           it was . . . some time around October 12, 1949."
Halley: "And you went up to the Gracie Mansion?"

Crane: "That's right."
Halley: "And you saw Mayor O'Dwyer?"
Crane: "Yes, sir."
Halley: "Were you alone with him?"
Crane: "Yes, sir . . . on the porch at Gracie Mansion."
Halley: "Will you tell the committee what transpired?"
Crane: "I told the mayor at that time that I had promised him the support of the firemen, and I offered him some evidence of that support on the occasion, in the form of $10,000."

Silence in the hearing room. Everyone leaned forward, all eyes on the witness.

Halley: "Was that in cash?"
Crane: "That was in cash."
Halley: "Was it loose, or in a package?"
Crane: "I had it in . . . this type of envelope you have right here, the brown one."
Halley: "Did he say anything?"
Crane: "He thanked me. He didn't look in the envelope, or anything else."

The scene of a mayor of New York sitting on the porch of Gracie Mansion accepting a bribe in cash from a union for help in wage legislation was to linger a long, long time in the minds of New York's citizens.

And this is so even though many knowledgeable New York civic leaders who were active in those days make quite a different case than the Kefauver committee did. They believe that O'Dwyer was given the money not as a bribe but as a legitimate campaign contribution and that it was given directly to O'Dwyer only because the firemen's union did not trust his Democratic Party campaign staff, and refused to deal with them personally.

Nevertheless, the Kefauver hearings exposing O'Dwyer's taking of bribes for whatever reason, plus the revelations about Frank Costello's influence on New York politics, had one positive result: they killed Tammany Hall. In a few short years the influence of the hall would finally disappear, and the Democratic Party would fragment and become what it is today, a loose coalition of various interests.

Jim Moran, O'Dwyer's aide, went to prison; O'Dwyer went into exile in Mexico; Frank Costello suffered most of all. When he returned to the stand he refused once again to state his net worth, and was cited for contempt of Congress. But this was not his worst wound.

For in the wake of the hearings, Frank would lose his one great claim to office at the top of the Mafia: his ironclad hold on New York politics through Tammany. It was a weakening men like Vito Genovese, the New Jersey don who was ambitious to unseat Frank, would quickly exploit. And, on the other side, the law was ready to pounce on Frank from every direction. His life would turn into a nightmare of trials, prison sentences . . . and a shot in the night.

BOOK V
A Shot in the Night

THE GUNS

1

October 4, 1951. Willie Moretti tooled his white Cadillac convertible toward Joe's Elbow Room, a bar at 739 Palisades Avenue, across the Hudson River from Manhattan.

Willie had been complaining that he was tired of those holes out West where Costello had been sending him. He was hiding out like a con—and for what? Two days ago he had had an argument with Frank about it and again Frank wanted him to get lost. Willie had told him to shove it. He could take care of himself.

On the sidewalk in front of the restaurant a man named Vince was waiting for him. Vince had told Willie that he had a proposition that would take the heat off Willie and allow him to stay here in the East.

Willie shook hands with Vince who slapped him on the back with the other hand and said, "Hey *combare,* you look good."

Willie said, "Yeah, I got nothin' but tan sittin' out in the sun, thanks to Frank."

They walked into the cool, shaded restaurant, which was empty except for three of Vince's friends sitting at a table, waiting. Vince introduced them, and Dorothy Novack, the waitress, came to the table. "Get us some menus, baby," Vince said. "We're starved."

The waitress smiled and went back through the swinging doors to the kitchen to get silverware and setups. Precisely at that moment the man next to Willie grabbed Willie's red tie, jumped up, and pulled it, hauling Willie back in his chair, and Vince, his friend, was pointing a .38 at his head. Willie lunged to the left, off the chair, but it was too late. The gun roared, and roared again. Other guns fired into his chest and head.

Willie Moretti lay with his feet outspread, pointed toward the door, blood running from his chest and head. He would make no more wisecracks to Senate committees, and never again call Frank Costello, his guardian.

Everyone in the underworld knew that Frank was Willie's protector. The murder of Willie was a violent announcement that Frank's power as the king was under direct threat. And it did not take Frank long to find out who the next candidate was. Vito Genovese.

But Vito always had one problem with Frank: Frank was smarter than anyone else. And in this case Frank foiled Vito with a very simple move; he turned the other cheek, and said nothing, made no countermove, refused to begin a war.

Frank was so popular that Vito needed an excuse to strike at him directly. A war, a killing ordered by Frank, might have provided that excuse. None was forthcoming, and the bid for power by the frustrated Genovese was thus checked for years.

Frank could use the time. He was in all kinds of trouble with the law.

2

Perhaps the most potent weapon this democracy has is a televised congressional hearing. In this century there have been three major hearings, and each has had enormous consequences. The Army-McCarthy hearings effectively ended the spectre of McCarthyism, which some had felt would never be purged. The

Watergate hearings already have changed the balance of power between the Congress and the presidency, and constitutional questions inspired by them will affect the course of our political future for many decades to come.

The Kefauver hearings had an effect which is still felt throughout the country. Immediately it stopped underworld leaders on many fronts, checking the spread of gambling casinos with their attendant coteries of Mafia figures who were moving into many communities throughout the United States.

And its longer-lasting effect came from its exposure of organized crime as a reality, not just a myth, and the actual physical sight and sound of criminal leaders either taking the Fifth or running into trouble—as Costello did—because they elected to talk.

The old order was exposed, and within years many of its members would be dead or toppled from power because they could not function under the spotlight which the Kefauver hearings had fastened on them. The new leaders coming up would not have their prestige, power, or experience. Many politicians who had thought it routine to go to people like Frank for approval before election now would shy away. Investigative government agencies would begin intensive probes aimed at organized crime.

Frank Costello was a marked man, the leader whom everyone was out to destroy. Almost immediately he would find himself caught between two pincers: government investigators probing his affairs and ambitious underworld leaders seeking to replace him.

Both would find Frank a tough fighter. This was a man who had broken the law all his life, and had only once gone to jail, as a young man, in 1915. A famous bootlegger, he had beaten the rap. A citizen who had made millions and never paid his taxes, he was not sent to prison for tax evasion. A leader of the Mafia during a time when over a hundred gangland murders were committed, there had never been any evidence connecting him with any of them.

Frank covered his tracks, eschewed violence, supported and financed politicians, judges, district attorneys, and, where necessary, jurors. He always went free.

But now the word was out: "Get Frank Costello."

3

The first legal lance aimed in Frank's direction was contempt of Congress charges flowing from the Kefauver hearings. Surprisingly, we were in good shape to handle that one. Dr. Douglas Quick, who had been Frank's physician for many years, would testify that he had operated on Frank's vocal cords to remove a cancerous tumor many years ago. This would be telling evidence to at least some jurors that Frank definitely had a voice problem when he staged his celebrated walkout.

The other charges related to Frank's refusal to reveal his net worth, and there I knew I could show that Frank had answered so many other questions relating to his income that a jury might be persuaded he had, in fact, been cooperative in his testimony. Also, as a matter of law, he had a right to refuse to testify if he felt the answer would incriminate him.

Victor Feingold, my associate at the time, joined me in driving with Frank to the federal courthouse on Foley Square in Manhattan on January 7, 1952. Frank looked chipper and in good spirits.

The first day in court was given over to choosing jurors. The second juror selected was to become quite a figure of controversy: Houston A. Hiers, who identified himself as a sales manager from the Bronx.

U.S. Attorney Myles J. Lane was brief in his opening remarks, apparently believing that the facts spoke for themselves. I, on the other hand, spoke for more than an hour in a voice which, according to reporters, "at times assumed oratorical warmth." I do not deny it.

But I did start off quietly. "I have waited almost a year to bring out the real facts in this case, which have never been revealed; to bring them out in a real court of law under dignified circumstances, in a court such as this before twelve red-blooded American jurors."

I told the jury how I had represented Frank since 1943, and had always found him willing to cooperate with constituted authority.

"I had represented him in several matters. I learned to know him personally. I am not condoning any of his acts of the past, of which Mr. Costello himself is not particularly proud. But Mr. Costello contends that so far as connecting him with underworld leaders—there is no truth in it. He'd like nothing better than if he could get a hearing before a forum, a responsible forum. He would be glad to avail himself of that."

I told how I had arranged with Rudolph Halley, the Kefauver committee's chief counsel, to have Costello accept the committee subpoena in my law office on Madison Avenue the previous January; how I assured Mr. Halley that my client would cooperate with the committee within the limits of constitutional privilege.

"After the executive hearings, at which Mr. Halley and Senator Kefauver complimented Mr. Costello on his frankness and cooperation, I left the room feeling that that promise of exoneration was made in good faith; that it was the dawn of a new era for Frank Costello."

Then I spoke bitterly about the committee's release to the newspapers of the interim report, and quoted from it: "There is no doubt in the minds of the members of the committee that there do exist at least two major crime syndicates. There is one with an axis between New York and Miami headed by Frank Costello."

"When I read this report, I rushed down to Mr. Halley's office and said, 'Mr. Halley, what is this? What does your promise mean to give him an opportunity for exoneration?'"

The committee had publicly "convicted" Costello before Frank had even testified. Nevertheless he did testify in good faith, but when his voice began to fail they pounced on him. "Instead of contempt by this man, he was most scrupulously respectful and desired to cooperate."

My "oratorical warmth" was at a high pitch now and from the bench came a request from Judge Ryan not to raise my voice. I did lower my voice but I was angry again when I spoke about the committee's reaction to the certificate from Dr. Quick.

"They attempted to force him. The witness said, 'I cannot, and will not until I get a voice rest' . . . When they attempted this inquisition method—"

Judge Ryan interrupted again with a plea, in effect, that I lower my voice. I did—but I hoped I had scored a few points with the jurors.

If I had, those points would be needed, for Dr. Quick now turned against us to such an extent that I once called him "Dr. Quack" on cross-examination. Frank and I were both enraged at his testimony. Here was the physician who had, by his own testimony, treated Costello for a tumor on the left vocal cords in 1933, who, on cross-examination, admitted that subsequent formation of scar tissue on Frank's vocal cords had been a continuing problem. Now, on direct examination, he admitted that he was called to Frank's apartment during the hearings, and found Frank's throat inflamed and irritated and that he prescribed medicines.

In effect he confirmed Frank's defense for his walkout, but then in answer to the prosecutor's question: "Did you tell him he could testify that day?" he replied, "Yes, I did."

This was news to both Frank and me. It was I who had personally taken the doctor's certificate into the hearings asking for a delay for Frank because of the inflamed throat. Dr. Quick explained the contradiction by saying that, yes, he had told Costello he was to avoid strain and not to force his voice. But, the doctor added, "I told him he could testify for a couple of hours. I felt that amount could be tolerated."

But then I nailed the good doctor. I asked to examine the grand jury minutes of Dr. Quick's testimony and read to the court what he said to the grand jury:

"I told him [Costello] that he had been using his voice too much and I stressed that because, with the amount of inflammation present, I was fearful of the possibility of having to put a tracheotomy tube in his neck."

Dr. Quick indignantly said it was all a matter of interpretation, that he had not stressed the possibility of having to put in a tracheotomy tube, but had stressed that Costello had been using his voice too much.

The doctor left the stand in some confusion and Frank was

happy. "All the loot I paid him all those years and he turns on me," he said, as I rejoined him at the defense table.

The next witness was Dr. John D. Kernan, the physician the committee had appointed to examine Costello after he walked out. He should have been a more damaging witness against us, but my cross-examination had even more effective results than I had hoped. Under questioning, Dr. Kernan conceded that he detected a stiffness in Costello's vocal cords, the result of X-ray treatments for the cancer condition years ago; that he had exchanged only a few words with Costello during his examination —and that in somewhat similar cases he was apt to advise a regimen of complete silence for the patient, even complete body rest.

Dr. Kernan also conceded that if Costello had been subjected to more than two hours of answering questions it might have been "crowding him a little bit."

"Would you permit a patient to testify with a badly inflamed larynx, Doctor?"

"No."

From my point of view, both physicians' testimony had been hurt badly by their admissions on cross-examination.

Rudolph Halley was the next prosecution witness. Perhaps it was because he was newly married—his bride was in the audience —or perhaps he was destined to function best as a prosecutor and not as a witness—he was the worst witness I ever faced. I just could not get a straight answer from him. Time and again I demanded, answer yes or no. Time and again he would be off on a long-winded response that would avoid the issue. And this from the hard-hitting counsel who had caused dozens of witnesses to squirm as he demanded direct answers himself.

About all he added to the evidence was that he himself could hear Costello during the hearings, and detected no trouble in Costello's voice. I was amused by Frank's very human reaction to Halley. He didn't like that man. When Halley testified, Frank turned his face away and refused to look at him, even when the committee counsel was pointing him out for identification.

At this point in the trial, January 11th, I believed we were ahead on the facts. But the next day Judge Ryan turned us down on a question of law. He ruled that Costello did not invoke his constitutional privilege against self-incrimination in good faith when he refused to answer questions as to his net worth.

Years later, this ruling still puzzles me. At the time, in court, I angrily said that Costello had stopped short of stating his net worth when he realized that he might by his answers leave himself open to federal prosecution for tax evasion.

But the court held that Costello had given the facts concerning his income at earlier committee hearings without showing commission of any crime for which he might be prosecuted.

With that, the court made its ruling, taking the decision away from the jury, which now had only to decide on the question of Costello's walkout.

The jury, which had been out for hours, finally returned, and we were in trouble. On the evidence adduced at the trial from both physicians, there was no question that he did have an inflamed throat, which was the reason he gave for the walkout in the first place.

Nevertheless, eleven jurors voted guilty, one held out for acquittal, and the result was a hung jury. But a symbol of the public attitude toward Frank Costello was the fact that the lone juror, Houston Hiers, was pilloried in the press, and actually called before a grand jury to explain his vote of acquittal.

It was clear Frank Costello was now the chief Mafioso in the eyes of the public. The prosecution demanded and got permission for an immediate retrial.

Outside, the reporters were waiting with cameras and note pads, pencils poised. Frank strode through the line between them, with flashbulbs exploding, and myself following. One reporter shouted, "Are you happy?" For some reason Frank smiled. "I've never been *unhappy*," he said.

But despite that jaunty statement there was to be unhappiness ahead for both Frank and me. Frank went on trial again, and this time I was not at his side. I had been felled by the flu, taken a penicillin shot, and suffered an allergic reaction which kept me in bed.

With me out of action, Frank turned to Wall Street for legal help. Surprisingly, the prestigious firm of Spence, Hotchkiss, Parker and Wuryee agreed to defend him, causing considerable comment in the New York legal community. The senior partner himself, Kenneth M. Spence, was to lead the legal team.

It looked good in the newspapers, but I am afraid Mr. Spence, an esteemed and highly successful lawyer, did not realize what he was getting into. Defending Frank Costello, as I knew better than anyone else, was a rugged, gut-level business. The pristine air of Wall Street turned foul almost the minute Spence appeared in court with his famous underworld client. This was the verbal exchange when Spence asked for a few more days' delay.

Spence: "I still ask for . . . three days' delay, in view of the record, and I state that, and no judge has ever questioned my integrity."

"I do not question your integrity," Judge Sylvester Ryan answered.

"Well, I think you do. I can do nothing to influence Your Honor so I will just walk out and have to do the best I can. But I do not want any more arguments with the court."

The judge said, "Well, I do not think we are having any arguments, Mr. Spence—"

"I do."

"And I don't like your attitude," Judge Ryan snapped.

A great start with the judge. But Mr. Spence had made an even worse start with me. Judge Ryan had ruled against us in the first case on a question of law, but we had achieved a hung jury on the question of fact. Now Spence informed me that he could win the case on the question of law alone. As for the facts about Frank's inflamed throat, forget them. He would stipulate that the government had *proved* its case on the facts (in effect saying that Frank did *not* have throat problems) and rely instead on his own interpretation of the law to convince the judge.

At that point, while he was telling me that, I could hear the jail doors clang behind Frank for the first time in almost forty years.

4

The second trial, as I suggested—and as I warned Frank—was a disaster. Judge Ryan later said that he was puzzled that the defense had not relied, as in the previous trial, on testimony that Costello's throat was inflamed as a reason for his walkout. He asked Spence why he had stipulated that Costello, during the hearings, was physically able to answer questions.

Mr. Spence said a man might be "almost at the verge of death and still be able to answer questions." The judge seemed a bit taken aback by this reply, honest as it was. It didn't make much sense as a defense position.

But by the time this exchange took place the case was over anyway, as far as Costello was concerned. The judge had turned down Spence's interpretation of the law on claiming the Fifth Amendment, exactly as he had done at the first trial. Why Spence thought he could change the judge's mind on the law is still a mystery to me years later. And Spence's next act caused even more mystery to develop. When it came time to sum up, the indomitable attorney simply declined to do so. He was, as it was later said, carrying to the ultimate his contention that no issues of fact were involved in the trial.

Poor Frank. He went down the chute for thousands in legal fees to a high-priced Wall Street law firm, and didn't even have the pleasure of a passionate summation, like the one I had given him in the first trial when I spoke for two hours with Frank hanging on every word (and the jury hanging, too, eventually).

What he did get—incredibly—after all those years, was a jail sentence. Eighteen months, plus a $5,000 fine, the heaviest penalty ever imposed in New York for contempt of Congress.

5

August 16, 1952. Frank Costello, now sixty-one, was sitting on a bench in one of the four large ground-floor cells in the federal courthouse, a feeble dome light bringing out the shiny spots on his slick pompadour. It was a hot day; I was in my shirt-sleeves when I came in to visit him. Frank had something on his mind.

"Get me the deputy marshal, George," he said.

I went outside and brought in the deputy. Frank said to him, "Tell the boys I've come in to do my bit. Tell them I don't want no favors from nobody. Tell them I expect to be treated like anybody else without no special requests."

The deputy said he would do that and left. I looked at Frank and realized he was shaken. After all the violent years, after all the pressures and the touch-and-go battle for survival, to be brought to grief for a contempt of Congress rap. He didn't like it. And he didn't like the prison guard now walking in with a pair of handcuffs. "Hell, I don't need those," Frank said. But the guard insisted, and soon Frank found himself handcuffed and, what was worse, placed in a van with two young draft evaders, also handcuffed. Frank looked accusingly at the two young draft-dodgers, one of them stocky and swarthy, the other a tall youth with lanky blond hair and silver spectacles.

"You kids are making a mistake, not answering for the draft," Frank said. "You're foolish. You're ruining your lives, if you only knew it."

This patriotism from the nation's crime lord only brought stares from the two young men.

That night his custom-made suit went into the steam sterilizer, he was stripped clean for medical examination, received his prison denims, and was taken into a twenty-bed receiving dormitory. Frank Costello was now a number.

Frank went to Lewisburg, Pennsylvania's Federal Correction Center, and then was transferred to the government's prison in

Atlanta. But legal attacks now struck from another direction. On October 22, 1952, the government moved to strip him of his United States citizenship. The Department of Justice filed a petition in federal court to cancel Costello's naturalization on the grounds that he had not been of good moral character for the five years preceding his citizenship application.

The petition charged that Frank, in his application, had concealed his arrest and conviction for carrying a weapon. Also, that he had used a false name and that his two witnesses had testified falsely in his behalf. One of these witnesses, incidentally, was the Harry Sausser made famous as the "flying Sausser" during the Kefauver hearings.

Frank Costello asked me to fly to Atlanta.

I was allowed to interview him in a private room, and in a few minutes I was apoplectic, not the last time this was to happen in the chaotic years ahead. For I found Frank was not immediately worried about the deportation trial, which he knew could be stalled, but had come up with a legal move he wanted me to make to free him. It was so ridiculous I just stared at him.

He asked me to apply for a writ of habeas corpus on the grounds that the Atlanta penitentiary was not a jail. It seems he had read the text of his sentence and discovered that he was sentenced for three separate *misdemeanors* and therefore should serve the terms in a "common" jail, not a penitentiary such as Atlanta's.

Specifically, he had been sentenced for one year for refusing to testify before a congressional committee, and had been given two sentences of six months each, to run concurrently, for leaving the committee meeting and refusing to testify. Frank had dug up from his law-conscious fellow inmates a statute that says a sentence for an offense punishable by imprisonment of one year or less shall not be served in a penitentiary without the consent of the defendant.

I argued, I pleaded, but to no avail. Soon I was making a fool of myself assuring an amused federal judge that Frank wanted to be let free because he was not in a "common" jail. The judge turned me down, of course, and Frank, for his pains, found himself on a bus to the federal correctional institution in Milan, Michigan, which was a common enough jail to qualify.

About the only good news Frank had in that period was that Vito Genovese was also in danger of being deported. On November 21, 1952, the government filed a complaint in denaturalization proceedings against Genovese, accusing him—like Costello—of having concealed his criminal record when he applied for citizenship.

Frank, I believe, had already heard rumblings about what Genovese was doing now that Frank was behind bars. I have always believed that his puzzling request for habeas corpus on ridiculous legal grounds was in the hope that he could get free for at least a few days to mend some fences in New York. But he didn't get those few days, and Genovese managed to stay free.

6

Newspapers always speak with scorn of an underworld leader's "army of lawyers." But, believe me, never was an "army" more needed than in the case of Frank Costello, who spent the next five years from 1952 in and out of court (and in and out of prison), with every one of the cases going to the U.S. Supreme Court.

The whole mission, as I have said, was to "get" Frank Costello, after television had pictured him as the nation's top criminal, and citizens were loudly wondering why such a man was not behind bars.

In one case, the Supreme Court was accused of creating "bad law" with a decision which was to be rightfully overturned years later by the same Court.

That was in the tax case brought against Frank, a case which began with a check for $5.10, the only check involving Frank the Internal Revenue investigators had been able to turn up after years of digging. Frank scorned the use of checks, as we have seen in the taxicab incident. But the investigators did come across that small check which Mrs. Costello wrote to a plant nursery for flowers.

The nursery specialized in supplying flowers for cemeteries. The Internal Revenue soon found out the flowers had been bought for a mausoleum owned by Frank which cost $18,165.* Frank had paid in cash for the mausoleum plus $4,888 for a cemetery lot, also in cash.

And so the pyramid of expenditures in cash built and built until the special agents on Frank's case were able to recommend:

"that criminal prosecution be instituted against Frank Costello in violation of Section 145(b) of the Internal Revenue Code for attempting to defeat and evade his personal income taxes for the years 1946 to 1950, inclusive . . . The total additional taxes for the years involved, namely 1941 to 1950, inclusive, amount to $384,824.67, and the total penalties for the same period amount to $201,442.05, making a grand total of $586,266.72."

The "bad law" was created in the grand jury proceeding, where the federal attorneys called as their only witnesses the Internal Revenue agents who had developed the case. They told the grand jury the results of their interviews with various tradesmen who had received money from Frank in cash. But none of the tradesmen themselves were called. Thus the grand jury heard only hearsay evidence.

At this time we could not capitalize on the fact because there had never been a Supreme Court decision on whether hearsay evidence was admissable before a grand jury, and there were no applicable statutes, either.

By the time Frank's case came to trial in 1954, he was out of prison, his sentence completed for contempt of Congress. But things looked dark indeed for him. And I was angry, myself. I was the lawyer who had made up Frank's tax returns during some of those years, so I was subpoenaed by the government as one of its witnesses.

---

* On January 25, 1974, twenty-two years later, the mausoleum which gave Frank so much trouble was in the news again. One year after his death, a bomb was exploded, blowing off the huge granite tomb's bronze doors. Frank's crypt was untouched. Newspapers and police officials were baffled by the mysterious incident. Was Costello, one year after his death, still a potent force in underworld affairs? Incredible—and yet the day after the explosion police investigators were quoted as saying it was a possible symbolic warning of a new outbreak of warfare for control of the underworld. True or not, police and criminal experts had to smile when assessing the incident, for Frank, who was the most famous and most publicized criminal of his time, could still get television and newspaper space after he died. Fame had trailed him beyond the grave.

Because of that fact I could hardly appear in court as both a defense counsel and a government witness. This time I suggested another lawyer for Frank, Leo C. Fennelly.

Then for days I consulted the federal prosecutors and finally worked out a deal whereby my testimony would be stipulated, and I would thus not have to appear as a witness against my own client. But then Frank called me with an inside revelation which could turn the whole trial around.

7

Frank and I walked in the sun in Central Park on a hot day. A passionate young couple was grappling on the grass right by our path and Frank smiled down at them and said, "Give it to her, kid."

The boy sat up angrily. "Who says? Get lost!"

Frank laughed, and I did, too. We went down a path toward one of the roads which wound through the park, cabs nosing by horse-drawn carriages and bicyclists. A pretty day. Frank said, "What do you think, George?"

"Did Fennelly explain it to you?"

"Yeah, but I want *you* to tell me."

We found a bench that was empty and sat down beside a pond where children push toy sailboats across the water and wait for the wind to carry them back. I said, "The government uses the net worth theory. That means they figure out how much you spent, and figure from that just how much you earned. It's a new theory the Supreme Court just allowed."

"Great," Frank said. "Look at that beauty." He was watching a toy schooner with blue sails beating across the pond. Then he turned to me. "But this I don't understand. If I spent $100,000, it doesn't mean I earned $100,000 that year. I could have spent it from money I saved, couldn't I?"

"Right. But then you'd have to tell where *that* money came

from and they'd go back to that year and prosecute for fraud then."

Frank turned away and resumed his study of the kids by the pond. "What makes me mad," he said, "is this time the government is full of crap. I got that money from a guy in Chicago legitimately a long time ago, when I was in trouble on the Flamingo deal. He owed it to me."

"You can *prove* that?" I was excited. If the money was legitimate this could knock the government's case right out of court.

But Frank was smiling a little smile. "I can prove it, but I ain't ever going to say it."

I knew what he meant. Testimony about the money would get the man in Chicago in trouble, just as Frank had gotten into trouble. The money loaned to Frank, no doubt in cash, and no doubt unreported as income, would nail his friend.

But I was unwilling to let Frank cut off his defense so easily. I actually clutched his shoulder. "Frank, this is big. Five years! And they're going to do everything they can to make sure you're convicted. Now friendship is one thing—"

But Frank silenced me with a wave of his hand. "George," he said, wearily, "you don't understand *this* kind of friendship."

So the climactic trial of Frank's life began. Leo Fennelly did a good job defending against the tax evasion charge, but he was handcuffed. The law was so vague he couldn't attack it; and the net worth theory of the government could only be disproved if Frank would state where the money for the expenditures came from. This he would not do.

About the only time Frank smiled was when I appeared on the witness stand and started sparring with the judge. I was determined to get at least one good fact about Frank into the record: his generous support of charities of all kinds. I did manage to do this, in two days of testimony, including mention of the Salvation Army dinner, and commendations from various charities which Frank had helped support.

But I was supposed to be a government witness, and all my testimony was aiding Frank! Time and again the judge became angry at me. Nevertheless I stuck to my guns.

But the cards were stacked against Frank so high that he

could never win. The prosecution put dozens of tradesmen on the stand. Some of these tradesmen gave ridiculous testimony, in my opinion. For example, a Waldorf Astoria barber testified that Frank tipped 25 percent of his bill. Whether this was generosity, or stupidity, it certainly added little factual evidence of income tax evasion.

On May 13, 1954, Frank was convicted. He had expected the verdict, but still the decision shook him. When he came out of the courthouse I thought he looked close to tears. His hands were shaking when he lit a cigarette and faced the reporters. "What is there to say?" he replied to the shouting newspapermen.

Frank was always a favorite of the reporters. He had the charisma they loved. Now there was a strange occurrence: a silence fell over them. The questions stopped. Somehow they realized, in that moment, that the king was dead.

One of them stuck his hand out to Frank, saying, "Don't take it too hard, Frank."

"No, no, I won't," he said.

8

But Frank had not gotten where he was by being soft. The next day he was back in the public eye, looking chipper and fresh, and delighting the reporters once again. He was down at the courthouse posting bail, and when he came out he had some words of advice for the reporters. First, he wanted to clear up those reports that he had been near tears the day before. "The newspapers said that I was nervous last night. That was wrong. I have never been nervous in my life and last night I had the best night's sleep I had in the past six weeks."

Then he turned to the matter of his conviction. "I have no malice against anyone, but I will say that I think this is a political thing, a lot of guys trying to get ahead by climbing on my back, and that's the way the world goes."

His next statement really amused the reporters, few of whom

had Frank's income problems. "I want to give you fellows some advice," he told the newspapermen. "Remember this—when you spend money, spend cash and don't have any checks. If your wife has money have her declare it right away or they will be after you."

On May 17, 1954, Frank was sentenced to five years in prison and a $30,000 fine for income tax evasion.

A shock went through the underworld. Frank had reigned for almost twenty years, since Luciano went to prison. Now what would happen? Would he be able to retain his position even behind bars?

The Boss of all Bosses, the man who had magically kept the peace for almost two decades, would be missing at the sitdowns where decisions were made.

Two men, Albert Anastasia and Vito Genovese, stood ready to take over the throne as soon as Frank went to jail. Willie Moretti's murder left no doubt that violence would decide who would be the boss. Either Anastasia or Genovese would be murdered, unless Frank Costello could figure out a plan.

9

Frank Costello was still out on bail, while he appealed the tax decision, when Albert Anastasia came into the Italian restaurant on West 48th Street flanked by two bodyguards. One of the guards went right to the bar and sat on a stool, facing out, his eyes sweeping the restaurant constantly. The other guard took a position near the door.

Frank Costello was in a booth in the back. Anastasia leaned over, shook his hand, then sat down across from him. The handshake was symbolic: soon word from the boys in this restaurant would sweep across the city. Anastasia was Frank's boy.

"Vito is bad-mouthing me," Anastasia said, after he had ordered a Scotch, which the waiter brought on the run. "He's claiming I'm muscling in on the Cuba business."

Frank lighted an English Oval, and blew a smoke ring. The ring never made it, drifting apart almost from his lips. "So?"

"So I don't think Vito's worried about Cuba."

"I'll talk to him," Frank said.

There was a silence. Then Anastasia said cautiously, "I don't think that would be too good an idea, Frank."

Frank, who had always been able to talk to Genovese, looked at Anastasia and said nothing. He knew he had just heard his own death warrant.

10

Meanwhile, on the legal front, Frank was in just as much danger. While he was out on bond and appeals were being filed on his tax case, the government moved on the denaturalization proceedings. I studied the government's evidence, interviewed witnesses, and came to a sad conclusion. This was one case where Frank was guilty, and there was no getting around it. He had lied several times on his application for citizenship. It was right there, on paper, even a false name.

Frank greeted this news with fury. "If you can't beat this rap I'll get another lawyer," he said.

"I'm advising you to plead guilty, and hope for leniency, Frank. That's all I can do, as your counsel. You don't want me to lie to you."

Frank clapped his hand on my shoulder. "With you it's always truth and consequences. But get me a new lawyer, anyway. That will give us an excuse to delay the trial, at least."

"For a case like this the best man is Ed Williams," I said. "He'll come high."

"Let's get him while I can still afford him," Frank said.

Edward Bennett Williams was—and is—one of the most famous lawyers in America. He made his reputation taking difficult cases involving unpopular defendants, ranging from Senator McCarthy to Jimmy Hoffa. By 1954 his success was already a legend.

I was happy to introduce Ed Williams to the federal court in New York, as is the legal custom when out-of-town counsel is brought in. The judge agreed to the substitution of counsel, and —as we had hoped—allowed Frank a delay in the trial.

In the meantime, the U.S. Supreme Court agreed to hear Frank's appeal on the tax evasion case. Several points were raised but the high court agreed to hear only one. That was, as I have said, whether his indictment in the tax case had been based on hearsay evidence only. Judge Learned Hand, in the appeals court opinion, had held that it was immaterial whether only hearsay evidence was produced before the grand jury, despite the fact that other lower court rulings had barred hearsay evidence as the sole basis of an indictment.

The Department of Justice admitted that the grand jury acted solely on the basis of testimony by the three revenue agents, but argued that their testimony, summarizing results of investigations, was competent and admissible even though they had no personal acquaintance with Costello.

On March 6, 1956, the Supreme Court unanimously upheld the conviction and—perhaps to the amazement of the justices— was immediately denounced from many quarters for creating "bad law."

The very next day the American Civil Liberties Union filed an appeal with the high court as a "friend of the court," saying that the justices had not given full consideration to the fact that the indictment of Costello was based exclusively on hearsay evidence.

Frank was somewhat amused to hear another part of the ACLU's appeal, which solemnly stated that "federal prosecutors traditionally are appointed by the political party in power and are not wholly free from political influence."

The next day the Supreme Court reaffirmed its decision, and by May 15, 1956, he was on his way to prison.

11

Ed Williams did all—and more—that a lawyer could to obtain Frank's freedom. On the denaturalization case he got a break; the government admitted that part of its evidence was obtained by wiretaps, then illegal in federal court. The wiretaps were placed on Frank's phone at 405 Lexington Avenue, way back in 1925. Their evidence was only a small part of the government's case—but Williams shrewdly hammered at the commingling of evidence between what was "clean" or legally permissible, and what was illegal.

He also used those same wiretaps to launch an appeal on the tax case. On that same case he initiated a novel appeal, based on the Internal Revenue code itself.

Section 145 of the code provided a penalty of five years in prison and $10,000 fine for willful intent to evade income tax. Frank was convicted on that section. But Section 3616 of the same code provided a penalty of only one year and a $1,000 fine for filing a false return.

Williams contended that both sections of the code covered the same ground, and in such circumstance Section 3616 should prevail over a "general denunciation of attempting to evade taxes" such as Section 145 contained. Therefore Costello's penalty was too severe and should be the lesser sentence.

The Supreme Court agreed to hear this appeal. Ed Williams had won his point.

It was a legal victory which would bring Frank Costello within an inch of death.

March 11, 1957, Frank Costello was back in New York. The Supreme Court had decided to release him, pending his appeal.

That first night out of prison he went out to celebrate with some friends, including a man whom I shall call Jim Fielding, and his wife Laura, also a pseudonym.

Laura was pregnant, and the restaurant was stuffy. She turned to the others at the table and said she needed some air. Frank was planning to go on to the Copacabana with the Fieldings after dinner, and he suggested that they walk the three or four blocks, and see whether Laura would revive.

It was a dark moonless night in Manhattan, with cabs and cars vying for position as they raced for the lights. This was noise which all Manhattanites knew, an ambience that was part of their lives. The night was cool, fresh winds blew from the Hudson, and Frank was feeling good. "The first night out you want to stay up till morning," he said to Laura.

The three of them walked over to the Copa side by side. They entered the lounge, and Frank went ahead to talk to some of his old friends already seated at tables.

But one man called the Fieldings aside. He whispered, "Are you crazy? You shouldn't be with *him*."

The war was on to see who would take over Frank's position as head of the Mafia. The main target for Genovese, of course, was Anastasia, but Frank's sudden and unexpected reappearance in Manhattan threw everything out of kilter. There was no doubt that Frank's presence immeasurably strengthened Anastasia's hand, and Genovese did not want that.

Joe Valachi testified that it was Genovese who sent a killer after Frank. Peter Maas, who wrote the Valachi book that included this opinion, and who interviewed Costello shortly before his death, told me that he asked Frank who was behind the shooting, and Frank said, "The way you had it in your book was right."

It so happens I got Frank's opinion myself, as the result of a dramatic confrontation between Frank and Genovese in the Atlanta prison.

But that was later. On May 2, 1957, there would be a miracle.

12

On the evening of May 2, Frank Costello and friends, including Philip Kennedy, the manager of a posh modeling agency, were dining at an East Side restaurant.

Kennedy was a former semipro baseball player who moved among the "better" people that Frank fancied, and he was also a witty companion whom Frank enjoyed.

But after dinner, when the others suggested going on to another place for a nightcap, Frank, as usual, said he had to go home to make his phone calls.

Outside, Phil Kennedy and Frank hailed a cab. They drove in the dark to Frank's apartment house on Central Park West. A long black Cadillac pulled up behind them, and an enormous man with a hat pulled over his eyes scurried into the apartment house while Frank was saying good-bye to Kennedy.

When Frank walked into the lobby the fat man was waiting in the dark. He pulled a gun out of his pocket and said, "This is for you, Frank." Then he fired at point-blank range. Frank had thrown up his arm to protect his head, but instantly blood streamed from his scalp and he crumpled, while the huge killer fled.

Frank Costello was dead.

Or so the killer believed. He had fired from just a few feet away. Frank was in shock, but he was alive. The bullet had miraculously grazed his scalp instead of entering when Frank had instinctively turned his head away at the moment of firing.

But later, as he was hurtling through nighttime Manhattan traffic toward Roosevelt Hospital, Frank himself did not believe a miracle had occurred, he was sure he was going to die.

13

As the news spread, homicide detectives, policemen, and reporters streamed into Roosevelt Hospital. Mrs. Costello hurriedly left the Monsignore Restaurant, where she had gone with Frank's friends, to join him. At 11:08 P.M. Frank entered the emergency room for treatment. There doctors found that the bullet had struck just behind his left ear, furrowed under the scalp around the back of his head, and emerged close to his right ear. A miracle, indeed.

At 12:45 A.M. Frank emerged from the hospital, bloodstains on his shirt and jacket, with a white bandage around his head. The first thing he told reporters was: "I didn't see no one."

The precinct station on West Fifty-fourth Street, where Frank was taken, was a madhouse. Everyone who had dined with Frank that night was arriving by police request, plus the doorman of the building. The doorman described the killer as a heavy-set man about six feet tall, wearing a dark suit and black hat.

The next day Frank was back in his apartment and I was called to his side, where I remained, helping to deal with the police and reporters. I found Frank in a wry mood. When I asked him who had attempted to kill him, he gave me a reply which later became famous when he repeated it to detectives: "I don't know who could have done it. I don't have an enemy in the world."

Chief of Detectives James Leggett later commented, "Whoever this guy was, he had a very strange way of showing his friendship."

Frank was in his robe; he was feeling all right, accepting calls from various friends. The reporters were jammed in the lobby below, but all they got was me. I was Frank's spokesman, which was not an easy position to be in as I had absolutely no idea at the time what really had happened. Deputy Chief Inspector Edward W. Byrnes, who commanded the detectives in Manhattan West, called on the house phone from the lobby, and asked to speak to Mr. or Mrs. Costello.

"You take care of it, George," Frank said. "No one comes in here today."

So I met Mr. Byrnes in the hall outside of Frank's apartment, and told him that my client would cooperate, but that he claimed he had not seen the assailant, and had no idea who he was. Mr. Byrnes did not look too surprised at this announcement.

But he went into action. No less than sixty-six detectives were assigned to the case, and in the next weeks hundreds of witnesses were heard. Informers were questioned in bars and hide-outs throughout the city.

The underworld was in ferment. The ancient adage, "When you strike at a king, you must kill him," had failed, spectacularly. I later heard that Genovese retreated to his guarded mansion in New Jersey and called all who were loyal to him to his side.

As Genovese expected, Albert Anastasia stayed away out of loyalty to Frank.

Frank was soon called before a grand jury, but refused to talk and was sentenced to thirty days in the workhouse for contempt, one more jail sentence in those chaotic years for him. This was the most degrading of all; he was right there in the Tombs with the drunks and muggers and small-fry hoodlums.

But trouble was building, instead of decreasing. The police had gone through his pockets when he was shot and found a slip of paper which was very interesting. It said:

> Gross casino wins as of 4-27-57, $651,284.
> Casino wins less markers, $434,695.
> Slot wins, $62,844.
> Markers, $153,745.
> Mike, $150 a week.
> Jake, $150 a week.
> L. $30,000.
> H. $9,000.

Nevertheless, Frank was out of jail in fifteen days instead of thirty. There was no question that he had the right to take the Fifth Amendment protection on self-incrimination, especially in the light of the note which the police had found in his pocket and photographed. He was already out on bail on a tax case, and the slip could certainly have a bearing on that.

By June 6th of that year the detectives had discovered that the numbers on the paper in Frank's pocket matched to a penny the "take" from the gambling tables of the new Tropicana Hotel in Las Vegas. It just so happened that the Tropicana had been built by Frank's old partner from the slot machine days, Dandy Phil Kastel. But Kastel had been forced to "withdraw" after the Gaming Board had held up the license because of his criminal record.

Frank, who was under constant police surveillance, had a problem. He wanted to notify the underworld that he wouldn't talk, no matter what. I don't know how he accomplished this under the eyes of the police, but he did. And on July 17, 1957, a man walked into the West Fifty-fourth Street police station, accompanied by a lawyer, and told the police he was the person they were looking for in connection with Frank's attempted murder. His name was Vincent "the Chin" Gigante, a small-time hoodlum, but a hulking man who fitted the description.

The trial was short. I sat beside Frank and discovered something ironic. He seemed to *like* the man accused as his killer. The man he didn't like was Gigante's defense lawyer, Maurice Edelbaum, who, Frank said, "is trying to make his name over my dead body."

On the witness stand Frank said that he had seen nothing at all, and could not identify the assailant. This testimony should have satisfied the defense counsel but instead he continued to interrogate Frank.

"Do you know any reason why this man should seek your life?"

"None whatsoever."

"Is the reason you won't say you saw the man because you'll be indicted for perjury?"

"Absolutely not."

"Tell us the truth. Who shot you?"

Frank just stared at him. Then he smiled. "I'll ask *you* who shot me—I don't know. I saw no one at the time."

But he must have been inwardly seething, for a few minutes later he burst out at Edelbaum, "Please don't raise your voice."

The judge intervened to say, "I'll give the directions in this court."

But Gigante got his biggest break from the potentially most damaging witness, the doorman who had seen the killer rush in and out. This killer was the luckiest man who ever lived because it turned out that the doorman was completely blind in one eye and had impaired sight in the other.

Gigante was acquitted, and I remember the moment so clearly when "the Chin" came over to Frank after the verdict was announced, stuck out his hand to shake Costello's, and said, "Thanks, Frank."

And I must add that some time later my wife and I went to dinner at Frank's apartment, and there, as one of the honored dinner guests, was Vincent Gigante, the man who had allegedly tried to kill Frank at point-blank range.

Frank was too intelligent to hold that against Vincent, who was, if anything, an errand boy sent to do a job. Besides, he knew that the legal troubles harassing him would make him unable to function as the leader of the syndicate in his old role as boss. But he could not escape the fact that leaders such as Genovese regarded him as a stumbling block who must be removed anyway, especially as long as Albert Anastasia, Frank's longtime associate, was in the picture.

Frank had many, many friends in the Mafia—a lifetime of "playing straight" with others had earned him this respect. But the laws of the underworld are savage; they are based on fear. No underworld leader vying for the top position can feel safe if the boss is still alive.

Frank knew this; and Anastasia knew it too. But Anastasia nevertheless made a mistake.

He took one of the most famous shaves in the world.

THE GUNS

14

October 25, 1957. Albert Anastasia, the man called the Lord High Executioner of Murder Incorporated, had seen many men killed in his day. One thing he knew: they were always hit on deserted roads or in deserted restaurants. That was why he sauntered into the crowded barbershop of the Park Sheraton Hotel on Broadway at 57th Street with such confidence. Just in case, his bodyguard was at the door. But a barbershop was safer than a church; for one thing it had mirrors all around, no one could get in or out without being seen.

Frank had called Anastasia the previous night to warn him once again about Vito, but Anastasia was too big to scare. His visit to a public barbershop was a sign to Genovese that he could not be frightened and would continue to support Frank.

Anastasia walked into the busy barbershop and there was his favorite barber, Joe Bocchino, at chair No. 4. He sat down in the chair as Joe started to place the white cloths around him. "I'll take a shave and a trim, Joe," Anastasia said.

The barber tilted the chair to a reclining position and started to lather Anastasia's face. Outside, the bodyguard saw his boss in the reclining position, and looked at his watch. Two minutes to go.

Then the car squealed to a halt outside the front door of the shop, and the bodyguard sauntered down the street, leaving Anastasia unprotected.

Two men, one large and bulky, the other short and thin, walked into the barbershop with scarves over their lower faces and guns out. Somebody saw them and gasped. But they were running to chair No. 4 and the barber was turning away. The gunmen were firing directly into the back of Anastasia's head. Screams and tumult erupted in the barbershop, as Anastasia's body, propelled by the bullets, catapulted out of the chair, breaking the footrest and slamming into the shelf with bottles spilling and crashing in every direction. How could he be alive? Another bullet crashed into his back and he twisted to face his murderers and then plunged face down on the tiled floor.

The killers showed their ultimate respect for Anastasia: even now they stayed behind in a crowded barbershop pumping bullets into him on the floor, just to make sure.

Then they slipped outside and went into the subway entrance and were never seen again. All the witnesses, all the barbers with all the mirrors, somehow couldn't describe those men. Anastasia's barber, who was a foot away from the slaughter, told the police he didn't see anything. His back was turned. No mention of the mirror in front of him could change his statement.

But then Frank didn't need their identification because he didn't care. It was the man who had ordered the killings who was his concern.

15

This time, after Anastasia's murder, I was summoned within hours of the shooting. When I arrived at Frank's apartment, I found him and Anastasia's brother Tony clutching each other and sobbing.

I had never seen Frank show such emotion, and certainly I never saw him cry in front of others. What did he see at that moment? No escape from death for himself—and a war which would shatter all that he had built. Terror would reign in the streets again—and this time without Frank behind the scenes to counsel nonviolence, because Frank was the target.

There was no hope. As I stood at the door of his living room, Frank looked up, saw me, and said quietly, "This means I'm next."

I don't believe anyone but Frank could have survived. Anastasia's death left him without any apparent defense. The savage

Anastasia in the background had always been a factor any underworld leader had to consider if he wanted to attack the unarmed
Costello. Now Anastasia was gone.

But in this crisis Frank came up with the most brilliant idea
of his life. He knew that mere protestations that he would retire
would mean nothing; Genovese and his men would not be con-
tent with that. But suppose a nationwide conference of all underworld leaders was held, with Frank's blessing, where Genovese
would be officially crowned the new *capo di capo re?* It was an
idea which offered prestige and glimmered with good sense. And
it saved Frank's life.

Soon, more than a hundred criminal chieftains from all over
the nation were journeying to a little town in upper New York
State called Apalachin.

But somehow, without Frank Costello in charge, things didn't
go so well.

16

November 14, 1957. Sergeant Edgar Crosswell, a New York State
trooper, knew something funny was going on at the mansion of
Joseph Barbara, an upstate Mafia leader with no visible means
of support except money.

First off, the orders at the little butcher shop had been fantastic, 300 pounds of steaks, enough to feed an army. Other little
shops also reported enormous orders. More than a hundred
rooms in the area had been reserved by Barbara for guests unknown.

Crosswell drove by the mansion and saw what seemed to be a
limousine rally. Big black limousines were pulling into the driveway and lining up on the street outside, while very tough-look-
ing men climbed out, peering right and left.

Crosswell knew Barbara had underworld connections, but this
carnival was incredible. What was happening in Apalachin to
bring such a mob? Was Barbara dying and his friends arriving?

The young state trooper didn't know what was happening, but he did know *something* was happening. And he took a very simple action. He set up a road block outside of Barbara's house, which meant that everyone inside would be identified when he left. Within minutes an incredible scene began to unfold.

Out of the house charged none other than Vito Genovese, surrounded by guards, all of them climbing into his Cadillac limousine. Genovese was followed by such leaders as Joseph Profaci, the crime king of Brooklyn, Carlo Gambino, a future Boss of all Bosses in the Sixties, Joseph Bonanno, the Manhattan Mafia family leader, Gerardo Catena, the New Jersey Mafia leader.

The top leaders of the Mafia were rounded up by a state trooper who didn't even recognize them, a total of fifty-eight men from all over the country. And even more embarrassing, other great Mafia family leaders unwilling to be identified took off on foot through the woods and were picked up like common tramps.

It was a disaster of numbing proportions to the Mafia. Kefauver had written about national organized crime but he hadn't *proven* it. Now there they were, from every corner of the nation, gathered in one house for a conference.

Frank Costello, the last great boss, was not there because that was his deal with Genovese, who would announce himself as the new Boss of all Bosses at the conference. And he was angry too. The conference was his idea, but the idea of locating it in a small town in upper New York State came from someone else. Frank told me it was stupid. "Why didn't they just sublet the 17th Precinct Station in Manhattan for a day; that way they could have saved the travel," was the way he put it to me.

What made him more angry was that Genovese now surely was thinking he had been "had" by Frank. His crowning had certainly not been the social event of the season.

Frank's life was once again in danger.

17

One by one all of Ed Williams' ingenious appeals were turned down, and Frank was remanded to the Atlanta penitentiary to finish his sentence for tax evasion.

And it was there that the final confrontation between Frank and Vito Genovese, never revealed before, took place. It so happened I was in the middle of it, called there by Frank.

It was a situation fraught with tension. By chance, both Frank Costello and the man who had tried to kill him were in the same jail.

Genovese, not helped by the Apalachin publicity, had been trapped on a narcotics charge. (The man apprehended with him and called his "right hand man" was Vincent "the Chin" Gigante, perhaps enough proof right there for those who have doubts as to who ordered the attack on Frank's life.)

One day I got an anonymous call from a gentleman who said, simply, "Frank wants to see you."

I was on my way to Atlanta the next day.

Gray in the midday sun, the walls of the Atlanta prison looked formidable. I waited at the gate, and was surprised to get a message that the warden wanted to see me before I visited my client.

A few minutes later I sat in the warden's office, having a cup of coffee. The warden said, "We've got a problem."

"Frank?"

"No, Genovese. He's going to be killed."

I looked at him in surprise. If anything, the call to visit Frank had alarmed me about *his* chance for survival now that Genovese was in the same jail. The warden was saying, "The inmates here are angry at Genovese. They think he informed on Frank's tax stuff, and that's why Frank is in prison."

"That doesn't sound right to me," I said.

The warden sipped his coffee. Then he said, "Whatever it is, there's a war about to break in that yard, and almost all of them are on your man's side. We don't have enough guards in Georgia to save Genovese."

With that startling information, I was allowed to visit Frank. I found him looking thinner, older, in prison denims. But he gave me a warm handclasp. "Good old George," he said. "You come a long way for me. I appreciate it."

For this conference the warden had allowed us a room instead of the usual desk with wire separating us. I sat across from Frank and said, "The warden says Vito is in danger of being killed because the boys think he ratted on you on the tax case."

"That's bull," said Frank. "Vito wouldn't do that."

"So what's up? Why did you want me?"

"Vito trusts you. I want you to set up a meeting."

For the second time that day I stared in disbelief. We were in a prison, Frank was a prisoner—and here we were arranging a sitdown just as if there were no walls or guards or jailers. Frank was saying, "He appreciated it when you gave him that advice on his divorce. Especially after he didn't take your advice and got slaughtered."

(In one of the most puzzling divorce cases in criminal history, Vito had let his wife charge him in open court with criminal accusations of every kind, all of which were noted and followed up by various government agencies. I had advised Vito to pay his wife any amount she wanted, no matter what, to prevent a trial. Why he went through with it remains a mystery to everyone, although as we all know, the human heart, even in the underworld, can never be equated with logic.)

I said, "So what's the meeting supposed to do?"

"This thing is too dangerous," Frank replied. "Everybody's in a panic. I pass the word myself that Vito's all right, and it don't do no good. I want us to have a meeting in the warden's office with a photographer showing us shaking hands."

"But what does a photograph mean? Nothing!"

Frank stared at me, apparently surprised that I did not immediately grasp what he was trying to do. "George," he said in that rasping voice, "it ain't the picture. *It's the fact I'm calling the sitdown.*"

"Suppose Vito doesn't buy it."

Frank smiled. "He has to buy it."

I stood up. "I'll go back to the warden and arrange a meeting with Vito. But one thing I don't understand, and please don't look at me as if I'm stupid. Why are you so anxious to save Genovese's life?"

But Frank's eyes had that look again. He said to me, "Vito's my *friend*. You know that."

That afternoon I walked across the prison yard with the warden and saw hostile faces on every side. The tension in that prison was frightening. We found Vito in his cell, looking composed as ever, his thin lips tight. When he saw me he stood up, shook my hand, and said to the warden, "What's the action?"

The warden said I would explain and left us alone. I told him what Frank had in mind, and Vito looked at me a long time in silence. Then he said, "George, between you and me, Frank is something. He is so smart I'm always wondering what's behind everything he says and then I find he's talking straight and I'm the jackass. He even warned me about holding that meeting in Apalachin and I didn't listen."

"So?"

"So tell him we'll have the sitdown."

I stood up. "Good," I said. "I'll arrange it with the warden right away."

I went to the cell door and Vito followed me. As it was being opened by a guard, he said to me, "Tell Frank the picture will be sent to New York."

Within a few minutes I was out in the sunlight again. The prison grapevine had already been humming, the tension seemed less taut, some prisoners even smiled as if they knew who I was, but I was seeing none of this. I was thinking of Frank Costello. What a waste to have that mind in a lawbreaker instead of a State Department diplomat (where his guile might have been used to good benefit for his country instead of Mafia intrigue, and Mafia survival).

For it was all clear to me now. Frank had just been given a lifetime pass when he got back to New York. Or, rather, he had earned it.

18

What is there to say about the rest of Frank's life? The drama was finished. Vito Genovese ruled from prison for many years, then other Mafia leaders took over. But no leader could be compared to Frank Costello. Families split; new Mafia men became prominent. Augie Pisano was killed; Joe Bonanno was kidnapped; Crazy Joe Gallo went on a rampage; Joe Colombo was cut down in front of television cameras; Crazy Joe got his in return in a restaurant in Little Italy.

But Frank was untouchable. His prison dealings with Genovese gave Costello the underworld's final stamp of approval on the man who was perhaps the most genuinely popular boss it ever had. Frank was allowed to live in retirement, make what money he could, and enjoy his life on Manhattan's East Side, a celebrity to be pointed out now in a historical sense, like Jack Dempsey or Joe Louis.

I do not know if Frank died a happy man. I hope he did. The Supreme Court threw out his deportation ruling on a legal technicality, and that made him happy. But Internal Revenue harassed him constantly throughout his last years, and often he came to my office to ask me to intercede with old friends, who owed him a favor, for a loan. But nowadays the boss was not boss—and the loans only trickled in.

But in the end this most unusual of men had created a legend; he was, somehow, Manhattan's gangster, a living monument that people always seemed happy to see. Knowing Frank as I did, I know this recognition pleased him. He had yearned all his life to be accepted by the "better" people. Other criminal leaders had built great mansions in the suburbs, and sought to be accepted as Frank had. But they all had failed.

Frank succeeded. You could see it whenever he entered an East Side restaurant. People smiled and nudged each other. No one recoiled as you would expect from the man who had been the head of the underworld.

And part of this was due to the fact that, by the time of his death at eighty-two, authorities were discovering that Costello, alone among the Mafia leaders, had been a spokesman for non-violence all these years. This knowledge was gradually communicated to the public in various books, including Joe Valachi's.

The other part was just charisma. Frank had it. The man who had once commanded more fighting ships at sea than Lord Nelson, and as many guns on land as a Marine division, had that quality of excitement born of experience.

He was the last of his kind, the last of the truly all-powerful bosses, and, alone among all of them, he died peacefully in bed in his home.

It was the underworld's ultimate sign of respect.

19

February 21, 1973, a mournful silence in the small chapel of a funeral parlor at 81st Street and Madison. Mrs. Costello is ushered in by Phil Kennedy, the man who had been with her husband when he was shot. Only fifty close friends have been invited; the ceremony is private.

Sitting in the chapel, my mind goes back to Willie Moretti's funeral: limousines in parade, massed banks of flowers, hundreds of guests in mourning, FBI men with cameras, the great gangland funeral of the past. Frank wouldn't have wanted that.

A simple prayer for the repose of his soul is being said. The words drone through the chapel. Mrs. Costello bows her head in tears, and I am thinking of what Frank said about his life, the man at the wheel of a car who suddenly finds his brakes are gone . . . and so many memories. Then the casket is being carried up the aisle, and I whisper "Good-bye, Frank."